Woodrow Wilson and the Great War

UNIVERSITY OF VIRGINIA PRESS
CHARLOTTESVILLE AND LONDON

Woodrow Wilson the and Great War

Reconsidering

America's

Neutrality

1914–1917

Robert W. Tucker

European wars, for it was only in such wars that America's rights as a neutral might expectedly be seriously challenged. Yet it was just such conflicts that posed the real test not only of neutrality but of isolation as well. If isolation worked only in periods of relative European stability and quiet, or at best in wars involving small powers and fought for limited stakes, its utility was distinctly limited.

A resolution of the conflict between isolation and neutrality evidently required the substantial modification of one or the other. Either the policy of isolation from major European wars had to be seriously qualified, if not simply given up, or the expansive version of neutral rights the nation had always insisted upon had to be compromised, if not abandoned, when put to the real test. In the long period stretching from the end of the War of 1812 to World War I it did not much matter that the conflict between isolation and neutrality was not resolved. So long as the circumstances conditioning this conflict did not arise, it could be, and was, left in abeyance. But these circumstances did arise again in 1914, and they were once more to lay bare the contradiction that had always been at the basis of America's policy of isolation.

Nor did the parallel between 1812 and 1914 escape Wilson's notice. Colonel Edward Mandell House, Wilson's confidant, recorded in his diary a conversation with the president early in the war, when the British were already moving to shut off all neutral trade with Germany, in which Wilson read from an account he had once written on the origins of the War of 1812. The earlier conflict, Wilson remarked to House, "was started in exactly the same way as this controversy is opening up." The president had written that "Madison was compelled to go to war despite the fact that he was a peace-loving man, and desired to do everything in his power to prevent it, but popular feeling made it impossible." Wilson went on to observe: "Madison and I are the only two Princeton men that have become President. The circumstances of the War of 1812 and now run parallel. I sincerely hope they will not go further."[3]

There was indeed a parallel between the circumstances of 1812 and those of 1914. But there was also a great difference, one that went far toward qualifying, if not invalidating, the parallel as Wilson had drawn it. The power of America relative to that of the European states had changed, and radically so, in the intervening century. If Wilson confronted the same basic dilemma Jefferson had once faced, he did so from a position of power that bore little comparison with that of his predecessor. Jefferson had believed that Great Britain's commercial dependence on America would assure respect for neutral rights. The threat of "peaceable coercion," a threat that found expression in Jefferson's embargo, rested on this belief. But experience showed this belief to have been wrong. A young America did not have sufficient economic power to compel Great Britain to concede the several issues on which the two countries differed. By contrast, the America of World War I undoubtedly had sufficient economic power, and from the outset British policy not only recognized that preeminent power but was prepared to submit in serious controversies over neutral rights rather than run the real risk of a break with the United States. That this risk did not arise, or even come close to arising, in the first year of the war was the result, not of a British willingness to concede to American positions on freedom of neutral commerce, but of an American unwillingness to press London on the measures it took to control neutral trade.

The parallel with 1812 Wilson thought he saw was in reality less one of parties than one of positions. The dramatis personae remained the same (once Germany was substituted for Napoléon's France), but their roles had changed. In 1914 the United States did not view Great Britain as having the role she had had in 1812. Despite the tensions that eventually came to mark Washington's relations with London by the summer and fall of 1916, it was still Germany rather than Great Britain that was seen as the putative enemy. But if the roles had changed, the position taken by Jefferson and Madison in moving toward war with Great Britain bore a close resemblance to the position taken by Wilson in moving toward war with Germany. Jefferson and Madison had put themselves in a position from which retreat was very difficult. Issues of neutral rights had been given an independent standing and then equated with interests that could not be compromised.

Wilson would put himself in the same position. Yet he would do so for reasons that were not nearly as compelling as those that had moved his predecessors, who still vividly remembered the struggle for independence. The measures at sea taken by Great Britain seemed to Jefferson and Madison nothing so much as a reenactment of the earlier struggle for independence. To a people still uncertain of the outcome of the venture in nationhood on which they had only recently embarked, and even more to its Republican leaders, the measures taken by the former mother country raised almost primordial fears. Even if one concedes that in taking the course they did Jefferson and Madison erred in underestimating the threat to the balance of power, and ultimately to America's security, held out by Napoléon, considering their past and the fears this past had instilled in them their actions were understandable.

In Wilson's case, on the other hand, the fears that had moved Jefferson and Madison were not apparent. In the conflict with Germany over neutral rights, the invocation of honor, prestige, and independence had to respond to something quite different. To what it responded, however, was never very clear. Unlike Secretary of State Robert Lansing, for example, Wilson appears to have entertained little real fear over the consequences a German victory held out for American security (an outcome that, in any event, he did not expect, and particularly in the earlier period of the war).[4] Conventional security considerations apart, there was still the concern over America's future role in the world. Had Wilson not responded roughly as he did to the challenge the submarine posed to neutral rights, could it be said that the United States was a great power entitled to play a major role in shaping the postwar international order? If this, at bottom, was the consideration that led Wilson to equate the defense of neutral rights with the nation's honor, prestige, and independence, it still may be seen as a concern for security.[5] Even if it is so seen, it was evidently a concern of a quite different order from the fears that moved Jefferson and Madison.

Between 1812 and 1914 not only the circumstances of the American position but also the nation's outlook changed. The change in outlook was in large measure the result of the change in circumstances, above all the growth of American power. While the prevailing outlook of the nation in 1914 remained decidedly isolationist, it was nevertheless the isolationism of a people increasingly aware of the nation's growing power relative to that of the nations of Europe. That awareness was all-important, for it marked isolation's transformation from the necessary to the simply desirable. The policy that a century earlier had presumably responded to the nation's core security was no longer deemed indispensable, for the same reason. Henceforth, for as long as isolationism persisted as a serious force in the nation's political life, its justification would be the impregnability of the Western Hemisphere and the adverse domestic effects of an interventionist foreign policy.

Woodrow Wilson was clearly sensitive to the change that had occurred and on more than one occasion gave idealized expression to it. In a memorable Fourth of July address on the eve of the war he declared: "Our independence is a fact so stupendous that it can be measured only by the size and energy and variety and wealth and power of one of the greatest nations in the world." America had come to its "majority," and the questions this stupendous fact raised were, "What are we going to do with the influence and power of this great nation? Are we going to play the old role of using that power for our aggrandizement and material benefit only?" In asking these questions, Wilson had Mexico most immediately in mind. Yet he also made clear that he was referring, not only to Mexico or even to the Western Hemisphere, but to the world. America had been established "to vindicate the rights of man." U.S. independence "is not a selfish thing for our own exclusive private use. It is for everybody to whom we can find the means of extending it." His dream, the president concluded, was of the time "that America will come into the full light of the day when all shall know that she puts human rights above all other rights and that her flag is the flag, not only of America, but of humanity."[6]

This was, to be sure, Fourth of July oratory. But it was also something more: it expressed a vision of national place and mission in the world that Wilson deeply believed in. It also goes far in explaining why there was never an easy fit between Wilson and neutrality. The "stupendous fact" of America's recently gained wealth and power, when taken together with the vision of a nation whose flag of freedom was not only her own but humanity's as well, gave rise to a novel and difficult problem in a world that was suddenly overtaken by the crisis of World War I. There was, in fact, no precedent for the position in which Wilson found himself. A century earlier, in another great European conflict, his predecessors had also entertained a vision of America as freedom's exemplar. But the stupendous fact that Wilson enjoyed was not theirs. For this reason alone, neutrality did not pose the same problems for them that it did for Wilson.

The difficulty of Wilson's position began with the recognition that the European war was not just another conflict but one that would determine the future order of the world. The normal indifference of neutrals toward the outcome of the wars of the nineteenth century, an indifference that rested on the assumption of the limited consequences of war, no longer held. In the case of the smaller neutral states of Europe, this consideration might be acknowledged, yet, in view of their weakness, considered irrelevant. In the case of a great power, even one separated from Europe by an ocean and long committed to a policy of isolation from Europe's politics, the response had to prove more difficult. The fate of a civilization of which America was a part could not simply be viewed with indifference, particularly given the role that Wilson had assigned to the nation. The responsibility imposed upon America by a world in crisis was one that inescapably followed from her power and ideals. America could not be indifferent to the war and its consequences, content merely to observe it from afar and relieved not to be involved. At the outset, it is true, this was by far the prevailing reaction. Even the president seemed momentarily to share in it. But it could not, and did not, last for a nation of immigrants whose ancestral ties to the several belligerents were still very strong. Even less could it have lasted in Wilson's case. If America was to occupy the status of a neutral, there would have to be a justification for neutrality that went well beyond what Wilson's predecessors had invoked a century earlier on behalf of a nation of only modest power.[7]

Although foreshadowed by statements made very early in the war, it was not until almost eight months following the outbreak of war that Wilson fully set forth his thoughts on neutrality and on America's vocation as a neutral. The basis of neutrality, the president explained, "is not indifference; it is not self-interest. The basis of neutrality is sympathy for mankind. It is fairness, it is good will at bottom. It is impartiality of spirit and of judgment." The commitment to neutrality did not stem from "the petty desire to stay out of trouble" but from the conviction that "there is something so much greater to do than fight: there is a distinction waiting for this nation that no nation has ever yet got. That is the distinction of absolute self-control and self-mastery." For America, in stark contrast to the nations of Europe, which had abandoned their respective fates to the arbitrament of armed force, the president coveted "this splendid courage of reserve moral force." America's vocation was to be the mediating nation of the world, if only by virtue of being a nation "compounded of the nations of the world. We mediate their blood . . . their traditions . . . their sentiments, their tastes, their passions; we are ourselves compounded of those things. We are, therefore, able to understand all nations; we are able to understand them in the compound, not separately as partisans, but unitedly, as knowing and comprehending and embodying them all." It was in this sense, Wilson explained, that America was a mediating nation, a nation without a past that impelled it in a fixed direction, a nation that had no "hampering ambitions" to take what did not belong to it. The president put what was for him no more than a rhetorical question: "Isn't a nation in that position free to serve other nations, and isn't a nation like that ready to form some part of the assessing opinion of the world."[8]

Until the decision to intervene in the war, the address of April 20, 1915, to the Associated Press remained Wilson's most significant statement on neutrality. At the time, the nation's neutrality policy, which markedly favored the Allied cause, was for all practical purposes set. America's pro-Allied bias had been privately acknowledged by Wilson's advisers in the winter of 1914–15. Though their candid admission was not unknown to the president, he did not reproach them. Two months prior to the April address, the stage had been set for the confrontation with Germany over the submarine. In responding as he did to the initial German declaration of a war zone around the British Isles, Wilson had left, whether by design or by inadvertence, almost no room for compromise. The act that would bring Germany and the United States to the brink of war—the sinking of the *Lusitania*—occurred less than three weeks after the April speech. Even at the time it was given, an incident had already occurred—the *Falaba* sinking—that, while resulting in the loss of but one American life, clearly indicated the difficulties ahead if the German and American governments held to their respective courses.

It was in the context of these developments that Wilson made his statement on neutrality. There is no reason to doubt that the president made it in all sincerity and good faith and that it afforded an accurate expression of his convictions. For as long as the nation remained a nonparticipant in the war, the principal themes of the speech—America's desire for service to a warring world, the nation's complete disinterestedness, her unique qualities as a mediating party—would find repeated expression. Only the moral equivalence of the belligerents would later find prominent expression, and even this theme was at least implicit in the April statement.

What stands out in Wilson's statement is a view of neutrality that was equated above all with spirit and intentions rather than with actions. Although such an equation came close to reversing the traditional understanding, Wilson seems to have taken it for granted. The equation accounts in part for his conviction, one otherwise so baffling yet one he steadfastly held to, that he had followed a quite neutral course. What mattered most was his spirit and intention, not the letter of the law. Wilson *knew* he was neutral. He knew it not only because he wanted to remain out of the war, a desire that became ever more intense with time, but because from almost the beginning of the war he had wanted a compromise peace. What better test was there of neutrality as Wilson had defined it—of sympathy for mankind, of fairness, goodwill, impartiality of spirit and judgment—than this support of a compromise peace, a peace without victory? Compared with differences arising from conflicting interpretations of the law of neutrality, these differences seemed almost inconsequential. Nothing else can explain Wilson's surprise and chagrin when, in January 1917, the German government declined to put its faith and fortunes in the hands of the American president and agree to the course outlined in his December 1916 peace note.

Wilson equated America's neutrality with a noble vision. Yet it was manifestly a vision that also expressed what Wilson believed to be the nation's interests. The president saw no conflict between the two.[9] The advantages neutrality conferred upon the nation were ultimately advantages to the world as well. America's "reserve moral force" might, it was hoped would, one day help to bring peace with justice to a war-torn world. That task could only be undertaken by a great power that preserved an "absolute self-control and self-mastery." The financial benefits that accrued to America by virtue of the war would facilitate this high undertaking. In his April 1915 statement Wilson noted: "Our resources are untouched; we are more and more becoming, by the force of circumstances, the mediating nation of the world in respect to its finance." This was the Wilsonian version of Jefferson's earlier view of a general European war that enabled the United States "to become the carriers for all parties" at sea, thus enabling the new world "to fatten on the follies of the old."[10] What to Jefferson was benefiting from Europe's infatuation with war and conquest was to Wilson the prospect of inheriting the position of world leadership by staying out of the war. To Edith Bolling Galt he wrote in August 1915: "Yes, I think the [newspaper] clipping about America now standing as likely heir to the influence and power hitherto possessed by England and her continental neighbors and rivals does contain a thought . . . and is it not a pretty safe prediction, always supposing we succeed in keeping out of the deadly maelstrom ourselves?"[11] The expectation of an exhausted Europe incapable of resisting a neutral America's growing influence and power persisted to the end of the period of neutrality. In mid-February 1917, during the final days of Wilson's crumbling determination to remain out of the war, the president reportedly said that "he is not in sympathy with any great preparedness—that Europe would be man and money poor by the end of the war."[12] It was by then a familiar calculation.

This is not to say that Wilson saw only advantages resulting from neutrality. From the start he was mindful of the possibility that by remaining neutral he might be excluded from playing a significant, even dominant, role in shaping the postwar order. The Allies might emerge impoverished from the war, but if they were nevertheless victorious, they might still be able to severely limit American influence. The point was made to Wilson on a number of occasions by his ambassador to London, Walter Hines Page, as well as by House, and this undoubtedly had an effect on the president. The prospect of being excluded from the peacemaking helps to account for the neutrality policy Wilson fashioned in the first year of the war. Keenly aware as they were of Wilson's desire to be a peacemaker, the British made full use of it. In July 1915 Sir Edward Grey wrote to House of his belief that if America did enter the war, "the influence of the United States on the larger aspects of the final conditions of peace will prevail [but] I am very doubtful whether anything short of being actually involved in the war will stir your people sufficiently to make them exercise, or enable the President to exercise, on the terms of peace all the influence that is possible."[13] Grey's words were not lost on Wilson.

The president found other liabilities attending neutrality. As the war progressed he came to fear that if the conflict led to a real deadlock, the resulting destruction might prove to be irreparable. Yet against this prospect Wilson repeatedly invoked the consideration that if the United States were to abandon neutrality and enter the war, there would be no disinterested party left capable of mediating the great struggle. "It would be a calamity to the world at large," he wrote to House in August 1915, during the *Arabic* crisis, "if we should be drawn actively into the conflict and so deprived of all disinterested influence over the settlement."[14] During the *Sussex* crisis, in March 1916, House recorded in his diary Wilson's fear that if the United States were to break relations with Berlin, "war would go on indefinitely and there would be no one to lead the way out."[15]

The unavoidable conclusion is that while Wilson did see liabilities attending America's neutrality, they were far outweighed by the advantages he found in remaining out of the war. Given his view of the relationship between the war and American interests, it could scarcely have been otherwise. Wilson was not blind to the prospective threat of a triumphant Germany to the nation's security interests.[16] He appreciated that a German victory, even if it were not immediately to give rise to a challenge to the Monroe Doctrine, might eventually impose a burden of military preparedness, which the country had been able to escape in the past. He realized that a German triumph might carry with it a threat to many of the values that defined American and, indeed, Western civilization. These considerations, however, were not sufficiently compelling to overturn long-held views about the nature and basis of American security. Despite a later concern over the possible consequences a German victory held out for American security, Wilson could never bring himself to view those consequences with the seriousness needed to prompt the abandonment of neutrality. Whatever fears he may have entertained of a German victory, he nevertheless continued to see America's security as essentially unconditioned by events in Europe. And to the limited extent that he did draw a connection between the two, what weighed heavily in his calculations was not the threat to the nation's security that *might* arise in a distant future when a victorious

Germany had recovered from the devastating effects of war but the threat to America's institutions and well-being that, he was utterly persuaded, *would* arise were it to become a party to the war. Between what he saw as a distant and hypothetical threat and what he considered an immediate and real danger, he had little difficulty in choosing.

Wilson's determined hold on neutrality, then, had the simplest of explanations: he wanted to stay out of the war. He wanted to stay out of the war because, as he said on numerous occasions, the people relied on him to keep the nation out of the war and because he himself believed to the very end that participation in the war held out the greatest threat to the nation's democratic values and institutions. Yet though Wilson's neutrality was ultimately rooted in his profound fear of war's effects, he was nevertheless unable to candidly avow the compelling reason for his determination to remain out of the war. Instead, that reason had to be disavowed as one unworthy of a great nation committed to the ideals Wilson had set out.

In this his task was greatly facilitated by a view of the war that found right and justice on neither side. Against a growing chorus of criticism at home and abroad that his neutrality was self-serving when it was not simply driven by fear, Wilson replied that the war offered little, if any, grounds for moral choice. The theme of the belligerents' moral equivalence, of the war as being simply a struggle for power, was Wilson's last line of defense on behalf of his neutrality. The view that the war was devoid of moral significance was one the president had come to only some months after the outbreak of hostilities. In the beginning he had appeared to think otherwise and even to privately endorse Allied claims respecting the causes and objects of the war. But it soon became apparent that whatever his initial reaction, his studied position was one of skepticism toward the moral claims of the belligerents.

Not unexpectedly, the British were the most upset by Wilson's moral neutrality. They found inexplicable what they came to see as his lack of moral sympathy for the Allied cause. During the first year or so of the war their indignation was contained, partly because the suffering imposed by the war had yet to test their endurance but also partly because Wilson had yet to give unguarded expression to his position. In 1916 what had earlier been little more than intimated by the president was increasingly given open expression. In his epochal May 1916 address to the League to Enforce Peace, Wilson declared of the war: "With its causes and its objects we are not concerned. The obscure fountains from which its stupendous flood has burst forth we are not interested to search for or explore."[17] These sentences evoked an immediate and indignant reaction from London. House saw them as virtually canceling out the good effects of the president's commitment to participate in a postwar security arrangement.[18] But Wilson was not to be deterred from voicing his view of the belligerents' moral equivalence. While disclaiming that he was passing any moral judgment on the war, he continued to do just that. To a peace group that visited the White House in late summer 1916 he observed that all he had meant in his May address "was that we hadn't had any part in starting the conflict . . . and that, not having any part in starting it, and not having any direct interest in what was being settled, if anybody knew what it was that was being settled, we had nothing to say in the way of judgment as to how it started or anything about it." And to make sure that his small audience grasped his point, he went on to note, in response to the belligerent charge "that the United States is so cold-blooded that it doesn't care what is going on in Europe," that "now, in one sense we don't care for what the quarrel is about, because we don't know, partly because nobody knows what the quarrel is about. It is just a fight . . . to see who is strong enough to prevent the other from fighting better. I don't see anything else that is involved."[19]

This refusal to see any moral significance in the conflict found repeated expression in Wilson's campaign speeches during the fall of 1916. "The singularity of the present war," he stated in Omaha on October 5, 1916, "is that its origin and objects have never been disclosed. They have obscure European roots which we do not know how to trace."[20] Three weeks later, in Cincinnati. he asked: "Have you ever heard what started the present war? If you have, I wish you would publish it, because nobody else has."[21] These were expressions of a president seeking reelection. Yet they bear a close resemblance to his most considered utterances as a statesman. Once the campaign was over, Wilson turned to his last and greatest effort to bring the war to an end. The December peace note to the belligerents was preceded by the November prolegomenon to a peace note, Wilson's private memorandum to himself on the meaning of the war.[22] In that memo, which reflected the quintessential Wilson, the president averred that the war had no meaning save its immense suffering and utter futility, that neither side's claims could be endorsed, that German militarism and British navalism had been equally important as causes of the war, and that a lasting peace could not be obtained by accepting either side's position. The prolegomenon is an essay on the moral enormity of the war, an enormity that is above all the result of the war's purposelessness. It had no object or purpose save victory, which in Wilson's eyes meant that it had no object or pur pose at all. It was essentially the same message that, in diplomatic terms, ran through Wilson's December peace note, in which the belligerents were asked to avow "the precise objects which would, if attained, satisfy them and their people that the war had been fought out."[23]

That Wilson believed in the view he expressed of the war there is little reason to question. He was not alone in this view. After all, the ever-pragmatic House took very much the same view. House too came to believe that the Allies had no higher, that is, "disinterested," purposes in waging the war than to prevail over the enemy. To an English friend he remarked in June 1916 that it was "tiresome . . . to hear the English declare they were fighting for Belgium and that they entered the war for that purpose."[24] House had discovered in the spring of 1916 that "no class of people are more ruthless as a rule in their dealings with one another than are governments."[25] But House's discovery was balanced by other considerations. He had never questioned the desirability of an Allied victory, though he had desired it to be a moderate victory. Nor had he ever doubted that such a victory was vital to American interests. If this meant America's eventual intervention in the war, he had been reconciled to that prospect since the summer of 1915.

Wilson was a very different case. He did not share House's view of interest, and even if he had, it is likely that he would have remained unreconciled to the eventuality of America's intervention. His basic judgment on the meaning of the war was not balanced by the considerations that moved House. But then House had never looked upon American participation in the war with the dread that this prospect evoked in Wilson. What to House was a practical matter of weighing costs against benefits was to Wilson something profoundly more difficult, given his conviction about the nature of the costs. The view Wilson took of the war's meaning, though sincerely held, was a reflection of this conviction. His insistence on the belligerents' moral equivalence was proportionate to this sense of vulnerability in the face of Allied criticism that despite his noble professions, he was in fact blind to the issues of right and wrong that the war raised and indifferent to the fate of a suffering world.

Considered in isolation, Wilson's belief that the war was no more than a struggle for power might well have proved a sufficient justification for his continued neutrality, whatever the outcome of the war. But, of course, it could not be considered in isolation. The neutrality to which the president had long been committed, and from which his efforts to escape proved unavailing in the fall of 1916, was pushing him inexorably toward war. Wilson's awareness of his deepening predicament was reflected in two themes that emerged in this period: the intolerableness of neutrality in modern war and the need for a cause in defense of which Americans would be willing to undertake the sacrifices of war. In a campaign speech in late October 1916 he elaborated on the first theme: "[This] is the last war of the kind, or of any kind that involves the world, that the United States can keep out of. I say that because I believe that the business of neutrality is over. Not because I want it to be over, but I mean this—that war has now such a scale that the position of neutrals sooner or later becomes intolerable."[26]

That neutrality had become intolerable did not mean, however, that Wilson had become reconciled to intervention in the war. Instead, he was registering his experience with neutrality, particularly his sense of entrapment in a policy that he could see was leading to war. Still, if neutrality had become intolerable, this did not mean that war had become tolerable, let alone desirable. It might be both if only a worthy cause for fighting could be found. "It has been said," he observed in an address at Shadow Lawn mansion, in Monmouth, New Jersey, on October 14, 1916, "that the people of the United States do not want to fight about anything. That is profoundly false. But the people of the United States want to be sure what they are fighting about, and they want to be sure that they are fighting for the things that will bring to the world justice and peace. Define the elements. Let us know that we are not fighting for the prevalence of this nation over that, for the ambitions of this group of nations as compared with the ambitions of that group of nations. Let us once be convinced that we are called into a great combination to fight for the rights of mankind, and America will unite her force and spill her blood for the great things she has always believed in and followed." What Europe must realize, the president went on to declare, was that "we are saving ourselves for something greater that is to come. We are saving ourselves in order that we may unite in that final league of nations in which it shall be understood that there is no neutrality where any nation is doing wrong, in that final league of nations which must, in the providence of God, come into the world, where nation shall be leagued with nation in order to show all mankind that no man may lead any nation into acts of aggression without having all the other nations of the world leagued against it."[27]

The statement was representative of Wilson's public utterances in the fall of 1916. What did it mean? Clearly the most reasonable interpretation was one that supported the Allied view that the president was indifferent to, even condemnatory of, the objects and purposes of the war. The "rights of mankind," the cause "in which it was a glory to shed human blood," as Wilson said on another occasion,[28] were never expressly defined. But one definition did emerge by implication. It was the right of the peoples of all states to be free of armed aggression. Wilson had proclaimed this right in his address of May 27, 1916, to the League to Enforce Peace, saying that "the world has a right to be free from every disturbance of its peace that has its origin in aggression and disregard of the rights of peoples and nations," and had declared America's willingness "to become a partner in any feasible association of nations formed in order to realize" the right of peoples to be free of aggression.[29] However, if this was the meaning of his statement, it referred to the future , not the present. America would shed her blood in a cause to which a future league of nations was to be dedicated, not in a cause, the war, intent on establishing the dominance of one group of nations over another. In that future league neutrality would have no place; for the present, neutrality, though intolerable, would be held to as long as honor permitted.[30]

Wilson would hold to neutrality, though intolerable, until Germany rendered his hold impossible. He would hold to it not from an attachment to the institution but from dread of the alternative. Despite his early effort to idealize neutrality, he had never found the status congenial. The outlook of the neutral was not Wilson's outlook. "Neutrality," he once said, "is a negative word. It is a word that does not express what America ought to feel."[31] Wilson's neutrality, like every state's neutrality, was determined by interest, yet Wilson was driven to disavow interest in explaining the nation's policy. Again, neutrality was primarily a matter of actions, yet Wilson insisted on considering neutrality largely in terms of spirit, intention, and ideals. Then, too, neutrality was the expression par excellence of an international system that sanctioned the absolute right of a state to resort to war, yet almost from the start Wilson set himself against this system, though, curiously enough, he continued to extol the legal order that embodied this right. Above all, neutrality was a modest position, one scarcely undertaken to save the world, yet Wilson insisted upon seeing America's neutrality as the promise of salvation to a warring world.

In the end, these disparities between reality and vision would lead Wilson to the renunciation of neutrality. In his war address the president declared: "Neutrality is no longer feasible or desirable where the peace of the world is involved and the freedom of its peoples, and the menace to that peace and freedom lies in the existence of autocratic governments backed by organized force which is controlled wholly by their will, not by the will of the people. We have seen the last of neutral-

ity in such circumstances."[32] In the new order, the war address proclaimed, there would be no place for an institution that was based upon
the refusal to distinguish between the just and unjust resort to armed
force. Wilson would later say, in defending the League of Nations, that
"international law has been the principle of minding your own business, particularly when something outrageous was up." But the covenant of the League made "matters of that sort everybody's business."[33]
In the new system there was to be no place for neutrality.

Until the winter of 1917, however, Wilson was still in the old system.
Neutrality had become intolerable for him, but not so intolerable as to
lead him to accept the alternative. There is sheer pathos in his repeated
call in the fall of 1916 for "some cause which will elevate your spirit, not
depress it, some cause in which it seems a glory to shed human blood,
if it be necessary."[34] What Wilson desperately searched for, he must have
known he could not find. There was no cause that, once recognized,
would free him from the dilemma that was in no small measure of his
own making. Only the German decision to pursue unrestricted submarine warfare could do that.

1

Woodrow Wilson and His Advisers

The war that burst on an astonished world in August 1914 was the first general European conflict in a century. In the wars of the French Revolution and Napoléon (1792–1815) a young America had sought to preserve its neutrality, while insisting on a broad interpretation of its rights to trade with the belligerents. The effort had not been successful. The new nation had enjoyed nowhere near a rough equality of power with either France or England. Nor was this inequality compensated for by Thomas Jefferson's strategy of "peaceable coercion." Based on the assumption that the advantages of trade with America would force the belligerents to concede to America's demands as a neutral, Jefferson saw in peaceable coercion an effective substitute for war. But events showed that Jefferson's belief in a new diplomacy that avoided war and its corruption had been misplaced and that America could not escape the travails of a neutral state attempting to preserve its commerce in a hegemonic struggle of the great powers.

The European conflict that began a century later raised very much the same stakes as had the Napoleonic Wars. Once again, the European balance of power was the central issue on which the conflict turned. And once again the United States sought to remain outside the war while continuing to trade with the belligerents. In the intervening century, however, a great change had occurred in the power of the United States relative to the European states. Whereas Jefferson had only dreamed of the day when America might "shake a rod over the heads of all,"[1] Wilson could be excused for believing that that day had come. In 1914 America had a population of more than 90 million people. Its economy was almost twice that of its nearest competitor, Germany. Its rate of growth was such as to make virtually certain that the nation's economic primacy in the world would persist into the indefinite future.

By these standards America was not only a great power; it was the world's greatest power. But the resources of a state did not of themselves determine its status. In the then European-dominated state system the critical test of power was the efficiency and determination with which a state's resources could be mobilized and employed for war. The European great powers, A. J. P. Taylor once observed, "were organizations for war. They might have other objects . . . but the basic test for them as Great Powers was their ability to wage war."[2] In 1914 the United States had yet to be seriously tested. The 1898 war against Spain could scarcely be considered a serious test. Since that time the country had not undergone a meaningful trial by arms. Nor had it shown any desire to do so. When war broke out in 1914, it had a military establishment smaller than that maintained by a European power of second rank, let alone by a major European power. The modesty of its military establishment corresponded to the disposition of the nation's government and people. A deep reluctance to bear that most demanding of collective sacrifices— war—had always been a characteristic of the nation's foreign policy.

These considerations notwithstanding, the importance of America in affecting the course and outcome of the war was apparent almost from the outset. Even assuming that the country remained a nonparticipant in the struggle, an assumption taken largely for granted in the early stages of the war, the character of its neutrality was seen as critical, particularly by the Allies. In undertaking the blockade of Germany, British statesmen were keenly aware of the significance of the American reaction. The great object of diplomacy, the British foreign secretary, Sir Edward Grey, stated in his memoirs, "was to secure the maximum of blockade that could be enforced without a rupture with the United States."[3] An effective blockade of Germany might not alone guarantee an Allied victory, but it would make a German triumph very difficult. In turn, the effectiveness of the Allied blockade depended, the submarine apart, on the American government's reaction to it.

America, then, despite its neutral status, was the holder of the balance of power in the world conflict by virtue of the scale of its productive resources and the decisive importance of access to them by one side or the other. In turn, the individual holder of that balance was the nation's president, Woodrow Wilson. He was so if only by virtue of the power over foreign policy a president possesses in the American constitutional system. Wilson believed in that power, and to a greater degree than had most of his predecessors. The president's power over the initiation and conduct of foreign policy, he had written some years before becoming president, was "very absolute." Although the president cannot conclude treaties without the Senate's consent, "he may guide every step of diplomacy. . . . He need disclose no step of negotiation until it is complete and when in any critical matter it is completed . . . whatever its inclination, the Senate may feel itself committed also."[4]

On becoming president, Wilson put this view into practice. The result was soon apparent in his conduct of diplomacy with Mexico. Only when war threatened between Mexico and the United States did a shaken president seek to enlist the support of a Congress that had been kept largely ignorant of his diplomacy. Although quickly given by the House, the resolution of support requested by the president was approved by the Senate only after a debate marked by dissatisfaction over the position in which Wilson's actions had put that body.

Wilson's actions toward Mexico were indicative of a pattern of action he would follow throughout his presidency. In the great battle over the peace treaty in 1919, it would lead to disaster for him. In the years between the beginning and the end, it would often result in a relationship with Congress that was more difficult than it need have been. Nearly all presidents have seen in Congress a threat to their power over foreign policy, but Wilson was more zealous in this respect than most. Nearly all presidents have kept Congress in the dark about their diplomacy, but Wilson was more secretive toward Congress than most. If he saw little reason to defer to the Congress on matters of foreign policy, this simply reflected his settled belief that the legislature had no real role in such matters, the power of the Senate over treaty making apart. Ironically, that limited power proved sufficient in the end to defeat the capstone of Wilson's policy.

But the final battle with the Senate over the peace treaty was preceded by years of victories. In the period of neutrality Wilson generally had his way with Congress in foreign policy. An important reason for his almost unparalleled dominance must be found in the remarkable affinity between the president's outlook and that of the public. Wilson's neutrality policy enjoyed widespread support because his waverings and uncertainties reflected the public's waverings and uncertainties. Even his opponents acknowledged this. No other public figure at the time mirrored the nation's mood; none voiced the nation's hopes and fears as did the president. Oddly enough, given his deeply held conviction that the popular mind was in conformity with his own, Wilson sometimes seemed unaware that in characterizing the former he was also depicting the latter. A revealing episode took place in the summer of 1915, in the midst of the *Lusitania* crisis, when a wavering president wrote to his secretary of state: "Two things are plain to me, in themselves inconsistent, viz. That our people want this thing [the *Lusitania* sinking] handled in a way that will bring about a definite settlement without endless correspondence, and that they will also expect us not to hasten an issue or so conduct the correspondence as to make an unfriendly issue inevitable."[5] This was indeed the prevailing outlook of the public, who wanted to uphold the nation's rights and stay out of the war. It was Woodrow Wilson's outlook as well.

The affinity between Wilson and the public meant that where the public was either uncertain or deeply divided in its certainty, Wilson had a decisive influence. He was, in Patrick Devlin's words, "not only the President: he was the casting vote of the nation."[6] At home as well as abroad, he held the balance of power over the issues of war and peace. The crucial decisions were his alone to make, for his was the only voice the nation as a whole listened to during the years of neutrality. In reaching these decisions, Wilson kept to a position of virtual isolation as few presidents have. It was a position he seemed almost to celebrate. In an address on Abraham Lincoln in September 1916 Wilson commented on Lincoln' s isolation in terms he must have felt were almost equally applicable to himself. They are worth quoting at length:

> I nowhere get the impression in any narrative or reminiscence
> [of Lincoln] that the writer had in fact penetrated to the heart of
> his mystery, or that any man could penetrate to the heart of it.
> That brooding spirit had no real familiars. I get the impression that
> it never spoke out in complete self-revelation, and that it could
> not reveal itself completely to anyone. It was a very lonely spirit that
> looked out from underneath those shaggy brows and compre-
> hended men without fully communing with them, as if, in spite of
> all its genial efforts at comradeship, it dwelt apart, saw its visions
> of duty where no man looked on. There is a very holy and very ter-
> rible isolation for the conscience of every man who seeks to read
> the destiny in affairs for others as well as for himself, for a nation as
> well as for individuals. That privacy no man can intrude upon. That
> lonely search of the spirit for the right perhaps no man can assist.[7]

The "very holy and very terrible isolation" that Wilson saw in Lincoln, he evidently saw in himself as well. That isolation was dictated not only by the "lonely search of the spirit for the right" but also by character. Wilson's character was such that it could not have accommodated a strong figure able and willing to engage the president on the great issues of war and peace. It could not do so for the reason that Wilson believed he found Lincoln unable to do so: the inescapable isolation of the prophet, of the "man who seeks to read the destiny in affairs for others as well as for himself." Prophetic visions are not achieved through the bureaucratic routine that marks the normal functioning of government. They are not achieved through committees that operate by consensus. They are reached alone, in communion with the self. Once reached, they are not subject to analysis and criticism.

The crucial decisions Wilson made during the years of neutrality often seemed to partake of the prophetic vision. This is not to say that they were made without prior consultation with advisers, though occasionally it came close to this. Nor is it to say that Wilson's small circle of advisers was without any influence on the decisions the president finally made. No man, not even the iron-willed prophet, is an island unto himself. It is to say that there were strict limits to the give and take over policy Wilson would tolerate from the few who did assist him. House came the closest in testing these limits. But even the colonel's willingness to engage the president on matters Wilson felt strongly about was never pushed very far for fear of jeopardizing a unique position. Unlike Washington, Wilson would not have tolerated a Hamilton. Once, House records, he observed to Wilson that a mark of Washington's greatness was the role he allowed Hamilton to play in his administration. Wilson agreed and remarked that "he [Wilson] always sought advice." "I almost laughed at this statement," wrote the one man who did presume to advise Wilson, though usually with due caution.[8]

Wilson's unwillingness to seek advice, his disinclination to hear what was unwelcome to him, and even more, his penchant for taking an immediate dislike to those who told him what he did not wish to hear were traits recognized by all who served him.[9] Unlike Jefferson, to whom he may in many respects be compared, Wilson did not have a Madison or a Gallatin. Wilson's ambassador in London, Walter Page, an acute observer for all his pro-British bias, noted in the fall of 1916, on his first visit to America since the outbreak of the war, that Wilson "has no real companions. Nobody talks to him freely and frankly. I've never known quite such a condition in American life."[10] What Page observed, others had as well. Wilson's isolation was without parallel among American presidents. Had the case been otherwise, had Wilson been disposed to treat with others on the basis of give and take, the outcome of this critical period in American and world history might have been quite different.

The centrality of Wilson in the history of World War I is a commonplace. The story of America's journey from neutrality to war to a failed peace is largely the story of Woodrow Wilson's journey from neutrality to war to a failed peace. Winston Churchill memorialized for later generations Wilson's position in declaring that it was "upon the workings of this man's mind and spirit to the exclusion of almost every other factor" that the "history of the world depended, during the awful period of Armageddon."[11] What Churchill wrote several years after the war was recognized at the time. What does Wilson think? What will the president do? Those questions were asked repeatedly both at home and abroad during the years of neutrality. They were asked in May 1915, when a German submarine sank the Cunard Liner *Lusitania* and 124 Americans perished, and they were asked in every subsequent crisis brought on by German acts at sea that were seen to violate America's neutral rights.

They are still asked today, and not only because of the enormous power Wilson wielded in so critical a period of history. They are also asked because of the assumption that this period of history might have turned out differently than it did. The continuing fascination with Wilson is difficult to account for without this assumption. After all, if the course events took was determined by the operation of great and impersonal forces, why should we be particularly interested in what prompted Wilson to act as he did? Apart from setting down what he did, our interest would be directed to analyzing the forces that presumably determined his actions. Yet this has not satisfied historians despite the prevailing conviction in post–World War II historiography that Wilson's neutrality course could scarcely have been other than it was. The search for the essential Wilson belies that conviction, at least in part, and is to be accounted for by the belief, however inarticulate, that events might well have turned out otherwise. Certainly, the small circle of assistants around Wilson thought so on more than one occasion. They did, for example, during the critical period in December 1916, when the prospect that the United States might find itself siding with Germany against the Allies seemed to them very real. Had the German government played its cards differently, had it responded to Wilson's peace note differently and postponed its decision to undertake unrestricted submarine warfare, the fears of Wilson's advisers might well have been realized. The American government might have found itself ranged against the Allies.

If the choices Wilson made were determinative, it is nevertheless the case that the "workings of this man's mind and spirit" remain in many respects as obscure today as they were to contemporaries who worked closely with him. There are significant limits to what we know about the inner man and the deeper springs of his actions. Wilson left no diary. Nor did he leave much in the way of private memoranda. The unpublished prolegomenon to a peace note, written at the end of November 1916, is a rare example to the contrary. Wilson's correspondence with the small circle around him dealing with foreign policy provides some insight, but often not enough for the student to be confident of what it was that moved him to a given act or policy. Wilson seldom revealed himself to those who served him. On a number of occasions, it is true, he did so with House. But even with House his intimacies had distinct limits. The love and support Wilson needed and expected from the few male friends he had in his life do not seem to have evoked the self-revelation that is normally associated with real friendship. One of House's recurring complaints is that Wilson seldom told his closest counselor what he really thought and was going to do. "The President is consulting none of his immediate entourage," House recorded in his diary during the *Sussex* crisis, in April 1916, and those around Wilson were "as ignorant of his intentions as the man in the street."[12] It was a familiar refrain in the critical months leading up to the decision to intervene in the war.

Occasionally one may get an insight into Wilson's "mind and spirit" through the letters he wrote to friends, particularly to women friends. His letters in the fall and winter of 1914 to Mary Hulbert, for example, reveal a man who remained terribly lonely and depressed following the death of his first wife, Ellen, in August 1914. "My own individual life has gone utterly to pieces. I do not care for anything that affects me."[13] His outlook was to change radically in the spring of 1915 after he met Edith Galt, whom he married in December of that year. But the period from August 1914 to March 1915 was very important in setting America's neutrality policy. Thereafter change would prove difficult. In some measure, Wilson's letters in this period point to a president unable to give neutrality policy the clear and unremitting attention it warranted. The many love letters written to Edith Galt in August and September 1915 are still more informative and significant in the light they throw on the president's outlook during the *Arabic* crisis. They show a Wilson who plainly dreads the prospect of war but who is unwilling to back away from a position that has brought him to the brink of war.

There are, of course, Wilson's public addresses. A case may be made that Wilson revealed himself as much in his public utterances as he did privately. It may even be that he revealed himself more in speaking to the public. Wilson's authorized biographer, Ray Stannard Baker, a journalist who knew and admired the president, wrote that Wilson "could be more intimate and confidential with five thousand people than with one."[14] With one person or a few Wilson was normally quite reserved and even diffident. Only seldom did he appear open and forthcoming. Again it is House who testifies to this. In a conversation with Wilson in December 1916 House put forth a suggestion on how to deal with the indemnity issue in a treaty of peace. "This interested him," House recorded in his diary, "but he did not express an opinion; something he seldom does."[15]

When he addressed the public, however, Wilson gave a quite different impression: he seemed to be at ease and more forthcoming. No doubt this was due in large part to his great gifts as a public speaker. In an age that still placed a high value on oratory, Wilson was without peer among public figures. The stories about how his words moved audiences are legion. They moved those who thought themselves sophisticated and even those who heartily disliked him. Whether they provided lasting instruction as well is another matter. Had they done so, the public would not have been as confused as it undoubtedly was in the end over the reasons for America's intervention in the war. Walter Lippmann, a brilliant young member of editorial board of the *New Republic,* who went from skepticism to admiration to opposition toward Wilson, was on the mark when he wrote in his skeptical period: "His mind is like a light which destroys the outlines of what it plays upon; there is much illumination, but you see very little."[16] But even Lippmann was moved more than once by Wilson's public pronouncements.

The question remains how much Wilson revealed when he addressed the public. His adversaries regularly accused him of dissembling, and never more so than over neutrality, but the charge is difficult to credit. That Wilson imputed an exaggerated sense of idealism to the nation, that he appealed to the vanity of the American people as few presidents have done, and that he benefited politically from the flattering portrait he repeatedly drew is certainly the case. Yet he did this with what almost seemed to be a transparent sincerity. Indeed, Wilson probably dissembled less when dealing directly with the public than did most political leaders of the period. This was almost certainly the case with respect to issues of concern in these pages. As already remarked, on the great questions of war and peace Wilson's views were close to the public's views. Even if he had been given to dissembling, there was no need for him to do so. This was not the case with his principal political adversaries, Theodore Roosevelt and Henry Cabot Lodge. Given their pro-interventionist position, they had a need to dissemble to a public that to the end of the neutrality period did not share their outlook.

Wilson's public candor had its limits. Why he acted as he did in many instances must, in the end, remain little more than speculative. The record, written and spoken, takes the student only so far, often not nearly far enough. There is irony in this, since Wilson appears to have been meticulous in keeping as much as possible of the written record of his presidency. Yet the man who saved nearly everything left of himself very little.

Wilson's foreign-policy assistants made up a small circle. When the war broke out, it included Colonel Edward M. House, who held no official position; William Jennings Bryan, the secretary of state; and Robert Lansing, the counselor to the State Department and second in command to Bryan. Among the envoys to the principal European states the most important was Walter Hines Page, Wilson's ambassador to London. Apart from the departure of Bryan in June 1915 and the addition of Frank L. Polk, who took over the number two position at the State Department after Lansing was appointed secretary, the composition of the circle of advisers did not change.

A group that seldom numbered more than three or four, then, either saw or communicated with the president on a fairly frequent basis. In the White House there was no one who assisted Wilson on foreign policy, the staff comprising the president's personal physician, Cary T. Grayson; a private secretary, Joseph P. Tumulty; two assistant secretaries; and several persons who performed clerical functions. Grayson was close to Wilson, who treated him in many ways like the son he never had, but played no role in affairs of state. On infrequent occasions Grayson did venture an opinion to House about his powerful patient, but this was all. Tumulty, on the other hand, did occasionally intrude into the realm of foreign policy, particularly when diplomatic issues had a strong impact on domestic politics. Tumulty, in addition to controlling access to the president, was Wilson's principal link with Congress and the press. He informed the president, often gratuitously, of the state of public opinion. And he was in constant touch with officials in the party. As might be expected, Tumulty's "advice" on foreign policy was generally conditioned by his reading of the political scene at home. Though he was an important member of the president's entourage, he was in no real sense concerned with diplomatic affairs. Considered from the perspective of a present-day observer, Wilson can be said to have had no staff that dealt with foreign policy on a continuing basis. Nor was the absence of a White House staff compensated by the State Department, then a modest establishment befitting a second- or third-rate power.

Although Wilson inherited an inadequate foreign-policy establishment, the question persists whether he would have made effective use of one more satisfactory. He seems to have made little use of the resources the State Department did have to offer. During the period of neutrality he took virtually no steps to create a more adequate mechanism for the conduct of foreign policy. At the outset of the war, Lansing constituted a joint State and Navy Neutrality Board to deal with the technical issues of neutrality. For the rest, almost nothing was done. Wilson did not create, for example, an advisory body that could help him on substantive issues of policy. He did not do so for the simple reason that he would have had little use for such a body, just as he had little use for the body he did have, his cabinet. Wilson worked alone for the most part. When he was faced with a difficult foreign-policy issue, an advisory group would only have been an unwelcome distraction. In a great crisis his need for isolation became all the more pronounced. What was necessary and sufficient was that he think through the issue and satisfy himself that the right solution had been reached. He might seek the advice, more often really the support, of House. In the closing months of the neutrality period he even appeared to rely less on House's support. In undertaking his peace initiative of December 1916 he acted quite alone. So, too, in late February and early March 1917 he reached his decision on intervention in isolation.

If Wilson worked largely alone, he nevertheless required some assistance. Since he often did not clearly grasp the legal issues of neutrality, he had need to call upon Lansing and the State Department's legal experts. Since he was disinclined to treat directly with the representatives of the belligerent states, and only rarely did so, yet was also loathe to use normal diplomatic channels for some of his most important initiatives, he had need of a trusted agent. House was that agent. And, of course, House was also the person with whom he could, when so disposed, exchange views and from whom he sought sympathy and reassurance in his otherwise lonely position.

House apart, Wilson was seldom content with his small circle of assistants. Not long after the war began, he complained to House that Bryan was unsuitable for the office of secretary of state, though he did not know what could be done. Perhaps Bryan would resign because of some policy disagreement.[17] Bryan did eventually do so in June 1915. His successor, Lansing, scarcely proved more satisfactory to Wilson. Wilson's unhappiness with Lansing was apparent by spring 1916 and would grow. The president's ambassadors were equally unsatisfactory to him. Page, in London, was increasingly a source of irritation and frustration to Wilson because of his strong identification with the Allied cause and because he openly voiced disagreement with Wilson's neutrality policy. By the summer of 1916 the president refused even to read his ambassador's letters, delegating this unwelcome task to his wife. Wilson's unhappiness with Page was exceeded only by his impatience in dealing with his ambassador in Berlin, James W. Gerard, whom he considered a complete incompetent. Whereas Page was unwilling to represent Wilson, Gerard was incapable of doing so.

Only House seemed to remain above criticism. But there are signs that by the spring of 1916 Wilson's confidence in the judgment of even his "dearest friend," as he addressed House in letters, had begun to wane. The president could not have been pleased with the results of House's mediation efforts in London. Those efforts had eventuated in an understanding, embodied in the famous House-Grey memorandum, that committed the United States to the Allied cause far in excess of what the president was prepared to accept. Although the understanding was never acted upon, Wilson's view of House in all likelihood underwent a subtle though significant change. The relationship between the two men at the close of 1916 was not what it had been only a year earlier. In drafting his peace note of December 1916, Wilson proceeded without the colonel. In his letters to House, "dearest friend" became "dear House."

The singularity of Wilson's experience with his advisers is striking. In the case of perhaps no other president in the nation's history can there be found a real parallel. Even so, was Wilson justified in the judgments he made? The answer has seemed clearest in the case of Bryan. Bryan was unsuitable as secretary of state. Political necessity had led to his appointment. He had no qualifications for the position. As secretary he was often an embarrassment to Wilson, given his startling ignorance of diplomatic issues and his insistence upon continuing to give public lectures for pay. The press made Bryan an object of ridicule, as did the Washington political community. Wilson, though defending Bryan in the beginning, finally came to agree with those who called for Bryan's resignation.

The president changed his mind about Bryan, however, only after the war began. The record shows that prior to the war he and Bryan had had no serious disagreements over policy and, indeed, had worked together rather well. Bryan's idealism appealed to Wilson. As idealists they were quite close, but as practical men who had to come to terms with the world as it was, not as it ought to have been, they differed greatly. At least Wilson thought so. Bryan was an idealist, absolutely sincere but utterly naive. This was presumably what made him dangerous in the end. By contrast, Wilson, as he thought of himself and as his admirers then and later have thought of him, was the model of the practical idealist.

Yet the contrast did not seem too glaring or burdensome to Wilson before the outbreak of the war. It was the travail of neutrality that brought the differences between the two men to the surface and led Wilson to voice his dissatisfaction with Bryan to House in December 1914. Bryan's great object, one to which he was ready to subordinate all else, was to remain out of the war. "He suffers from a singular sort of moral blindness," Wilson wrote to Edith Galt shortly after Bryan's resignation in June 1915, "and is as passionate in error as in the right courses he has taken."[18] Wilson meant that Bryan was ready to sacrifice neutral rights in order to stay out of the war. It was true.

At the same time, it was also true that Bryan advocated positions Wilson was subsequently to take. It was Bryan who urged mediation on the president at the outset of the war and, in doing so, articulated the idea of a peace without victory.[19] It was Bryan as well who urged a course upon the president in the first year of the war that was essentially the course Wilson followed in his peace initiative of December 1916.[20] Bryan's abortive efforts to find a modus vivendi in the belligerents' conduct of the war at sea, one that would obviate the threat to American neutrality held out by the submarine, were ill-founded and clumsy. His occasional diplomatic indiscretions violated the first rule of the diplomatist. Yet he saw almost from the start, as others did not, where the Wilson administration's initial response to Germany's war-zone declaration, of early February 1915, would ultimately lead. It was Bryan, alone among Wilson's close advisers, who argued in the spring of 1915 that the administration's position, if persisted in, ran the strong risk of war with Germany since it required, in effect, that Germany abandon her manner of conducting submarine warfare against Allied shipping.[21] Unalterably opposed as he was to a course that ran a strong risk of war with Germany, Bryan urged Wilson to refrain from demanding German observance of neutral claims—principally the claimed right of American citizens to travel in safety on Allied vessels—that were in any event a matter of uncertainty and dispute. When the crisis brought on by the sinking of the *Lusitania* resulted in the American note demanding that Germany abandon the use of the submarine altogether, Bryan, unwilling to sign the note, resigned.

If ever a cabinet resignation resulted from a difference in principle, and one that reflected the deepest convictions of the departing official, this was it. Bryan had not wanted to leave. To the contrary, he had wanted to remain as secretary of state. Nor did he leave because Wilson had repeatedly rejected his advice in favor of his subordinates' counsel. Whatever his many faults and shortcomings, and some were monumental, Bryan was not a small man. Generous to a fault, he bore no resentment toward the man who had successfully opposed his position before the president and who would succeed him. Bryan was always disposed to forgive and forget, always ready to give the other, whether friend or foe, his due. In these respects, as in so many others, he differed greatly from Wilson. Critics who decried Bryan's ignorance and his boundless naiveté nevertheless liked him personally in a way they did not and could not like Wilson.

Bryan's resignation was transparently a matter of principle and conscience. If anyone could be expected to honor and appreciate that, it was Woodrow Wilson. Yet Wilson did not take the resignation well. To Edith Galt he wrote: "The impression upon my mind of Mr. B's retirement is a very painful one *now*. It is always painful to feel that any thinking man of disinterested motive, who has been your comrade and confidant, has turned away from you and set his hand against yours; and it is hard to be fair and not think that the motive is something sinister. I have been deserted before. The wound does not heal, with me, but neither does it cripple."[22] Wilson wrote these words six months after he had told House he wanted Bryan out. He wrote them after months of repeatedly rejecting Bryan's counsel. House, not Bryan, had been Wilson's confidant, as Bryan well knew and told Wilson upon resigning. Why Wilson could not simply acknowledge that Bryan's resignation was the result of an honest and serious difference is difficult to understand. Perhaps it only reflected the well-known Wilson trait of finding in any and every conflict unworthy motives on the other side's part. Earlier that year, in a struggle that had arisen in Congress over legislation to permit the government to acquire interned German ships, Wilson had written to a friend, "You cannot know to what lengths men like Root and Lodge are going, who I once thought had consciences but now know have none."[23] Bryan had a conscience, and a large one. Wilson knew this as well as anyone, yet he found it hard to believe that Bryan's motive in resigning did not hide something sinister.

Bryan was the first and the last of Wilson's close foreign-policy assistants to resign. He was not the last, only the first, to entertain serious differences with Wilson over the nation's neutrality policy. But Bryan was quite open in voicing his differences with Wilson, just as he was candid in saying what he thought would be the consequences of the neutrality policy the president had adopted. Wilson's other advisers would be less forthcoming when in disagreement. Even Page would not be as straightforward over his differences with Wilson, though in the end he would still lose all influence. House, though also differing from the president over his neutrality policy, and increasingly so as time went by, was almost always circumspect in voicing these differences, for he knew better than anyone Wilson's limited tolerance of disagreement. Perhaps the most circumspect of all was Bryan's successor, at least at the outset. In time Lansing would come to openly entertain differences with Wilson that were almost as great as those the president had entertained with Bryan. Indeed, on the continuum from nonintervention to intervention, Lansing would stand to Wilson as Wilson had stood to Bryan. Nor would the irony end there. Unlike Bryan, Lansing would not resign over differences with the president. He would only occasionally threaten to do so in his private memoranda to himself.

Wilson had appointed Bryan out of necessity. His political debts to Bryan, Bryan's standing in the Democratic Party, the need for party unity, and Bryan's ardent wish to be secretary of state had led to his appointment. In Lansing's case these considerations were absent, even desire, since Lansing had not thought he would be a serious candidate for so high an office. Wilson had not wanted him at first. House, though he scarcely knew Lansing, had quietly urged his appointment. Aware that Wilson did not think Lansing "big enough" for the job, House wrote to the president that Lansing "could be used to better advantage than a stronger man." A stronger man might have ideas of his own and be intent on pushing them. Lansing, the colonel thought, would be "a man with not too many ideas of his own and one that will be entirely guided by you without unnecessary argument."[24] In finally approving Lansing as secretary, Wilson agreed that he was "practically his own Secretary of State and Lansing would not be troublesome by obtruding or injecting his own ideas."[25] To both men Lansing's appointment seemed convenient. House would get rid of his "Bryan problem," no longer having to look over his shoulder when usurping the functions of the secretary of state.[26] Wilson would get over *his* "Bryan problem," no longer having to contend with a secretary who disagreed with his neutrality policy and who still had a substantial political following.

To the outside world, Bryan's successor seemed to fulfill House's and Wilson's private expectations. Even within the Wilson cabinet, let alone the Washington community, Lansing was seen as little more than the president's obedient law clerk. The impression was deceiving. Although in public and even in cabinet meetings Lansing was generally quiet, reticent, and even diffident, he was also a man of strong convictions, as his confidential memoranda show. Foreign diplomats Lansing found guilty of some transgression could also attest to this. In appearance retiring,

Lansing was in fact stubborn to the point of being willful. Unlike the pragmatic and pliable House, Lansing seldom abandoned a position.

The widespread belief that despite his high position Lansing was unimportant arose in large part from his concentration on, some thought obsession with, legal issues. Again in contrast to Lansing, House was seen to deal with the larger political issues. But Lansing's concerns went well beyond the narrowly legal. And to the extent that they did focus on the legal, they were more important than was commonly perceived. Neutrality was, after all, a legal institution, defined by certain legal rights and duties. A neutral's conflicts with belligerents, whatever the political interests at stake, had to be expressed in legal terms, that is, in the form of legal claims and counterclaims. A neutral government might contend, as the American government often did, that its honor and dignity were at stake in a dispute with a belligerent; even so, these interests were at stake because the neutral's rights had presumably been violated and the alleged transgressor had refused to make proper redress. In America's case, legal issues were particularly significant given the president's essential position throughout the period of neutrality. Wilson did not raise the issue of the nation's security during this period, at least not in a way that tied security to the course and outcome of the war. He also refused to see any difference between the moral claims of the two sides. Humanitarian issues aside, this left America's rights and duties as a neutral to contend with the belligerents, and although the violation of rights was seen to raise larger issues of honor, dignity, and prestige, it did so through the medium of the law—such as it was.

In becoming secretary, Lansing thus had a built-in though frequently overlooked advantage. He had been counselor to the Department of State. He was acknowledged to be an expert on international law, not enjoying the renown of his illustrious predecessor, John Bassett Moore, but still having a solid reputation in the field. He had spent most of his earlier years in international legal work. During the months following the outbreak of war the legal issues of neutrality had been critical, and although his positions did not always carry the day, they did so often enough. While he started off on the wrong foot as counselor by insisting that the United States call upon the belligerents to accept a still unratified codification of naval warfare, the Declaration of London, he recovered quickly enough. His elaborate defense of America's neutral position in late 1914 against charges of partiality toward the Allies pleased Wilson, as did the hard view he took at the outset toward German claims to the right to establish extended war zones within which submarines might take reprisal measures against Allied shipping. Whether the fateful American response of February 10, 1915, to the German announcement setting forth such claim was Lansing's doing, including even the term *strict accountability,* is not clear from the historical record. At the least, he played a significant role in drawing up the response. In the period between the February note and the crisis that arose in May over the sinking of the *Lusitania,* Lansing's was the voice Wilson listened to for instruction on America's rights as a neutral. That voice had little doubt that Germany's conduct of the war at sea was not only wanton and indiscriminate but a deliberate affront to the United States.

In appointing Lansing as secretary of state, Wilson had nevertheless chosen someone whose views were opposed to his own. Although Wilson had earlier approved of most of counselor Lansing's legal positions on America's neutral rights, he had not done so on the assumption that they would sooner or later lead to war with Germany. This had been Bryan's position, not Wilson's. What Wilson might have done had he thought the course he was following would eventuate in intervention must remain speculative. Certainly his subsequent behavior strongly suggests that he would have been much more hesitant to take positions from which retreat would later prove so difficult. Lansing was another matter. Quite persuaded that the defense of neutral rights was identical with the nation's honor and dignity, Lansing had also reached the conclusion by the late spring of 1915 that American intervention on the Allied side would prove necessary should it once become apparent that Germany was gaining the upper hand in the struggle. "I have come to the conclusion," Lansing wrote in a private memo shortly after becoming secretary, "that the German Government is utterly hostile to all nations with democratic institutions because those who compose it see in democracy a menace to absolutism and the defeat of the German ambition for world domination." A German triumph would threaten democracy everywhere. Even a war that ended in a draw would vindicate the German cause, since it would establish Germany as the equal in power to the rest of Europe. The danger was great, but the remedy was plain: "It is that Germany must not be permitted to win this war and to break even, though to prevent it this country is forced to take an active part. This ultimate necessity must be constantly in our minds in all our controversies with the belligerents. American public opinion must be prepared for the time, which may come, when we cast aside our neutrality and become one of the champions of democracy."[27]

These words summed up Lansing's credo with respect to the war, one that with the passage of time would be ever more tenaciously held. Wilson had chosen a secretary of state who was a determined interventionist. Lansing did not always act consistently with his stated convictions on the deeper significance of the war. The president was, after all, a man whose views required a measure of dissimulation on the part of those who served him. As time went on and Wilson became more intent on remaining out of the conflict, this need for deception increased. A substantial degree of deception was, in any event, built into Lansing's position by virtue of his conviction that public opinion demanded an apparent impartiality in dealing with the belligerents. Lansing was sensitive to what he considered the requirements of public opinion. His presumption of expertise in gauging these requirements more than once angered the president.

An ingrained habit of seeing issues in legal terms also led to positions that at times appeared to contradict Lansing's commitment to the Allied cause. The secretary's pursuit of "cases," as Page contemptuously characterized Lansing's approach, was often directed against Allied transgressions of America's neutral rights and presented in a heavy-handed way that ignored Allied sensibilities. House, who more than once defended Lansing to Wilson, thought him lacking in tact. In fact, it was more than that: Lansing seemed to be afflicted with a kind of schizophrenia; he appeared to live in two worlds, the legal and the "other" world. His defense was that his duty did not permit him to overlook violations of the nation's rights, even violations by the Allies, and that the public would not have sanctioned such a course. There was a good deal to be said for this defense, particularly when considered alongside Lansing's habit of submitting protest notes to the Allies in which "everything was submerged in verbosity"[28]—an art in which Lansing was expert— and nothing was brought to what might prove a dangerous head. Even so, there are occasions that can scarcely be accommodated, if at all, on these grounds and must be seen either as gratuitous or as attempts on Lansing's part to placate his all-powerful client.

Lansing's lapses notwithstanding, his strong Allied sympathies are apparent, as are the pro-Allied policies he nearly always urged Wilson to follow. The war, he was persuaded, was a great struggle between freedom and absolutism, democracy and autocracy. In this struggle nothing must be spared to defeat the German drive for world empire. Lansing immediately feared German designs in Mexico, Haiti, Santo Domingo, and elsewhere in Latin America. But a German victory would have much broader consequences. A Germany that was not utterly defeated would soon seek to renew the struggle by allying its forces with Russia and Japan, the two empires that were almost as hostile to democracy as

Germany and entertained similar ambitions of territorial expansion. The three great empires "would constitute an almost irresistible coalition against the nations with republican and liberal monarchical institutions. It would be the old struggle of absolutism against democracy, an even greater struggle than the one now in progress." The success of such a coalition would mean a new division of the world and "the turning back of the hands of human progress two centuries."[29]

This dark vision of a future consequent upon a German victory was sketched out in July 1915, shortly after Lansing became secretary of state. It was written as a private memorandum, an exercise in self-edification. Lansing had no apparent reason to persuade himself that the stakes of the war were greater than he indeed believed them to be. Unlike Wilson, he did not look with dread upon America's intervention in the war. He appears to have shared almost none of the president's fears with respect to the domestic consequences of war. Wilson had a profound psychological and spiritual need to find a special justification for going to war. Lansing had no comparable need. It was not that he somehow gloried in war and thus welcomed it. It appears that he genuinely believed in what he thought to be the threat held out by a German victory, or for that matter a peace without victory.

Lansing's reputation has been that of a realist par excellence. One side of him was just that, but the other side was that of the ideologue, and it is this side that appears to have been dominant. Considerations of power were never excluded, but they were subordinated to ideological considerations. In his desire to see Germany utterly beaten, there was no apparent concern on Lansing's part about the effect this might have on the future balance of power in Europe. He evidently believed that Europe's peace and security were dependent primarily on the kind of government the European states had after the war, not upon the balance of power that would emerge. In a world made up of democratic states the balance of power would be reduced to a minor role since democracies were neither aggressive nor unjust. The essential of peace—permanent peace—was not that power should be balanced but that all nations should be politically liberalized.

Lansing was to make almost a litany of these themes. House too emphasized the need to see in democracy an essential condition of permanent peace, but he was also sensitive to balance-of-power calculations. Page's position was closer to Lansing's, though Page saw the "war for democracy" theme almost entirely in terms of an Anglo-American partnership. That Wilson did not embrace Lansing's view was a matter of wonderment and anxiety to the secretary. "The amazing thing to me,"

Lansing noted in a September 1916 memorandum, "is that the President . . . does not seem to grasp the full significance of the war or the principles at issue. . . . That German imperialistic ambitions threaten free institutions everywhere apparently has not sunk very deeply into his mind. For six months I have talked about the struggle between Autocracy and Democracy, but do not see that I have made any great impression. However, I shall keep on talking."[30]

Lansing did keep on talking, to Wilson's growing annoyance. The president was never as oblivious to the principle that preoccupied Lansing as the secretary believed. As early as December 1914 Wilson had expressed the view that even though responsibility for the war was not Germany's alone, one condition of the war's settlement was that "the Government of Germany must be profoundly changed."[31] Whatever the precise meaning to be read into this statement, it evidently carried the implication that Germany's government was in some measure a cause of the war. If it did not go nearly as far as Lansing, this was because Wilson wanted above all else to remain out of the war. To a mind of Wilson's cast, this desire could only be jeopardized by accepting the distinction Lansing drew. If that distinction were once fully embraced, Wilson's view of the belligerents' moral equality would have to be abandoned. But abandonment would in turn dictate taking sides, at any rate in moral terms. In Wilson's view, this step would threaten to undermine his entire position. Once the war was seen as Lansing saw it, how could the president act as an impartial mediator? If the struggle were one between the forces of oppression and the forces of freedom, how could he champion a peace without victory? Indeed, if the moral judgment was the ultimate judgment, as Wilson believed, how could the abandonment of moral equivalence fail to result sooner or later in America's intervention?

If even House seems not to have appreciated the reasons that bound Wilson to his stand on the moral equivalence of the belligerents (House persistently treated the matter as one on which Wilson might readily yield), it is hardly surprising that Lansing did not do so. House was more sensitive than Lansing. Moreover, House knew Wilson as Lansing did not. Even if this had not been the case, it is doubtful that Lansing would have behaved very differently. Over time, Lansing became not only an ever more ardent interventionist but one apparently willing to pay any price to see Germany decisively beaten. He had almost none of Wilson's deep anxieties about the costs of going to war, though he thought these costs would be considerable. On the eve of the nation's entering into the war, Lansing wrote to himself: "Things have turned out right and the days of anxiety and uncertainty are over. . . . It may take two or three years. It may even take five years. It may cost a million Americans; it may cost five million. However long it may take, however many men it costs we must go through with it."[32]

Nor did Lansing share Wilson's aspiration to reform international society by the inauguration of a new diplomacy. Despite Lansing's conviction that the great essential of permanent peace was the political liberalization of all nations, his view of diplomacy and of America's interests was thoroughly conservative and conventional. He was a nationalist in the American grain, quite content to retain the historic bases and interests of the nation's foreign policy. His devotion to international law and the strict observance of treaty commitments was not such as to stand in the way of interest. His commitment to the Monroe Doctrine, and accordingly to American predominance in the Western Hemisphere, was complete, though he was not opposed to Wilson's and House's modest efforts to multilateralize the Monroe Doctrine so long as its essential character remained unchanged. An acute sensitivity to what he perceived as any infringement on the nation's honor and dignity marked all of Lansing's actions. He too believed that America was the last and best hope of the world. Yet this belief did not lead Lansing, as it did Wilson, to dream of America serving as order giver to the world. Lansing thought that Wilson's "dream of possessing a beneficent domination over the nations, both belligerent and neutral, had become apparently the great underlying impulse to Mr. Wilson's future course of action" but that it was entirely futile. The secretary opposed the president's efforts to create what he later termed "a world federation to preserve international peace."[33]

If these were in outline Lansing's views, they were coupled with what became soon after his appointment a possessive regard for his position. Lansing believed that *he* was secretary of state, in fact as well as in form. His awe of the office and of his suddenly elevated position lasted only several weeks. Appointed in early July 1915, by late August he was intent on pursuing a course toward Germany that went further than Wilson intended. In the crisis that arose in late August over the German sinking of the British liner *Arabic,* in which two Americans perished, Lansing showed an independence that scarcely conformed to the picture of the obedient law clerk intimidated by his high office. Intent on forcing the German government to capitulate on the submarine issue, Lansing informed the German ambassador that unless Berlin "frankly declared that there would be no more surprise attacks on vessels carrying passengers, and lived up to that declaration, the United States would certainly declare war on Germany."[34] The warning, indeed ultimatum, was given without the president's authorization. Its failure, as Lansing acknowledged in a private memorandum written two days earlier, might well have led to his disavowal by Wilson. Lansing had taken this course because he was convinced that it was "the only way to avoid national humiliation." But, he added, "we cannot enter the war with the country divided as it is at present. So if my declaration is challenged I cannot make good."[35]

As matters turned out, Lansing's bluff was not called. His good fortune was to have had a German ambassador, Count Johann von Bernstorff, who proved to be very cooperative because he was determined to avoid war. In this context, the significance of the episode is to be found, not in the terms by which it was settled, terms that left unresolved most of the issues that had brought the two states to the brink of war, but in Lansing's behavior. The secretary presumably had acted as he did to avoid national humiliation. Yet if his bluff had been called by Berlin, the choice would have been either war or national humiliation. Wilson was not prepared to go to war. Though the president endorsed a course of action that clearly ran the risk of breaking relations with Germany, he did not equate a break with war. Lansing was considerably in front of Wilson. He knew this, yet he acted.

The *Arabic* crisis revealed a secretary of state with a propensity for sailing close to the wind and determined to pursue a course he considered required by the nation's interests even if the president was not, or not yet, so persuaded. Lansing's action foreshadowed a pattern that before the period of neutrality had come to an end would border on insubordination. Yet it seems that he did not see his acts for what they were. Even in the case of Wilson's peace initiative of December 1916, Lansing, both at the time and subsequently, refused to acknowledge that he had sought to undermine the president's chosen course, though any other interpretation of his behavior is difficult to credit. Perhaps he was sincere in this. If so, it was a sincerity based on the belief—an illusion, to be sure—that in acting independently he was doing what the president would have wanted done had the latter better understood the situation.

If Lansing indeed thought he was only slightly ahead of the president when acting on his own, he was not entirely to blame. In the first eight months of the war Wilson had given him no little encouragement for so thinking, having endorsed most of counselor Lansing's positions. Then, too, in the *Arabic* and *Sussex* crises the new secretary of state was the official out in front, constantly urging a harder position on a president who, now increasingly sensitive to the direction in which his neutrality course was taking him, had begun to hesitate and to entertain increasing unease over the wisdom of that course. But the *Arabic* and *Sussex* crises ended in victories for the United States, victories due in no small measure to positions an unyielding Lansing had urged. Wilson, though willing enough to accept these victories, was nevertheless left ever more uneasy by them. Yet he was locked into a neutrality that could be substantially modified only with the greatest of difficulty, a neutrality that he had earlier committed himself to in terms that allowed little latitude.

In this simple fact lay Lansing's principal advantage and chief strength. He had only to act on the logic of the positions that defined the nation's neutrality after the spring of 1915. It was Wilson who increasingly sought to escape from what had become for him a labyrinth affording no satisfactory way out. Wherever he turned, he saw not only the belligerents but his secretary of state blocking the exits.

Lansing's role in Wilson's diplomacy has generally been underestimated. By contrast, House's role, though considerable, has often been overestimated. Certainly it was so at the time. The picture drawn of House by contemporaries was that of the publicly withdrawn but all-powerful friend and adviser whose dominant influence extended in almost every direction. The press referred to House as "The Silent Partner." House seldom failed to discourage the attention given him, for he sensed that sooner or later it must jeopardize his altogether distinctive standing with Wilson. Yet in the beginning, at least, the president seemed to encourage the popular impression of the colonel's position. To a journalist who questioned whether House had faithfully represented him on a given matter, Wilson famously replied: "Mr. House is my second personality. He is my independent self. His thoughts and mine are one."[36] In the twentieth century, no president so equated his persona with that of an assistant. But then in the twentieth century there was no relationship comparable to the relationship between Woodrow Wilson and Colonel House.

A Texan who had served as an adviser to several governors of that state, House had become a figure of some standing in the national Democratic Party. He had met Wilson in November 1911, at a time when the future president, then governor of New Jersey, was considering making a bid to be the Democratic Party's standard bearer in the 1912 presidential elections. The day following the meeting, House wrote to his brother-in-law: "He is not the biggest man I ever met, but he is one of the pleasantest and I would rather play with him than any other prospective candidate I have seen." House, having grown tired of Texas politics, was looking for a larger stage to satisfy his ambition. Unable himself to play the part he nevertheless aspired to, he had come to realize the necessity of doing so through someone who could. In Wilson he at once saw that he had "found both the man and the opportunity."[37]

A close relationship between the two men soon formed, a relationship Wilson appears to have entered into as eagerly as did House. By the time Wilson had become the president-elect, a year later, House had become his principal assistant and trusted adviser. As such, the colonel played an important part in helping Wilson fill the positions of his forthcoming administration. House took a hand in some of the diplomatic appointments. The ambassador to Great Britain, Walter Page, though a friend of Wilson's, was under a special obligation to House for his position. In time House's role, as measured by those in his debt, would grow. It will be recalled that when Bryan resigned, it was House who urged Lansing's appointment as secretary, something Lansing must have eventually learned, in all likelihood from House. Lansing's successor, Frank Polk, was a House man. The same was true of two assistant secretaries, William Phillips and Breckenridge Long. By late 1915 the upper reaches of the foreign-policy establishment bore House's imprint.

House served Wilson in a variety of roles. Viewed from the vantage point of today, he was the functional equivalent of what would be today the president's chief of staff and his national-security adviser. But House was also Wilson's chief diplomatic agent for treating with the European belligerents, a task that in turn led to his role as a principal collector and evaluator of intelligence on developments relating to the war. It was House who had direct relationships with the leading statesmen of Europe through his several European trips as well as through his considerable correspondence. With the British foreign secretary, Sir Edward Grey, he communicated directly in secret code, a practice that appealed to his penchant for intrigue. With the head of the British Naval Intelligence in the United States, William Wiseman, he enjoyed close personal contact. From London and Berlin, Page and Gerard wrote frequently to House, and House reciprocated.

House maintained an apartment in New York, where he lived except for summer months spent in New England. To the casual observer he might have appeared to lead a quiet life. In reality, virtually every European visitor to America of consequence made it a point to visit House. So also did the Washington diplomatic community when the need arose and House was unavailable in the capitol. In the course of the successive crises with Germany, Bernstorff became a frequent visitor. Not surprisingly, perhaps, House came to believe that *his* was the vantage point from which a war-torn world might best be seen. "I cannot begin to outline here what happens from day to day," he noted in his diary in March 1916, "how information from every quarter pours into this little unobtrusive study. I believe I am the only one who gets a view of the entire picture. Some get one corner, and some another, but I seem to have it all."[38]

The "little unobtrusive study" was roughly four hours by train from the Oval Office. With rare exception, House made the trip only when specifically requested by the president. Moreover, his trips to Washington were usually quite brief, House staying only long enough to confer with Wilson and to see those administration officials who might need his counsel. From May to October, he was absent altogether from the capitol, pleading his physical inability to suffer Washington weather. There is more than one exchange of letters in which Wilson laments House's absence from Washington and House pleads in reply reasons of health. Whether House's modus operandi was simply a subtle version of the conventional wisdom that absence makes the heart grow fonder (or advisers seem more valuable), it seems to have worked with the president. Wilson did not appear to consider House's curious routine— curious, at least, from the perspective of today—as a sign of disinterest or withdrawal. To someone as withdrawn as Wilson, the colonel's physical absence may even have been considered normal. The two men communicated with frequency by mail, the form of communication most congenial to the president. If the written word took time, this seemed less important than its greater precision. Besides, it was a different, more leisurely age. The frantic pace of the later twentieth century had yet to take hold.

How prepared was House for the roles he came to play? Although he had never graduated from any of the several colleges he attended, his early biographer, Charles Seymour, wrote that for House, in contrast with a presumably more parochial Woodrow Wilson, "foreign affairs were always of the first interest and importance" and that during his earlier years in Texas "he had never ceased to study current diplomacy."[39] The depth of House's study is not clear. What is clear is his interest in foreign affairs and his determination very early in the Wilson administration to concentrate on diplomatic matters. House belongs to the twentieth-century tradition of public-spirited men of independent means for whom domestic affairs came to hold little attraction but who found fulfillment in foreign policy. Still, a desire to participate in great affairs of state, to engage in momentous undertakings, did not thereby qualify House for the roles he sought and eventually gained. Though intelligent and perceptive, in dealing with those for whom diplomacy was a profession House was often at a disadvantage, something he seems not to have appreciated. His diary entries for his 1913–14 European trips are full of "successes" he enjoyed in talks with the statesmen of the great European powers. House saw himself instructing Europeans about matters on which he found them singularly obtuse. He frequently recorded the "conversions" he made to his point of view. When war came in the summer of 1914, he recalled his earlier predictions to the British of impending disaster and noted in his diary: "It was hard for them to think I was diagnosing the situation correctly. I take it I will have some reputation as a prophet with Sir Edward and his confreres."[40]

It was the first of House's mistaken judgments about a man whose mind he thought ran "nearly parallel" with his own. "I know in advance, just as I know with the President, what his views will be on almost any subject," he said of Grey.[41] Wilson apart, House's most important relationship during the years of neutrality was with Grey. From the outset, House was much taken with him. Only Page exceeded the colonel in his admiration for the British foreign secretary. "I feel complimented beyond measure," House once confided to his diary after an intimate conversation with Grey, "that he has such confidence in my discretion and integrity."[42] Grey was a person of considerable charm. Even more, his quiet demeanor and grave manner conveyed a man of great integrity. He had a way of persuading a listener that the latter enjoyed his complete confidence. To House, Grey's defense of the positions taken by London, whether on the need for the Allied blockade or the obstacles to mediation, was usually persuasive. A critic of the House-Grey relationship has wittily written: "One can imagine him [Grey] deploring some British action, but since this was the way the world worked, it had to be done. Grey could talk engagingly about sin without taint of sin himself, yet give the impression that human weakness was not alien to him. He fortified House's pro-Ally feelings."[43] It was not until quite late in the neutrality period that House began to take Grey's real measure. Grey had played an intricate game with him and had won. The British had sustained their blockade while putting off American schemes of mediation.

Even so, if Grey took House in, it was in part because House wanted to be taken in. For the most part, the colonel was a shrewd observer. His judgments, faithfully recorded in his diary, bear this out. He was wrong in his initial appraisal of Lansing, but then he hardly knew Lansing. He was close to the mark on many others. The composite portrait drawn of the president over many pages of the diary remains one of the most valuable we have. House was not an unkind or intolerant man. His comments on others show a considerable degree of empathy and understanding, even for those, like Page and Sir Cecil Spring Rice, the British ambassador in Washington, who became thorns in his side (and whom he urged Wilson to act against). On more than one occasion he interceded on behalf of those, such as Gerard, who had incurred the president's displeasure. He defended Lansing to the president when the secretary's relationship with Wilson had reached a precarious point. He even defended Bernstorff to Wilson by noting how difficult the ambassador's position had become. In turn, Bernstorff not only was grateful to House for the personal consideration House had shown him but became quite fond of the colonel. It was a tribute to House's role-playing ability—or, more generously, to his ability to separate the personal from the diplomatic side of a relationship—that to the very end Bernstorff seems not to have suspected that the man he dealt with most, and liked best, in the administration took positions toward Germany scarcely distinguishable from those of Lansing, with whom Bernstorff had a poor personal relationship.

While the intimacy between House and Wilson was very real, it was rooted in inequality. Although Wilson might occasionally speak of it almost in terms of a partnership, nevertheless if it was a partnership, it was one between unequals. Wilson was the dominant partner, for his was the power. House entertained no illusions on this score, at least not in the beginning. He knew his place and appreciated that he had to keep to it or risk losing all. He appreciated that Wilson could not be urged, let alone pressured, beyond a quite modest point. Advice had to be given with care. Wilson would never tolerate being lectured to, no matter what his state of ignorance on a given matter. If an idea or course of action could be insinuated in such a way as to lead the president to believe it was his own, so much the better. House records in his diary occasions in which his suggestions to Wilson turn up later as the president's.

At the outset, the inequality marking the relationship between the two men seems to have presented little difficulty for House. He looked upon Wilson with genuine respect and admiration as the authentic voice of liberal reform at home. Then the war began. By the summer of 1915 House had clearly begun to entertain serious doubts about Wilson's course, to question not only the substance but the methods marking the president's diplomacy. He became critical over what he deemed to be Wilson's failure to appreciate the importance of foreign policy, to take adequate measures of preparedness, and to determine upon a policy and remain steadfast in pursuing it. When the *Arabic* crisis broke in August and the president asked for House's advice, the colonel, who favored sending Bernstorff home and recalling Gerard, wrote in his diary: "I am surprised at the attitude he takes. He evidently will go to great lengths to avoid war. He should have determined his policy when he wrote his notes of February, May, June and July. . . . If we were fully prepared, I am sure Germany would not continue to provoke us."[44]

In the following months, these and yet other criticisms of the president by House grew more insistent until the moment, in the fall of 1916, when the flag of rebellion was covertly raised against a president no longer considered capable of carrying out his tasks. "The President must be guided," House reports saying to Frank Polk, "for he has no background of the European situation. He has always been more interested in domestic problems than in foreign affairs and I have never been able to get him to devote sufficient time to inform himself so as to act intelligently."[45] House had reached the point where he believed he knew better than Wilson, that he understood Europe and the war as the president did not.

House's rebelliousness reflected more than a mounting concern over the course taken by Wilson in late 1916. It may also be seen as an attempt, albeit an unconscious one, to seek a greater measure of equality in his relationship with the president. By the time of Wilson's reelection the colonel had begun to take the notion of partnership seriously, something he would never have done in the beginning. But then in the beginning he had seen Wilson in a different light. In the more than two years that had followed the outbreak of the war Wilson's stature had diminished in House's eyes. He still thought, as he wrote in June 1915, "that Woodrow Wilson is the greatest asset the world has."[46] He still supported and shared the president's lofty ideals and goals for reforming international politics. Even so, he now saw what he had come to believe were Wilson's shortcomings as a statesman. At the same time, his sense of his own importance increased. When he was leaving Great Britain for the United States in early June 1915, the British government assigned a naval convoy to accompany the ship on which House had taken passage. In his diary House wrote: "I can understand why my life seems of so much value to them at this particular time. It is well known in both France and Great Britain that my influence has been steadily thrown on their side. If I should disappear from this picture they are fearful of what may happen."[47] This was scarcely the musing of a man who saw his role as simply the voice of the president, charged with conveying to the governments of Europe no more and no less than what Woodrow Wilson thought.

House's estimate of his role had begun to grow as his doubts over Wilson's conduct of foreign policy had begun to find expression. "The truth of the matter is," he wrote in July 1915, "that the President has never realized the gravity of our unprepared position. I have urged from the beginning that the country prepare for eventualities. . . . If we had gone actively to work with all our resources to build up a war machine commensurate with our standing among the nations we would be in a position today to enforce peace. If war comes with Germany because of this submarine controversy it will be because we are totally unprepared and Germany feels that we are impotent." Wilson had not acted on House's advice. Given his self-described "one-track mind," the president "does not seem able to carry along more than one idea at a time." Part of the problem, House thought, was that he, House, was absent from Washington so much of the time. "From the first of May until the first of October, I see him practically not at all and I find that I cannot stir him to action unless I am with him in person and undertake the prosecution largely myself."[48]

A good deal of this sort of thing may of course be discounted. Just as Lansing was more courageous in his private memoranda to himself than in his actual dealings with Wilson, so, too, House was in all likelihood less direct and less urgent in tendering advice to the president than his diary often suggests. Still, the diary may be taken accurately to convey House's aspirations, and if these aspirations are often confused with reality, they nevertheless remain significant for the light they throw on his desire for a greater measure of equality. There is no evidence, however, that this desire was ever met. Wilson was liberal, even lavish, in his praise of the colonel's efforts, at times mystifyingly so in view of the results. But he remained unprepared to admit his friend to a status of greater equality. What endeared House to Wilson perhaps above all else was what the president perceived to be the colonel's complete self-effacement. House's role was to help the president achieve the right and to do so as unobtrusively as possible. House's reward would be precisely that of having helped Wilson achieve the right. Nor was this perception of House's role and reward so different from House's initial perception of it. If Wilson and House were from the beginning a "perfect fit," as indeed both men initially thought, it was because both had seen their relationship in these essential terms. The difficulty was that in time House's perception of the relationship changed, whereas Wilson's did not.

We have one candid appraisal of House by the president during the period of neutrality. It was written in August 1915, in response to a letter from his bride-to-be, Edith Galt, in which she had ventured to observe that she could not "help feeling he [House] is not a very strong character," especially in comparison with the president.[49] Edith Galt had not yet met House. Her remark was apropos of nothing save that she had just read a letter that House had written Wilson (the president having unfortunately begun the practice of sending her state papers presumably for her edification but on which she also made frequent comment). In reply, Wilson wrote the following of his friend:

> House *has* a strong character—if to be disinterested and unafraid and incorruptible is to be strong. He has a noble and lovely character, too, for he is capable of utter self-forgetfulness and loyalty and devotion. And he is wise. He can give prudent and far-seeing counsel. He can find out what many men, of diverse kinds, are thinking about, and how they can be made to work together for a common purpose. He wins the confidence of all sorts of men, and wins it at once—by deserving it. But you are right in thinking that intellectually he is not a great man. His mind is not of the first class. He is a counsellor, not a statesman. And he has the faults of his qualities. His very devotion to me, his ardent desire that I should play the part in the field of international politics that he has desired and foreseen for me, makes him take sometimes the short and personal view when he ought to be taking the big and impersonal one— thinking, not of my reputation for the day but of what is fundamentally and eternally right, no matter who is for the time being hurt by it. We cannot require of every man that he should be everything.[50]

While this is a generous appraisal of House's character, what Wilson found most commendable in House was his "utter self-forgetfulness and loyalty and devotion." If House is depicted as a man of considerable abilities, above all as an exceptional facilitator, those abilities are nevertheless seen as limited. Even within their limits they are marred by an excessive concern for the president's momentary reputation, a concern that presumably leads House at times to choose the expedient at the expense of the eternally right. But then one cannot require that House be everything. It is not quite the appraisal one would ordinarily expect from a "dearest friend," even one holding the high position Wilson did.

And it is clearly not the appraisal of one who thinks of friendship in terms of anything resembling real equality.

House's increased sense of independence reflected only in part an attempt to achieve a greater measure of equality in his relationship with the president; in part it was rooted in the unspoken differences that had developed between the two over the war and the American interest in its outcome. Wilson's great objective, never more pronounced than in the several months preceding American intervention, was to stay out of the conflict if at all possible. He also desired, it is true, that the war be brought to an end by a peace without victory. Still, if a choice had to be made between these two objectives, it is likely that he would have chosen to remain out of the war even had this meant the acceptance of a German victory. Not so with House, whose strongly preferred outcome was a moderate Allied victory. If this outcome were not to prove feasible, House was prepared to accept an Allied victory that resulted in a harsh peace. What he was not prepared to accept and was ready to go to war to prevent was a German victory.

There was, then, a simple yet critical difference between Wilson and House, one that in the closing months of the neutrality period came close to overshadowing the many things on which they were in agreement, especially in their conviction of the need to reform the international system and in their views on the nature of the reform needed. Had there not been a close correspondence of outlook, House could never have enjoyed Wilson's trust and played the part he did. They differed, not in ideals and aspirations, but in the compromises they were willing to make and in the price they were willing to pay to achieve their shared objectives. The record makes all too plain that in compromising principle Wilson was much less pliable than House. That Wilson was less willing to pay the price required for establishing a new relationship with the world is equally clear. Although he had long before disavowed isolationism, Wilson nevertheless retained the traditional fears of the isolationist. His view of the origin and causes of the war, with its emphasis on the moral equivalence of the belligerents, testified to this. House was not immune from these fears. The view that the belligerents were all selfish and that, unlike America's, their actions were "interested" is one of the diary's pervasive themes in 1916. "We were the only nation that desired nothing," he exclaimed to an English official in the spring of 1916. "The part we had taken [in the war] and the part we intended to take was entirely unselfish."[51] These convictions, shared by Woodrow Wilson, expressed the old American fears about the dangers of political entanglement with Europe. But Wilson's fears went much deeper

than those of his adviser. House was willing, if necessary, to accommo-
date to a selfish world to an extent that Wilson was not. And House was
reconciled to paying the price required for effective participation in Europe's politics, whereas until March 1917, at any rate, Wilson was not.

By the summer of 1915 House believed America's participation in
the war on the Allied side to be all but inevitable. With the passage of
time this belief was to harden. Still, House's interventionism differed
from that of Lansing and Page. While he too saw the war as a struggle
between autocracy and democracy, House tempered this view with a
concern for reestablishing a balance of power in postwar Europe, a
concern that dictated a *moderate* Allied victory. House was never as
unqualifiedly committed to the Allied cause as Page. Nor did he share
Lansing's hard-line position toward Germany. He was still ready to
explore the possibility of bringing the war to an end without America's
active participation, for he did not desire such participation. Yet he also
did not dread this prospect, as Wilson did. Believing as he did that war
was the nation's likely fate, he was prepared to make the most of it.

The difference that thus developed between Wilson and House over
the war seems never to have been brought fully into the open. The
agreement House concluded in February 1916 should have forced
recognition of the difference. The House-Grey memorandum, after all,
outlined a plan for America's military intervention on the Allied side in
the event that Germany either refused to attend a peace conference
called by the president (though at Allied initiative) or, having accepted
the president's call, proved unwilling to accept peace terms "not unfavorable" to the Allies. That plan was a striking departure from the
president's position as defined in a letter to House before the latter's
departure for Europe in late December 1915.[52]

Yet Wilson did not remonstrate to his friend when shown the agreement. Instead, he simply inserted the word *probably* in several places in
qualification of the obligation to enter the war against a German government that refused to attend a peace conference or that behaved
unreasonably at such a conference. At the time, House took no notice
of Wilson's additions. In turn, Wilson expressed pleasure at the results
of House's labors; House's diary entry about the meeting records the
president as saying, "I cannot adequately express to you my admiration
and gratitude for what you have done.[53]

It was a bizarre accounting. Given his essential position toward the
war, Wilson could not possibly have approved of House's handiwork.
On the other hand, House could not have reasonably believed that he
was faithfully carrying out the president's wishes. The episode has been

pointed to by some as the prime example of the gulf of misunderstanding that had always existed between Wilson and House. Ray Stannard Baker was persuaded that there had never been a "clear, sharp understanding between the two men. It was House's practice to approve everything, or almost everything, the President said: and Wilson assumed that House completely understood his mind. . . . It was the fatal flaw in their relationship and led to infinite confusion and thwarted effort." Wilson's lifelong error, as Baker saw it, "was to suppose that men whom he accepted as his friends—sorely needed intimate friends—not only loved him, but understood completely his clear and swift-running mind, and agreed with him in all things."[54]

This was the view of a Wilson admirer and a House critic. Baker did not raise the question why House approved of "almost everything" Wilson said and thereby presumably misled the president. House was not a mere sycophant, whatever his other failings, yet experience had taught him that candor with Wilson could prove dangerous, and argument more so. Wilson was not even receptive to the efforts of others at "clarification." And since he assumed, as Baker emphasized, that his friends completely understood and agreed with him, there was no need to make special efforts with intimates to achieve clarity so as to ensure that there was a meeting of minds on a given issue. The several exchanges between the two men that form the background of House's mission often have an ambiguous and inconclusive character. Did Wilson's silence signify agreement, as House more than once thought? Were key terms, such as *intervention,* used on both sides with the same meaning? In retrospect, it is apparent that House and Wilson were often like two ships passing each other on a dark night.[55]

Yet after these considerations are duly taken into account, the facts remain that the president's instructions to House were clear on the points that mattered most to Wilson and that House simply ignored them. Perhaps he did so because he had come to believe that the president had placed the negotiations with the belligerents entirely in his hands and that he was virtually a free agent in conducting them. In place of Wilson's scheme of mediation, one that was as evenhanded and impartial as his neutrality policy was partial, House had substituted a thinly disguised plan for intervening on the side of the Allies. Why had Wilson not voiced his disappointment, even his displeasure? Was this not proof that House not only disagreed with the president but had subverted his policy?

That Wilson's response was to praise House for his work said a great deal about the relationship between the two men. Reproof, Wilson may well have thought, would seriously alter his friendship with House, perhaps even destroy it. This he could not bring himself to do at the time. Besides, he must have felt that House had acted with the best intentions. At any rate, it was done. Friendship apart, the agreement could not be rejected, and House virtually disavowed, without incurring considerable cost diplomatically. Wilson could only dilute the force of the undertaking stipulated in the agreement, something that he promptly did. He could also attempt to turn the agreement House had concluded to his end of stopping the war, for Wilson was persuaded that if the war could once be stopped, for whatever reason, the belligerent governments would never be able to restart it. But Grey showed little disposition to cooperate in an undertaking he had probably never taken very seriously, and the exchanges of the spring and summer of 1916 were altogether barren of result. The Allies no longer had much confidence in Wilson's promises. Even had this not been the case, they would have resisted proposals to end the war, for they were intent on gathering the fruits of complete victory. House's terms of moderate victory, even had they been assured of Wilson's support, held little attraction.

The House-Grey memorandum marked the high point of House's influence during the period of neutrality. In Wilson's eyes, the colonel had supped once too often with the devil and had lost. In the following months, Wilson's latent distrust of Allied motives rose to the surface, there to remain. Determined more than ever to stay out of the war, he moved slowly toward the peace initiative that House had earlier managed to shunt aside. In this Wilson acted as consistently as did House, who quickly recovered from his initial disappointment over Grey's lack of response and again took up the Allied cause with an increasingly deaf president. The record of their exchanges of late fall 1916 shows how far apart they had moved.

Wilson's unhappiness with his advisers has no simple explanation. Certainly they made mistakes, some quite serious. Yet their mistakes must be seen against the background of the difficulties of serving a president who was often withdrawn and uncommunicative. Both Lansing and House complained of frequently being kept in the dark about the president's wishes and intentions, though Lansing's complaints were the more insistent. Nor were their complaints without justification, for Wilson did frequently fail to provide clear guidance to his subordinates. In Lansing's case, this failure was largely the result of an increasingly poor relationship and the president's growing distrust of his secretary of state.

But it was also the consequence of Wilson's almost congenital reluctance, bordering on inability, to plan for the near future. This was a serious defect, especially in the circumstances of the neutrality period. Yet Wilson could not seem to remedy it, as he admitted in a letter to Edith Galt. "The fact is, I never have had any patience with 'ifs' and conjectural cases. My mind insists always upon waiting until something actually does happen and then discussing what is to be done about that."[56] Wilson's refusal to plan how to meet the crises that lay ahead was of recurring concern to Lansing and House. "There is another thing I cannot bring the President to realize," House wrote in his diary on March 29, 1916, during the *Sussex* crisis, "and that is the importance of making ready to meet the crises which may fall upon him any day. He was compelled to go into Mexico at a moment's notice. The same will happen in the European situation and yet we are inert as if it were a remote possibility of some future age. I have urged him ever since the war began to make ready and we are no more ready today than we were two years ago."[57] It was not easy to serve a president who dreamed of the millennium but was unwilling to consider the possibilities of tomorrow.

Wilson's unhappiness with his advisers was often reciprocated, then, by their frustration with him. This mutual dissatisfaction, moreover, had roots that went beyond differences in the method and conduct of diplomacy. What the president wanted from his advisers was something they could not give him and would not give him even if they could. At bottom, Wilson's unhappiness was not so much with his advisers as it was with the plight in which he increasingly found himself. What he wanted from those serving him was not merely competence but deliverance from a difficult and perilous position. Yet there was no apparent way to satisfy this desire, particularly after the summer of 1915, for Wilson's position was rooted in a contradiction that could not be resolved. There was no apparent way to maintain America's established neutrality without incurring an ever-increasing risk of war with Germany. Wilson's anger over the additional blockade measures taken by the British in the summer of 1916 reflected this sense of entrapment, for these measures did not significantly alter a system of control over neutral trade to which he had in effect long given his consent.

By 1916 the president's assistants could not have devised successful schemes for significantly altering the terms of neutrality even had they wanted to do so. Yet they clearly did not want to do so, for those terms favored the Allies, and they had long been committed to the Allied cause. While they followed Wilson's efforts in the fall of 1916 to pressure the Allies to abandon the most irksome of the blockade measures, they did so only reluctantly. Lansing, though he could not quite bring himself to abandon his old habit of acting as the president's faithful legal adviser, wrote in a private memorandum of September: "Nothing in our controversies with Great Britain must be brought to a head. . . . I will never sign an ultimatum to Great Britain."[58] House apparently shared this view.

The gulf separating Wilson from his advisers was never more apparent than in the closing months of the neutrality period. It was vividly illustrated in the events that led to and attended the president's peace note of December 1916. The peace note was pure Wilson. It expressed his deepest convictions. In calling upon the belligerents to declare in specific, not general, terms what they were fighting for and what they meant by victory, Wilson acted from motives that were utterly devoid of any favoritism toward either side. The peace note was the public expression of the thought that he had developed in his unpublished prolegomenon (which he apparently showed to no one) and that made clear his belief that the war had no meaning save "untold human suffering," that neither side's contentions could be supported, and that between German militarism and British navalism there was little to choose. Yet the war might still serve a great purpose if it could be used to destroy the psychological and political bases for future wars. For this a peace without victory was indispensable; nothing else would drive home the lesson for future generations that war was the Great Illusion. The peace note was intended as the first step down the road marked out by the prolegomenon. Wilson was determinedly prepared to entertain a favorable response from either side. If Germany were forthcoming, he was ready to exert the greatest pressure he could on the Allies to reciprocate, a prospect that filled his assistants with apprehension and against the risks of which they came close to rebelling. Even after Wilson moderated his course, in response to their objections, his secretary of state sought to subvert the initiative.

A case can be made that Wilson's advisers were never really candid in their dealings with him, that their counsel often obscured their real convictions, and that if the result was not to deceive the president, it was at least to mislead him. Even Page, the most open of Wilson's assistants, was occasionally guilty of voicing apparent convictions that in all likelihood he did not hold to. But Lansing and House made a regular practice of doing so. Never once did Lansing reveal his true position to the president. Instead, a strong interventionist intent was invariably presented in the disguise of legal issues that were equated with the nation's honor, self-respect, and regard for the dictates of humanity. House was only slightly more direct. Only toward the close of the neutrality period, when Wilson was plainly intent on pursuing his peace initiative even at the risk of a possible break with the Allies, did House depart from his strategy of indirection in dealing with the president. For this momentary candor he paid the price of exclusion from Wilson's confidence in the latter's preparation of his peace note.

If Wilson's advisers were less than forthright in their dealings with him, it was not because they had a common character defect. They knew that were they once to strongly urge Wilson to a course he was averse to taking, let alone openly argue with him, they might lose altogether what modest influence they had. They increasingly opposed the president's course as time went by and believed it would lead to unfortunate results were it not abandoned. Given Wilson's temperament, their recourse was to disguise and, if necessary, to mislead. The necessity of that recourse would persist even in the wake of Germany's declaration, on January 31, 1917, of unrestricted submarine warfare. Only Wilson's decision for war in March would bring that necessity to an end.

2

Isolation and Neutrality

The world at the outset of the twentieth century, it is well to recall, was still very much a traditional one. The balance of power provided the central ordering principle of international society. Such stability and moderation as the balance brought rested ultimately on the threat or use of force. War remained the essential means for maintaining the balance of power. Despite a growing movement that looked to the amelioration of state relations through greater legal regulation, international law depended for its effectiveness, as it had always depended, upon the maintenance of a balance. Given this dependence, war remained the indispensable prerequisite for the realization of an effective legal order. At the same time, war undertaken to maintain the balance was an insurmountable obstacle to realizing an effective legal order. The customary liberty accorded states to resort to war in order to maintain the balance of power formed only the most notorious justification of their primordial right of self-help. In fact, it was scarcely necessary to place this liberty in a separate category, since it was readily encompassed by the more general "right" of self-preservation that states took for granted.

This was the world in which Woodrow Wilson, along with others at the time, called for the abandonment of isolation.[1] In doing so, he made no apparent effort to speculate on what such abandonment might mean for the United States. There is no record that he ever seriously considered the relationship an America that had once abandoned isolation might have to the European balance of power. Nor is there any indication that he ever gave serious consideration to how the abandonment of isolation might affect the relationship between the English-speaking peoples on the opposite shores of the Atlantic, even though Wilson had always been an ardent Anglophile. These issues had long been of deep concern to Theodore Roosevelt and his circle of intimates. The need to work for an ever-closer relationship of cooperation with Great Britain—though given the public's prejudices, a relationship that fell short of formal alliance—was common currency among them. So, too, was the conviction that an Anglo-American partnership of interest and power held out the best hope of preventing the destruction of the European balance of power and the emergence of a power supreme on land and sea. There is no evidence that Wilson gave sustained thought to these issues.

In view of these considerations, the question arises whether Wilson's early call for the nation to abandon isolation had much significance. Clearly, for him the abandonment of isolation meant America's economic expansion. But the search for foreign markets was unending. Belief in the desirability and, indeed, the necessity of America's foreign economic expansion had been taken largely for granted since well before the turn of the century. It was not in the economic but in the political sphere that the tradition and policy of isolation found expression. And it was not everywhere, but primarily in Europe, that isolation found political expression.

Despite his early call for abandoning isolation, it is more likely that Wilson in fact shared the prevailing view that continued to support America's political separation from Europe. Certainly nothing he said in the intervening years before coming to the presidency indicates the contrary. Nor is there any real indication of a change in outlook after he took office. On the contrary, in the period prior to the outbreak of war his few utterances that bear on America's tradition of isolation confirm, if anything, a continued attachment to that tradition. A revealing instance of this may be found in a speech Wilson gave in May 1914 on the meaning of the American Revolution. That meaning, he declared, was "that America might be free to make her own life without interruption or disturbance from any other quarter . . . that America had a right to her own self-determined life." What were the "corollaries," Wilson asked, that followed from this? "What does it mean that America shall live her own life?" The first corollary had been seen by Washington when he wrote his Farewell Address:

> It was not merely because of passing and transient circumstances that Washington said that we must keep free from entangling alliances. It was because he saw that no country had yet set its face in the same direction in which America had set her face. We cannot form alliances with those who are not going our way; and in our might and majesty and in the certainty of our purpose we need not and we should not form alliances with any nation in the world. Those who are right, those who study their consciences in determining their policies, those who hold their honor higher than their advantage, do not need alliances. You need alliances when you are not strong, and you are weak only when you are not true to your-

self. You are weak only when you are in the wrong; you are weak only when you are afraid to do the right; you are weak only when you doubt your cause and the majesty of a nation's might asserted.[2]

This was Wilson's understanding of Washington's Farewell Address, not Washington's. It was no part of Washington's meaning that the nation must keep free from entangling alliances so long as other countries "are not going our way," that is, so long as they were not entertaining the same institutions and sharing the same high purposes and ideals. The Farewell Address had been directed to the distinctly political conditions that necessitated a policy of isolation. Wilson's reading of Washington virtually ignored those conditions, while concentrating on an ideological and moral justification of isolation.

Once the war began, Wilson's consistent refusal during the period of neutrality to participate in drawing up terms of a European peace settlement followed the timeworn injunction against implicating the United States in Europe's politics. Significantly, this refusal persisted even after Wilson committed the United States, in May 1916, to joining a universal organization for maintaining peace and security. While declaring that "the interests of all nations are our own also" and that "we are partners with the rest," America's interest and partnership was still not to require—or permit—more than the most modest degree of political intimacy with Europe.[3] The postwar organization for maintaining peace and security was to be, not an "entangling alliance," but a "disentangling alliance."[4] Only in his peace-without-victory address, of late January 1917, did Wilson venture to set out the general principles a peace settlement should observe.

In his desire to preserve America's isolation from the politics of Europe, Wilson did not evoke the outlook of Washington and Hamilton so much as that of Jefferson. Thus his insistence during most of the neutrality period on the moral equivalence of the belligerents was little more than a replay of Jefferson's theme during the Napoleonic Wars. In both instances an emphasis on the moral equivalence of the belligerents served to distinguish the higher moral standing of America and to point to the undesirability of compromising that standing by abandoning a position of isolation from Europe's politics. So, too, Wilson's identification of neutral rights with the "laws of humanity" was reminiscent of Jefferson's equation of neutral rights with "the law of nature on the ocean." In both, the quality of moral absolutism with which neutral rights were invested raised issues of prestige, honor, even independence, issues that in turn made almost inevitable an outcome—war—

that both Wilson and Jefferson deeply feared because they saw it as a threat to almost everything they held dear.

Neutrality, as earlier observed, was the corollary of isolation. A neutral state stood apart from the wars of others. In what now appear as the archaic terms of an earlier age, the neutral nation was the friend of both parties at war. At the outset of World War I, Woodrow Wilson invoked these terms in declaring that "the true spirit of neutrality . . . is the spirit of impartiality and fairness and friendliness to all concerned."[5]

Once so significant a part of the nation's diplomatic tradition, neutrality has since suffered the fate of isolation. Neutrality now stands as discredited as does isolation. The stigma that came to be attached to the one also came to be attached to the other. It did so in the first instance, not as a result of the nation's experience with neutrality in World War I, but as a result of the nation's interwar experience. The policy of isolation pursued in the period between the two world wars was later found to have been blind to the nation's vital interests and to have threatened disastrous consequences. So, too, the neutrality policy adopted in the mid-1930s was later seen to have encouraged the forces of aggression, thereby contributing to the onset of the century's second global conflict.

Other developments as well worked to discredit neutrality. In the two world wars, the practices of belligerents, including those of the United States once it entered the conflicts, reduced neutral rights at sea almost to a vanishing point. The conviction later gained acceptance that the two wars must be considered, in the treatment accorded to neutrals, the likely standard for the future rather than exceptional events of the past. Of equal importance was the change that occurred in the political and legal position of war itself. In marked contrast to the international system that prevailed until World War I, states are no longer considered at liberty to resort to war as a means of national policy. Instead, the dominant view in the second half of the twentieth century was that war could no longer be regarded as a legitimate means for resolving international differences. In the generally accepted view, the resort to armed force was forbidden save as a measure of legitimate self- or collective defense against a prior resort to force.

Given this change, one in which Woodrow Wilson played an early and important role, the traditional institution of neutrality also had to change. Once war is seen as being just or unjust, legal or illegal, the effect must be to deprive neutrality of its inner raison d'être. This is the case even if it is assumed that the changed position of war does not impose upon each and every state the duty to join in the active and forcible repression of aggressors. At the very least, the change must be seen to permit third parties the right to discriminate against the aggressor, or it can have little significance. But if this is the necessary consequence of the altered position of war, it is incompatible with the absolute impartiality that is—or was—so fundamental to the traditional institution of neutrality.

To these considerations must be added the radically changed position of the United States in the world. From the close of the eighteenth century to the 1914–18 war America played a critical role in the development of neutrality. That role was placed in lasting doubt when the United States, in April 1917, finally intervened in the European conflict and President Wilson declared that "neutrality is no longer feasible or desirable where the peace of the world is involved and the freedom of its peoples, and the menace to that peace and freedom lies in the existence of autocratic governments backed by organized force which is controlled by their will, not by the will of their people. We have seen the last of neutrality in such circumstances."[6] Wilson's forecast was very nearly correct. When the prospect of a second great European war arose in the 1930s, the United States did not follow the course it had taken as a neutral in the earlier conflict. Instead, a still prevailing isolationism momentarily gave rise to a neutral policy of self-abnegation. The neutral's traditional rights at sea were renounced in favor of a self-imposed isolation in war that went far beyond the requirements of international law.[7]

The neutrality legislation of the years 1935–39 responded to the experience of World War I and was based on the belief that in a future war American neutrality might be preserved by America's denying to itself the exercise of those rights whose defense had ultimately led Wilson to intervention. In fact, from the outset the renunciatory neutrality adopted by the United States had a hollow core of real belief. While it might have been suited to the circumstances of World War I, it was not suited to those of World War II. The America of the late 1930s could not evoke the innocence of an earlier period; the effort to do so was forced and unsustainable. The experience of World War I had left a permanent mark. Even had this not been the case, there was no denying the changed circumstances, political and technological, that set the later conflict apart from its predecessor. The Germany of 1939 was not the Germany of 1914. Once World War II began, the United States, though remaining outside the conflict, rapidly moved from a renunciatory neutrality to a policy of discrimination and to an open abandonment of neutral duties that found few parallels in the history of neutrality.

In the years that followed World War II, the prevailing American attitude toward neutrality reflected not only the nation's recent experience but, even more, its new role as principal guarantor of international security and order. In consequence, the country that had once been the ardent champion of neutrality became one of the institution's most severe critics. What had once been seen as a policy both moral and in the nation's interests was invested with an opprobrium altogether novel. During the 1950s a secretary of state could characterize the principle of neutrality as one that was indifferent to the fate of others. Derided by some at the time, John Foster Dulles's characterization of neutrality came close to expressing the post–World War II understanding. Neutrality, like isolation, has been equated with indifference to the fate of others and for this reason alone condemned.

The contemporary understanding would have surprised an earlier age. The indifference that characterized the traditional institution of neutrality was not considered to reflect the absence of a sense of community. The normal indifference of neutrals toward the outcome of war in the nineteenth century proved possible largely because the solidarity of international society was sufficiently great, even in war, not to make the outcome of an armed conflict a matter of deep concern to the nonparticipants. The decline of neutrality in the twentieth century was not the result of a growing sense of community but quite the opposite. That decline testified to the breakdown of the nineteenth-century international order. An integral part of that order, neutrality was not equated with an indifference between right and wrong. To so interpret the wars of an earlier era is to give to these conflicts a significance that would have escaped the comprehension of both the participants and the nonparticipants. America's neutrality policy in World War I cannot be properly understood by applying to it the perspective of the post–World War II period, a period so near in time yet so far in outlook. It is only by seeing that policy in the perspective of the past that such understanding may be achieved.

An important part of this perspective was legal. Neutrality was not only a political but a legal status, the status of a state in international law that stood apart from a war between other states.[8] To be sure, the decision to remain apart from a war was a matter of policy, determined by state interest. But once a government had decided upon nonparticipation in a conflict, it occupied a status of neutrality, the legal significance of which was to bring into operation a system of rules regulating the neutrals' relations with belligerents. To the question, then, that has so often been raised—why Wilson and his advisers took the legal issues of neutrality with the seriousness they did—the answer is that they simply assumed that they had little alternative but to do so. As long as the nation remained a nonparticipant in the war, it was neutral; as long as it was neutral, the issues attending neutral status were critical. The view of neutrality as a protean condition, compatible with varying degrees of discrimination toward belligerents, was a twentieth-century development that presaged the end of that institution. The traditional system did not admit of it.

Among the duties of a neutral, that of impartiality occupied a position of central importance. The principle of impartiality obligated a neutral state to fulfill its duties and to exercise its rights in an equal, or nondiscriminatory, manner toward the belligerents. Impartiality did not determine the contents of a neutral's duties and rights, only the manner in which they were to be applied. Nor did the duty of impartiality require that the measures a neutral might take bear with equal effect upon the belligerents. A neutral was under no obligation to adopt measures that sought to ensure the belligerents a factual equality of treatment—in most instances a difficult, if not an impossible, task. A belligerent had no legal grounds for complaint because a neutral state's position worked to its actual disadvantage. Even the unequal effect upon belligerents resulting from a neutral's discretionary exercise of its rights afforded no legal cause for complaint by a belligerent. The law of neutrality required only that the neutral refrain from discriminating against either belligerent in the actual application of those regulations it was at liberty to enact.

The duty of impartiality applied to the acts of a neutral state or government. Apart from certain limited exceptions, a neutral state was under no obligation to prevent its citizens from giving material assistance to a belligerent, though it might forbid such behavior at its discretion. Nor was the neutral state obligated to prevent its citizens from expressing moral support or sympathy for one side in a conflict. When President Wilson declared in August 1914 that "we must be impartial in thought as well as in action," he called upon the nation to meet a standard higher than that required of neutrals.[9]

Of equal importance with the duty of impartiality was the neutrals' duty to abstain from furnishing belligerents with a wide range of goods or services. A neutral state violated this duty if it provided a belligerent with arms, munitions, war materials of any kind, money, loans, or almost any form of assistance that would aid a belligerent in the prosecution of war. But although itself under a strict duty to abstain from furnishing belligerents with certain goods or services, a neutral state was under no obligation to prevent its nationals from providing most of these same forms of assistance. Occasionally, belligerents questioned this absence of obligation of the neutral state when the trade of private individuals conferred a decided advantage on one side. Germany and Austria-Hungary did so in 1914–17, complaining that private American trade with the Allies had reached such proportions and conferred so great an advantage on one side as to raise the question whether the continuance of this trade could be considered compatible with a neutral state's duty of impartiality. In rejecting the complaints of the Central powers the United States was undoubtedly supported by the traditional law, although the scale of the traffic in arms and munitions to the Allies was unprecedented. The recourse open to a belligerent so disadvantaged consisted in taking certain repressive measures against neutral traders engaged in furnishing assistance to an enemy. The law of contraband and blockade prescribed the permitted means for accomplishing this end. In turn, the neutral state was obliged to acquiesce to the repressive measures permitted belligerents.

Historically, the major disputes between neutrals and belligerents have arisen over the nature and scope of the repressive measures belligerents could take against the private trade of neutrals. It was common to characterize the problems attending neutral trade in terms of conflicting rights: the right of a neutral to insist upon the continued freedom of commerce for its nationals even in wartime and the right of belligerents to prevent the neutral's trade from affording assistance to an enemy's military effort. Whether or not these were conflicting rights, they were certainly conflicting interests. While the neutral's interest was to suffer the least amount of belligerent interference in the trading activities of its citizens, the belligerent's interest was to prevent neutral rights from compensating for an enemy's weakness at sea. The reconciliation of these opposed interests was never easy and, as the preamble to the 1856 Declaration of Paris stated, "has long been the subject of deplorable disputes . . . giving rise to differences of opinion between neutral and belligerent which may occasion serious difficulties and even conflicts." On more than one occasion marking the evolution of neutrality the attempt was made to find in the "general principles" alleged to govern maritime war criteria by which precise limits upon the belligerent's license to interfere with neutral trade could be set. Such attempts were vain. It was quite true that the neutral state had the right to demand that no repressive measure be taken by a belligerent against legitimate neutral commerce with an enemy. But from this general principle, it was scarcely possible to determine the character of the neutral trade to be regarded as legitimate. Experience pointed instead to a very different conclusion: that the practices establishing the rights and duties of belligerents and neutrals were dependent, not upon logical deductions drawn from general principles, but rather upon the concrete circumstances attending war's conduct in a particular historical period.

Among these circumstances, the relative power of neutrals and belligerents was critical. A rough equality of neutral and belligerent rights depended, in the first instance, upon an equality of power. Where neutrals did not possess an equality of power with belligerents their interests, and rights, usually suffered accordingly. The lesson taught by the Napoleonic Wars, which opened the nineteenth century, was in this respect quite clear. By contrast, in the century that followed the great contest between England and France a rough balance was struck between the conflicting claims of neutrals and belligerents, a balance that was duly reflected in the law of neutrality. If anything, the law inclined in favor of neutral interests, and in doing so it also reflected the experience of the century, which was one of limited warfare. The view generally prevailed that in maritime war the burden of proving the legitimacy of any kind of interference with neutral trade rested squarely upon the belligerent asserting it.

Certainly, this was the American outlook. That outlook had been given early expression in American diplomacy. Jefferson had been its most ardent advocate. "War between two nations cannot diminish the rights of the rest of the world remaining at peace," he once wrote as president to his minister to France. "The doctrine that the rights of nations remaining quietly in the exercise of moral and social duties, are to give way to the convenience of those who prefer plundering and murdering one another, is a monstrous doctrine; and ought to yield to the more rational law, that the 'wrong which two nations endeavor to inflict on each other, must not infringe on the rights or conveniences of those remaining at peace.'"[10] In accord with these sentiments, Jefferson had championed the doctrine that free ships make free goods and had wanted, if not simply to do away with the concept of contraband of war, then to limit severely its scope. And he looked to the time, as did most of his contemporaries, when the belligerent right in warfare at sea to seize the private property of an enemy would be abolished entirely.

Jefferson had confidently expected that the day was quite near "when we may say by what laws other nations shall treat us on the sea."[11] In this he was wrong. Yet the course of the nineteenth century did vindicate Jefferson's prophecy to a remarkable extent. By midcentury the European powers, Great Britain included, had accepted the principle championed by the United States that free ships make free goods. The 1856 Declaration of Paris provided that "the neutral flag covers enemy goods, with the exception of contraband of war." The acceptance of this provision in turn encouraged the belief that the way was at last open to the virtual abolition of the belligerent right to seize enemy property at sea, since a belligerent could now transfer his trade to neutral vessels and by doing so secure immunity from seizure. It was recognized that the significance of the change ultimately depended upon the scope afforded to contraband; a broad enough definition of contraband would largely negate the effects of the principle that free ships make free goods. The Declaration of Paris had not dealt with the issue of contraband. At the time, however, the law of contraband, as evidenced by the practice of states, appeared modest in scope and was to remain so throughout the century. Still, the failure of maritime states to satisfactorily address this controversial core of neutral-belligerent relations was noteworthy. If the consequences of failure did not seem portentous at the time, this was largely because the wars of the period did not provide a harsh test of neutrality as it had evolved over the long period since the last great European wars.

Ironically, it was the state most identified with the development of neutrality that posed the greatest challenge to this institution in the course of the nineteenth century. In the great trial by arms of the Civil War the United States, in blockading the Southern states, expanded upon the customary rights of belligerents. Still, the expansion was modest in character. That it could be employed a half-century later to justify the measures taken by Great Britain in shutting off American trade with the European neutrals would doubtless have come as a surprise to those who fashioned and passed legal judgment on it. In fact, the experience of the Civil War did not mark a significant break in the American tradition of support for neutral rights. In the period following the Civil War the United States continued to support the positions it had championed since the latter part of the eighteenth century. It continued to do so even at the close of the nineteenth century, when its naval power had grown considerably and navalists were calling for change in the nation's historic positions on neutral rights.

The 1900 United States Naval War Code testified to this continuity.[12]

Although formally revoked by the Navy Department in 1904, the Naval War Code continued to express the views of the American government in the following decade. American delegates to the Second Hague Peace Conference of 1907 and the London Naval Conference of 1908–9 were instructed to urge the states attending both conferences to look upon the code as a basis for formulating conventional law respecting neutral commerce. In respect to the principal grounds for belligerent interference with neutral trade, the code followed prevailing state practice.

Developed over a period of two centuries, the law of neutrality achieved its fullest expression in the years preceding World War I, a period in which the circumstances that had favored the growth of this institution were already eroding. In retrospect, neutrality in these years resembled the proverbial star that shines the brightest only before its eclipse.[13] Neutrality had flourished in conditions that were favorable to a certain kind of state and a certain kind of war. The conception of the state was not necessarily democratic, but it was of a state having only limited powers. The law of neutrality presupposed economic liberalism with a clear distinction drawn in war as in peace between the activities of the state and the activities of the private individual. On that distinction, the greater part of maritime law had been based, and belligerents had found it very difficult to wage wars that would necessitate drawing upon the full resources of their peoples. The conception of war was of a limited war, limited in terms of the parties involved, the fraction of the populations actively engaged, and the nature of belligerent war aims. A war that was not limited was almost by definition one in which a rough balance of interests between belligerents and neutrals would be difficult to sustain. The traditional law of neutrality was conditioned throughout by the assumption, as one observer has written, "that the greater part of the world is at peace, that war is a temporary and local disturbance of the general order, and that the chief function of law is to keep the war from spreading, and to minimize its impact upon the normal life of the world."[14]

Even when the circumstances favoring it were in the ascendant, as they were during much of the nineteenth century, neutrality was characterized by the weaknesses of an institution that formed a part of international law. Then as always, international law suffered from the difficulties endemic to its distinctive condition. The law of neutrality did so as well. In the absence of a legislative body competent to enact law binding upon states, the legislative function must of necessity be relegated to the states themselves, to be undertaken through custom or convention (treaty). In the case of neutrality, neither process of law creation proved very satisfactory. Customary law was not only the result of a lengthy process but nearly always attended by a substantial measure of uncertainty. The law governing carriage of contraband was an instructive example of the drawbacks that marked the process of law creation by custom, particularly when there existed no authoritative body competent to interpret customary law in a manner binding upon states. Although many of the uncertainties of customary law might have been removed by the conclusion of multilateral conventions, the development of the law of neutrality was attended by very few such conventions; in the nineteenth century the 1856 Declaration of Paris formed the only example of a multilateral convention on neutral commerce in war concluded and ratified by most of the maritime states. The inevitable result of this situation was that the law of neutrality remained characterized by a degree of uncertainty that as the nineteenth century drew to a close was further aggravated by the rapidly changing conditions of naval warfare. When World War I broke out, the stage was set for belligerents to take novel measures against neutral trade that were justified on grounds that had more than a semblance of plausibility.

The uncertainty that marked the customary law of neutrality is nevertheless a theme that has often been overdrawn, even by those who knew better. In his memoirs, the man Woodrow Wilson chose as legal guardian of the nation's neutral rights declared that when the war had come, "there was no definite code, no fixed standard, which could be applied to the relations between neutral and belligerent." Everything, Lansing later recalled, "seemed to be vague and uncertain by reason of the new conditions."[15] But among the new conditions, the most important by far in accounting for the fate of neutrality in the war was simply the character of the war itself. There had been, after all, a number of wars in the two decades prior to the Great War—the Spanish-American, the Boer, the Russo-Japanese, and the First and Second Balkan wars. Issues of neutral (and, of course, belligerent) rights had arisen in the course of these conflicts. While the law of neutrality had led to a number of disputes between neutrals and belligerents, it seldom if ever had occurred to any of the belligerent parties to contend that the law might be swept aside, or if not simply swept aside, then subverted through the operation of reprisals or the claim of novel circumstances. But then these conflicts had been limited in character. Neutrals had had both the power and the will to insist on their rights. Belligerents, in turn, had been confronted with the prospect of raising up new enemies if they sought to override the rights of neutrals.

World War I was very different. It was conducted with an intensity that had been unanticipated, and it soon became clear that if there was always a latent conflict between belligerent and neutral interests, even in a local war conducted with restraint and for limited purposes, the conflict between these divergent interests in a hegemonical contest of great powers was very nearly irreconcilable. Given the stakes of such a conflict, the primary aim of the belligerents in warfare at sea, an aim that was first apparent on the Allied side, was the shutting off of all enemy trade, the destruction or capture of all imports to or exports from enemy territory, without regard to whether this trade was carried in enemy or neutral bottoms. Yet the effect of the traditional law, if adhered to, was to make it very difficult for the measures a belligerent could take at sea against an enemy's economy to play more than a limited role in the pursuit of victory. This antagonism between the restraints the law imposed upon belligerents with respect to neutral trade and the importance of cutting off the enemy's seaborne trade if victory was to be achieved cannot be emphasized too strongly. The steady belligerent encroachment upon neutral rights at sea that marked the years 1914–17 must be attributed far more to this circumstance than to any other. Even had the customary law enjoyed greater clarity and its course been one of constant adaptation to the changing conditions of naval warfare, the belligerents would nevertheless have found this inadequate in World War I since it still would not have given them what they wanted.

At the same time, the marked belligerent inroads upon neutral interests in World War I often had a strong legal basis, such that neutral protests had no real legal foundation. The nineteenth-century balance between neutral and belligerent was reflected not only in law but also in the extralegal restraints that had characterized belligerent behavior. The importance of these restraints can be fully appreciated only with the advantage of hindsight. During the 1914–18 war many of the most effective measures taken by the Allied powers against neutral trade—measures that so angered President Wilson in the summer and fall of 1916 and against which he threatened reprisals—consisted of so-called "interferences by sovereign right." The essential purpose of the varied belligerent measures falling within this category was to cut off trade with the enemy by threatening to deprive neutral traders and shippers of certain advantages if they were found or suspected of aiding the enemy's cause. Despite strong neutral protests against measures that often reduced neutral trade to a position of near subservience to belligerent controls, there were no rules forbidding belligerents to subject the trade of neutrals to a strict control through the threat of interference by sovereign right. There was no law, for example, forbidding Great Britain from refusing bunker supplies or ship's stores to neutral ships in British ports throughout the world or from denying insurance (by British companies) to neutral shipping. The British made extensive use of these and other informal measures that were often more effective in controlling neutral trade than legal restraints. Neutral protests failed to acknowledge that a significant area of neutral-belligerent relations depended upon the character of hostilities and the restraints belligerents felt compelled to accept, not as a matter of strict law but for reasons of expediency.

Quite different considerations were raised by belligerent measures that clearly could be considered departures from the established law. In these instances, neutral protests against what were alleged to be belligerent violations of traditional neutral rights at sea required belligerent justification. In part, belligerents responded to neutral protests by maintaining that legally controverted measures taken against neutral trade merely represented a reasonable adaptation of the traditional law to the novel circumstances in which hostilities were being conducted. In part, belligerents attempted to justify measures whose legality could not otherwise be seriously defended by the claim that they formed legitimate measures of reprisal taken in response to an enemy's unlawful behavior.

The belligerent contention that novel circumstances justified novel measures was met by the neutral contention that once recognition was accorded this plea, it could be used as an instrument for subverting all law. This was the position taken repeatedly by the American government in rejecting the plea of novel circumstances. The belligerents did not strengthen their position by claiming the right to invoke the doctrine of novel circumstances in their own case, and (from the neutrals' point of view) for their own interests, though invariably rejecting the same doctrine when invoked by the enemy. Thus the unreserved British condemnation of the contention that allegedly novel circumstances could ever serve to release the submarine from any of the traditionally accepted rules governing seizure and destruction of merchant vessels was seldom viewed as hindering support for the contention that changed conditions justified the diversion of neutral vessels into port for visit and search. Admittedly, cogent considerations were put forth in support of the practice of diversion. Even so, there was little doubt that the practice was not permitted by the law as it stood at the outbreak of hostilities in 1914.

The Allies nevertheless contended that novel practices were justified, though constituting departures from established law, if they did not prove destructive of the basic purposes of the law but merely sought to adapt the latter to changed conditions. The argument took on added force once it was recognized that although the conditions of naval warfare did change, and particularly so during World War I, the history of neutrality was one in which states nearly always manifested reluctance to amend the law through express agreement. The result was that change, when it did come, often had to do so through what appeared as departures from the established law. These departures were to be condemned, the Allied argument ran, only if they struck at the basic purposes of the law, as did measures of unrestricted submarine warfare against neutral shipping. Departures were not, or not necessarily, to be condemned if they conserved these basic purposes, as presumably did the practice of requiring diversion for visit and search.

The argument was not without merit. Still, the dangers for neutrals in accepting it were clear. Once accepted, belligerent behavior was judged, at least in part, by the degree to which it conformed to the law's essential purposes (to the "spirit of the law"). But if it was always difficult enough to reach a clear statement of the law, it was next to impossible to state its essential purposes with an authority and clarity that would elicit general acceptance. Again, it is necessary to point out that the law regulating neutral-belligerent relations at sea can only be understood as the product of conflicting interests, informed at best by the spirit of compromise. And even if the traditional law reflected some measure of identity of purpose between neutral and belligerent, this was largely dissipated once hostilities began in 1914.

These considerations necessarily assume that the controverted measures taken by belligerents, reprisals apart, were readily acknowledged to be departures from the law. Usually, however, the novel measures resorted to by belligerents were viewed by the latter as adaptations permitted by, and taken within, the established legal framework of neutral-belligerent relations. This was the position taken time and again by the Allied powers, and in many instances their claims could not be simply dismissed as mere subterfuge for the justification of unlawful action. Whether at the time or in retrospect, it was all too easy to exaggerate the degree to which the maritime powers of the world had by 1914 settled upon the limits of the belligerent right to interfere with neutral trade. Many issues had remained unresolved throughout the preceding century. A case in point was the all-important question of trade in contraband, a question that, as noted earlier, had always provided the controversial core of neutral-belligerent relations.

In the years preceding World War I an attempt was made to resolve the various disputed issues. The 1909 Declaration of London laid down what was generally considered at the time of its conclusion to be a definitive code governing neutral-belligerent relations at sea.[16] Often considered to have reflected the interests of neutrals, this judgment is persuasive only when viewed from the perspective of subsequent belligerent claims. From the perspective of neutral interests in the prewar period, a different judgment must be drawn. Although the rules of the Declaration of London did not always "correspond in substance with the generally recognized principles of international law" governing naval warfare, as the preamble to that instrument stated, they also did not markedly depart from those principles. They were, in fact, a compromise both between belligerent and neutral interests and between Anglo-American and Continental views. The declaration certainly did not anticipate the claims to control over neutral trade that belligerents would make in the coming war and could not be reconciled with those claims. The same had to be said, though, of any reasonable interpretation of the customary law.

Despite the expectations attending the conclusion of the Declaration of London, the convention did not become law. Although Great Britain played a leading role in the events that led to the declaration, it subsequently refused to ratify the instrument. The other signatories followed the world's leading naval power. The declaration was without force in August 1914, when the American government, in the first week of the war, proposed that the belligerents nevertheless agree to accept the declaration as the law governing the conduct of hostilities at sea. While most of the belligerents announced their initial willingness to adhere to the provisions of that instrument, in the British case subject to significant reservation, it was only a brief period before the declaration was virtually abandoned by the belligerents. In effect, then, a number of the long-standing controversies over neutral rights at sea were never satisfactorily resolved.

Finally, to the difficulties that arose from the claim of changed conditions and the uncertainty that characterized a part of the traditional law must be added the intractable problem of belligerent reprisals. In the last analysis, a number of the most significant belligerent measures bearing upon neutral trade could not be reconciled even with the most liberal interpretation of the traditional law. Belligerents, determined to escape from the restraints the law imposed, therefore sought to justify these measures by the claim that they formed a necessary and permitted incidence of reprisal action taken in response to the unlawful behavior of an enemy. Even when, exceptionally, belligerent reprisal actions were taken in good faith and with the intent of enforcing compliance with the law, their overall effect was to subvert the traditional rules.

Yet there was no apparent solution to the issues raised by belligerent reprisals at sea. The right of a belligerent to take reprisal measures against an enemy persisting in unlawful behavior was itself unquestioned. But in naval warfare the problem of reprisals was almost always complicated by the presence of neutrals. Not surprisingly, the position of neutral states was consistently one of denying that reprisals between belligerents could serve to justify any infringement of neutral rights. Such infringement, neutrals contended, could follow only from a failure on the part of the neutral state to fulfill its duties. Belligerents, while not denying that reprisals taken in response to an enemy's misconduct should avoid, as far as possible, affecting neutral rights, nevertheless refused to concede that consideration for neutral rights constituted an absolute restriction upon belligerent measures of retaliation.

This disagreement between neutrals and belligerents was complicated further by the fact that unlawful acts charged to a belligerent by an enemy usually adversely affect neutral rights as well. In this situation, the injured belligerent contended that if a neutral would not or could not take the necessary steps to compel the lawbreaker to observe neutral rights, it could not complain if the other belligerent, in the course of retaliating upon an enemy, infringed upon neutral rights. Here again the reply of the neutral was to reject the belligerent's contention that the latter's obligation to respect neutral rights was dependent upon the effectiveness of the measures taken by the neutral to secure belligerent respect for these rights. In the notable exchange between Germany and the United States that marked the end of the *Sussex* crisis in May 1916, the German government, while promising that its submarines would thereafter abide by the rules of maritime warfare, made its promise contingent on the behavior of the Allies. "Neutrals," the German note read, "cannot expect that Germany, forced to fight for her existence, shall, for the sake of neutral interest, restrict the use of an effective weapon if her enemy is permitted to continue to apply at will methods of warfare violating the rules of international law."[17] The American government, however, dismissed the German contention that Berlin's promise could be conditional in any way upon American efforts to obtain Allied conformity with the law. The rights of American citizens upon the high seas, President Wilson wrote in reply to the German note, could not "in any way or in the slightest degree be made contingent upon the conduct of any other government affecting the rights of neutrals and non-combatants. Responsibility in such matters is single, not joint; absolute, not relative."[18]

The German position was not distinctive among those of the belligerents. The Allies embraced it as well. It was a British prize court that, in one of its best-known judgments on the Allied system of reprisals, rejected the argument "that a neutral, too pacific or too impotent to resent the aggressions and lawlessness of one belligerent, can require the other to refrain from his most effective or his only defense against it."[19] The practical effect of accepting this view, however, was to charge the neutral with the task of ensuring that belligerents behaved in conformity with the established rules. This imposed a heavy burden upon neutrals, even a neutral with the resources of the United States. Yet, to this burden was also added the liability resulting from belligerent disagreement over the rules regulating belligerent behavior, with respect both to the enemy and to neutrals. On the first opportunity, it was relatively easy for one belligerent to charge an enemy with the violation of neutral rights and, in the absence of an immediate cessation of the allegedly unlawful action through vigorous neutral response, to consider itself entitled to take appropriate measures of its own against neutral trade. The neutral, caught up in the belligerents' controversy, was made the common victim of belligerent differences.

Those who sided with the neutrals in the bitter controversies that arose in the course of the war at sea naturally stressed these considerations. Yet it was equally apparent that in endorsing the neutral's position a law-abiding belligerent—or, at any rate, a more law abiding belligerent—could be placed at a serious disadvantage. Nor could this disadvantage be characterized merely as one that deprived the belligerent of striking at an offending enemy "through the side" of the neutral. For in many situations the unlawful acts of an enemy, affecting belligerent and neutral alike, might only be effectively countered by acts bearing equally upon both the offender and the neutral. Legal considerations apart, there was much to be said for the positions of both belligerents and neutrals. It was for this reason that the entire problem of reprisals at sea appeared to many detached observers at the time as insoluble.

The conclusion seems especially compelling in the light of the essential function served by belligerent "reprisals" in World War I. Clearly, this function was not to preserve the traditional rights of neutrals. Instead, the evident intent of belligerents was to use reprisals as a means of breaking from the constraints of the traditional law. It was primarily for this reason that reprisal measures soon became not only a permanent but also the dominant feature of warfare at sea during the period of American neutrality. Where belligerents differed was not in their resolve to use reprisals as a means for shutting off all neutral trade with an enemy but in the distinctive methods they employed in pursuit of this aim. It was on the issue of method that the course of American neutrality ultimately turned.

3

Interpretations

The historiography concerning the period leading up to American intervention in 1917 was dominated, in the period between the world wars, by the revisionists. The revisionists appeared less clear about the causes of intervention than they were that intervention had been a mistake. In the major revisionist study of Charles Tansill, *America Goes to War*, the assumption that intervention had been a mistake is apparent throughout. Yet Tansill disclaimed any special insight into the causes of that mistake. "The real reasons why America went to war," he wrote early on in his lengthy work, "cannot be found in any single set of circumstances. There was no clear-cut road to war that the President followed with certain steps that knew no hesitation. There were many dim trails of doubtful promise."[1] In fact, this seeming modesty about the causes of intervention was less than candid. Tansill "knew," as did other revisionists, why the American government had pursued a course that was bound to end in war. It had done so because Wilson was surrounded by advisers intent on siding with the Allies and because Wilson, quite apart from his susceptibility to the influence of his advisers, also believed that Great Britain represented the cause of civilization and that a German victory would eventually pose a threat to American interests in the Western Hemisphere. The British had been adept in exploiting American sympathy and in turning it into substantive support for the Allied cause.

Once influential not only among the lay public but with many historians as well, revisionism fell into almost complete disrepute after World War II.[2] Yet it did not do so because of its insistence that Wilson had not followed a strictly neutral course and that he had not done so because he had sided with Great Britain against Germany. The historiography that succeeded revisionism in the period following World War II did not, on balance, take a substantially different view, though it did put forth a very different account of why Wilson had pursued a neutrality that objectively favored the Allied cause.

The sin of the revisionists that led to their fall from grace must instead be found in their insistence that American intervention in the war had been a great mistake. The revisionists had contributed to the disillusionment of Americans with Europe and its politics during the interwar period. In turn, this attitude had provided important support for isolationism. Not all of the revisionists were isolationists, though most were. Whether they were or were not, there was no doubt that their interpretation of the American experience in World War I provided support for the isolationists of the 1930s. Such support was not, to be sure, the necessary result of the revisionist view of America's earlier experience. The Germany of Hitler, after all, was not the Germany of the kaiser. What had been considered a mistake in 1917 need not have been so considered a generation later and indeed in some instances was not. But on the whole the burden of the revisionist effort was to the effect that the mistake that had once been made ought not be made again. Even revisionists who were not isolationists themselves were the objective allies of the isolationists. More than anything else, it was the de facto alliance of the revisionists with the isolationists of the interwar period that discredited them.

The revisionists subscribed to a voluntarist view of America's experience in World War I. They minimized the circumstances constraining neutrality policy. Wilson's actions were more often than not seen as having been virtually unconditioned. Having enjoyed freedom of action in his neutrality policy, he chose to exercise this freedom by supporting the Allied cause from the start. Too late did he come to realize that the course he had taken, a course that had been insistently urged upon him by House, Page, and Lansing, could have but one outcome.

The historiography of the post–World War II period all but reversed the assumptions and conclusions of the revisionists. In place of the freedom emphasized by the revisionists, the prevailing view of historians writing after 1945 was one that emphasized historical necessity. Looking at the course of events that ended in America's intervention, they drew the judgment that the outcome had been all but inevitable considering the circumstances that conditioned action—the nature of the American position, the outlook and disposition of the American people, the character of the war, the uncertainty of the institution of neutrality. Given these circumstances, an impressive consensus held, there was very little that Wilson might have reasonably done to preserve the nation's neutrality that he did not do, just as there were no promising diplomatic initiatives he might have taken as a neutral to bring the war to an end that he did not take. This being the case, the task of the historian was seen, not as one of torturing himself over what might have been in a crucial period in American history, but simply as one of explaining. As a leading representative of post–World War II historians

once declared, the focus of attention shifted from "what went wrong"—
the concern of the revisionists—to "what happened."[3] What happened,
however, was increasingly seen as what could scarcely have happened
otherwise. To explain became in effect to justify as well.

The seeds of the post–World War II historiography were in fact sown
before World War II in the work of Ray Stannard Baker. It was Baker
who traced Wilson's difficulties in fashioning a neutrality policy to America's distinctive position and power. "From the beginning," he wrote,
"the President of the United States, by virtue of his position and power,
became to an extraordinary degree the arbiter of the war." Baker insisted that Wilson had been neutral in attitude and spirit and that he
had preserved throughout a remarkable detachment about the rights
and wrongs of the war, finding blame on all sides and insisting that an
accounting be deferred until the end of the struggle. Wilson's dominat-
ing purpose, "deeper perhaps than any other aspiration, was . . . not
only to keep America out of the war but to be the instrument for making peace in the world."[4] In the end, however, he was forced to acknowledge that the two could not be reconciled and that neutrality would have
to be sacrificed to the vision of a new world order in which war would
be abolished.

Wilson's neutrality was doomed, in Baker's view, by circumstances over
which he had little or no control. Wilson had not intended that America become a base of supplies for the Allies. It had happened "by force
of circumstances and in consequence of the fortunes of war" (the British
enjoyed a favorable geographical location and superiority at sea). Once
it had developed, Baker wrote (echoing Lansing), any attempt to redress
it would have been inequitable, even a violation of America's duties as
a neutral. Moreover, to have broken the golden chains of commerce that
were soon forged with the Allied side would have resulted in a great
shock to an economy that had just as quickly become dependent on
traffic in war materials. Once deeply entrenched in the American economy, this traffic was probably beyond the power of government to
change.[5]

The same inevitability was seen to govern Wilson's acceptance of the
British maritime system in the fall of 1914. Wilson had initially shown
an inclination to resist many features of the developing Allied blockade.
But in the end, Baker asked, what could he have reasonably done in
response to measures taken by a British government desperately at war
and determined to do anything necessary to shut off Germany's seaborne trade? The sanctions a neutral might take to vindicate its rights
at sea, Baker noted, were war or economic embargo. The United States

was unprepared for war, a course, in any event, that Wilson ruled out. But an embargo, quite apart from its economic implications, might have proven as disastrous as war itself and, indeed, might well have eventuated in war, as it had done in the years before the War of 1812. Then, too, there was the consideration that the formal basis for any action Wilson might have taken, the law governing neutral-belligerent relations at sea, was itself characterized by great uncertainty. "There was no dependable law or code upon which the nations of the world agreed, or any organization to enforce such a code if one had existed."[6] America had itself taken advantage of this uncertainty during the Civil War, Baker observed (again echoing Lansing), when it had expanded belligerent rights, ostensibly according to law but in fact in response to necessity. The British had done the same a half-century later in establishing their system of contraband control.

All paths, then, led to a common destination. The circumstances that imposed themselves on Wilson and that constrained his actions pointed to an inescapable outcome. No diplomacy of neutrality, no matter how skillfully conducted, could have kept the United States out of the war, Baker concluded. "There was a kind of fatality about it all. . . . No human being could, once the crisis arose, do much to change the disastrous course of events."[7]

These themes became the common fare of historians writing in the post–World War II period. They too could scarcely imagine Wilson having taken, even during the critical initial period of the war, a neutral course very different from the one he did take, and for substantially the same reasons that Baker invoked. At the same time, they strengthened Baker's argument by drawing implications from it that he had not done. Baker had argued that given America's position and power, it was inescapably the arbiter of the war. But why had Wilson become the kind of arbiter he soon did? Baker's answer was that the other circumstances attending the conflict—geography, British naval dominance, the development of wartime trade, the absence of acceptable sanctions against early British infringements on neutral rights, the very uncertainty of neutral rights—had all but dictated Wilson's course.

Later historians, while also emphasizing these considerations, took Baker's explanation of Wilson's course still further.[8] Given America's position and power, they maintained, *any* course Wilson might have taken would have conferred an advantage, and in all likelihood a decisive advantage, on one side or the other. This being the case, the assumptions, however unspoken, that formed the very foundation of neutrality were largely irrelevant in the circumstances that marked the Great

War. But if neutrality as traditionally conceived was all but impossible, the only alternative to the course that was taken, one that admittedly favored the Allies, was one that sided with Germany. Had the United States insisted upon keeping open the channels of trade with both sides, Edward Buehrig argued, "Germany would undoubtedly have abstained from ruthless assault on world shipping for she would have accomplished her end through virtual alliance with the United States."[9] Trade with both sides meant alliance with Germany. Wilson's choice was between accepting the British maritime system and pursuing in effect an alliance with Germany. To have sided with Germany, however, would have meant the denial of vital national interests, both economic and political. "It is hard to conceive of alternative courses that Wilson and Lansing might have followed in 1914," Ernest May wrote in his now standard account of the period, "without sacrificing the national economic interest, violating their own moral codes, and deliberately rendering service to the Germans. It may not be too much to say, indeed, that the alternatives not only were unthinkable for the Wilson administration but would have been for any administration similarly situated."[10] May characterized Wilson's course as one of "benevolent neutrality"; it was a benevolence, though, that reflected the working of necessity far more than that of choice.

In the work of the premier Wilson scholar, the president's choice, if one may still call it that, is also seen as one between objectively favoring the Allies and objectively favoring the Central powers. Explaining Wilson's early adjustment to the British maritime system, Arthur Link concluded that "British sea power . . . was one of the important facts of international life in 1914. The American leaders could not have been substantially neutral, that is, as impartial as circumstances would permit, and deny that the British had a right to stop the flow of supplies and raw materials that were obviously essential for the easy functioning of the German war economy."[11] To have acted otherwise would have been to side with Germany, a course that, in its denial of vital national interests, was all but inconceivable. "Wilson could not have been unaware of the political results that would have flowed from an effective American challenge to British sea power—the wrecking of American friendship with the two great European democracies, the possible victory of the Central Powers, and the sure ending of all hopes of American mediation—all without a single compensating gain for the interests and security of the American people and the future welfare of mankind."[12] Nevertheless, Link did not deem Wilson's course one of "benevolent neutrality." Like Baker, he judged Wilson in terms of outlook and intention. "If any single conclusion comes out of the evidence," he wrote in the preface to the fifth and final volume of his monumental study of the life and times of Woodrow Wilson, "it is that Wilson tried sincerely to pursue policies of rigid neutrality toward the Entente allies."[13] Wilson had been as neutral as circumstances and interests permitted. His departures from neutrality in practice—as opposed to thought and desire—were beyond Wilson's, or, for that matter, any statesman's, control. But if this was indeed the case, could it be fairly said that Wilson had been unneutral?

Interestingly enough, Wilson himself may be invoked on behalf of both sides of the issue respecting his fidelity to neutrality. The Wilson who insisted on his strict impartiality throughout is of course well known. The Wilson who subsequent to intervention insisted on his partiality is less so. Yet he existed. The locus classicus of the shift is the war address. While the war address set forth the orthodoxy, it also pointed the way to a new version of the period of neutrality and the reasons for intervention. Wilson having once abandoned a view of the war that refused to find moral significance in its "causes and objects," having once disavowed the conviction of the belligerents' moral equivalence, what had been the moral basis of neutrality for him was overturned. In a conflict between freedom and despotism, democracy and autocracy, Wilson's new understanding of the war, impartiality was to be condemned. Henceforth in his reconstruction of the recent past Wilson had never been impartial. He had instead long held back from actively casting his lot in with those fighting for freedom, he told Theodore Roosevelt several days following the war address, only because the American people "were not awake to the need, and . . . he had to bide his time."[14]

The president had banished from memory his earlier, determined opposition to intervention and was never to readmit it. In August 1919, in the course of a memorable meeting with the members of the Senate Committee on Foreign Relations to discuss the Versailles Treaty, a senator put the following question to Wilson: "Do you think that if Germany had committed no act of war or no act of injustice against our citizens that we would have gotten into this war?" The president unhesitatingly replied: "I do think so."[15] Wilson was the fount of the orthodox version of why America intervened. He was also the first "revisionist."[16]

Might Wilson have followed a course that held out greater promise of issuing in a durable peace? His interwar revisionist critics did not really address this question. Their concern was not with what America's contribution to the postwar international order might have been but with whether America could have remained out of the war by pursuing what in their view was a neutrality of strict impartiality. Persuaded that no vital American interests had been at stake in the conflict, the revisionists contended that had Wilson pursued a strictly neutral course, which he presumably had been free to do, he could have avoided participation in the war. But this conclusion followed only by assuming that the defense of neutral rights, if necessary by force, would not have resulted at some point in America's participation in the conflict. It may be that had a more strictly neutral America been ready to use force in defense of its rights, and had this readiness to do so been made apparent to the belligerents from the start, the need to do so would never have arisen. Certainly there is reason for believing that this would have been the case with respect to Great Britain. Whether it would have been the case with respect to Germany as well is another matter. It might have been, though the evidence suggests otherwise.

In any event, revisionists had no way of knowing what the German response would have been to an America that hewed to a strict neutrality and was prepared from the outset to defend its rights. Nor had they any way of knowing whether such defense would not have eventuated in America's participation in the war. America's experience in the preceding century instead supported the conclusion that in a general European war, one fought over the balance of power, a readiness to defend neutral rights afforded no guarantee of avoiding participation in the war. Even more, it indicated that in a war involving the major European powers a policy of strict neutrality backed by force was in conflict with a policy of isolation (with its corollary of nonparticipation in such a war). Bryan, the hero to many of the revisionists, had instinctively recognized this and was prepared to resolve the conflict by the simple expedient of abandoning those neutral rights whose defense threatened to lead to armed confrontation. In this, Bryan was nothing if not consistent, whatever else may be said of his position. Bryan's logic led a generation later, in the 1930s, to the short-lived American policy of "renunciatory" neutrality, whereby traditional neutral rights at sea were renounced in favor of a self-imposed isolation in war that went far beyond the requirements of existing law.

The revisionists were wrong in insisting that a policy of strict neutrality would have kept the United States out of World War I. Whether it would have done so depended on the use the Germans made of the submarine and, of course, on America's response. Even so, revisionists were not wrong in insisting that Wilson had not followed a course of strict neutrality but from the outset had shown in his actions a marked partiality to the Allies. Nor were they wrong in contending that Wilson had not been constrained by circumstance to follow the course that he did. Doubtless revisionists often exaggerated the president's freedom of action. On balance, however, their depiction of a president at liberty to follow any one of several quite different courses seems closer to reality than the picture regularly drawn by the post–World War II historiography of a president confronted by circumstances over which he had but little control.

The course the president might instead have taken was one that combined a strict neutrality with measures of preparedness.[17] Its logic was simple enough and followed from Wilson's primary objectives, which were to remain out of the war and mediate an end to the war on the basis of the status quo ante. These objectives dictated, in turn, that the war be brought to an early end. As long as the conflict lasted, there was the danger of America's involvement. Then, too, the longer the war went on and the greater the destruction it wrought, the poorer the prospects were likely to be for a just and lasting peace.

Whether Wilson fully appreciated the importance of ending the war as quickly as possible is unclear. While he found the war itself shameful and odious, something open to "utter condemnation," it did not necessarily follow that once the conflict had begun, the most important consideration was to bring it to the earliest possible end. How it ended seemed to Wilson, at least in the beginning, as important as how soon it ended. Thus his hope, expressed in an interview with Herbert Brougham in December 1914, that the war would end in a deadlock, which would show the belligerents the futility of employing force to resolve their differences. The chance of a "just and equitable peace," Wilson believed, "will be happiest if no nation gets the decision by arms."[18] Yet he acknowledged in the same interview that an Allied victory would not "hurt greatly the interests of the United States." By contrast, a German victory would not be "an ideal solution." In any event, Wilson believed that the government of Germany "must be profoundly changed" as a result of the war. How this was to result from a deadlock, or even from a moderate Allied victory (which House favored), was left unexplained.

The Brougham interview indicates that four months after the war began, Wilson had yet to form a coherent position on how American neutrality might be used to further prospects of a just and equitable peace. The interview conveys a determination to keep the country out of the war, regardless of its outcome. This determination did not reflect an unwillingness to recognize that American interests would be affected by the outcome. Wilson may have underestimated the consequences for American interests of a German victory. House reports him as saying in November "that no matter how the great war ended, there would be complete exhaustion, and, even if Germany won, she would not be in a condition to seriously menace our country for many years to come."[19] Yet even this statement bears out Wilson's recognition that American interests dictated, if not an Allied victory, then a standoff that would leave Britain's naval supremacy intact. If he minimized the consequences a German victory held out to American interests, it was not because he was blind to the differences between a British and a German victory but because he believed that these differences, though significant, were nevertheless insufficient to justify America's participation in the war.

At the same time, Wilson's desire that the war end in a standoff, in what would later become known as a peace without victory, was not disinterested. To the contrary, it clearly expressed a distinctive view of the nation's interest. The evident result of a war in which "no nation gets the decision by arms" is a peace based on the status quo ante. To be sure, the president's conception of a just and equitable peace also equated the peace that would follow the war with a new international order, one in which states would be forbidden to resort to aggressive war. Even so, the new order would be based on the prewar status quo. Great Britain would retain her dominant position at sea, and Germany would at a minimum have to give up the lands her armies had occupied (and very likely have to submit to a measure of disarmament). The prewar balance of power, a balance that had been favorable to American security, would thus be restored and presumably even strengthened by virtue of the restraints the new order placed on the resort to force.

Still, the question that had to be answered was how the American government might mediate such a peace. For America to play the role of peacemaker required that American neutrality enjoy the respect and the trust of both sides in the conflict. But this requirement was never satisfied. After only several months of war, Wilson's neutrality had lost the respect of Great Britain and the trust of Germany. A strict neutrality, together with a readiness to enforce neutral rights by arms if necessary, might have gained the respect, even the trust, of both sides. And it might have resulted in securing the dependence of both sides rather than, as matters turned out, only of one. A measure of moderation and restraint might in consequence have been imposed on the belligerents' conduct of the war at sea and led to the deadlock on which the president had placed his hopes. Wilson's deadlock was a promising notion only if it issued from a war waged with moderation and restraint. Otherwise, it was an invitation, however unintended, to a warfare that in the end would prove contemptuous of any limits. That from this warfare would emerge the most promising chance of a just and lasting peace was surely one of Wilson's greatest illusions.

A strict neutrality would have denied the use Great Britain made of its sea power from the outset of the war. That Wilson could have imposed this denial, that he could have required Britain to conform to the provisions of the Declaration of London or, failing that, to a strict interpretation of the customary law, is not seriously contested by those who have found little fault with his neutrality. Instead, they have argued that any course other than the one Wilson in fact followed would have favored Germany. It would have done so by denying Great Britain the advantages that nation enjoyed by virtue of her naval supremacy. And it would have done so without, in Arthur Link's words, "a single compensating gain for the interests and security of the American people."[20] A choice had to be made, the familiar argument runs, between Great Britain and Germany. Wilson made the right choice, indeed the only choice a president so situated could have made.

It is not fatal to this view that it rests on a basic misunderstanding of the institution of neutrality. Nevertheless, it does do so in its virtual equation of power and law. The traditional system of neutrality was not simply the handmaiden of sea power. Its purpose was quite as much to constrain sea power as it was to provide for its effective use. This being the case, there was always an inherent and insoluble conflict between the law of neutrality and the interest of the dominant naval power to exploit its superiority without hindrance by neutral states. The traditional law of neutrality certainly did not express the irrelevance of sea power, but it did assert that this power, while undoubtedly significant in the development of the law, had to be exercised within certain limits. In 1914 these limits, had the American government insisted on their observance, would have prevented Great Britain from doing what it was clearly intent on doing after the first two weeks of the war.

To argue that American leaders could not have been expected to qualify the advantage Great Britain enjoyed at sea by virtue of its naval supremacy or to assert that President Wilson "could not have been substantially neutral . . . and deny that the British had a right to stop the flow of supplies and raw materials" essential to the functioning of the German economy[21] is to make neutrality and neutrals the pliant accomplices of the dominant power at sea. The British "right" to stop the flow of neutral trade to Germany was neither more nor less than the law of contraband and blockade permitted at the time. In September 1914, what this law permitted was plainly spelled out by the State and Navy Neutrality Board in its draft protest of the initial measures of contraband control taken by Great Britain, a draft that was rejected by Wilson.[22]

Neither geography nor Britain's naval dominance dictated the character American neutrality soon took. Wilson might have chosen to follow a different course, one that placed clear limits on the claims of Great Britain to control neutral trade and that, accordingly, kept open such trade with Germany as the Declaration of London, or the customary law, allowed. This course admittedly afforded no guarantee against America's eventual involvement in the conflict. Moreover, its effectiveness necessitated measures the nation was reluctant to undertake: an arms program of sufficient magnitude to impress the European belligerents with America's determination to defend neutral rights.[23] And its effect would have been to make Britain's position more difficult. Still, these considerations must be weighed against the consideration that a course of strict neutrality held out the only prospect of mediating an early end to the war on the basis of the prewar status quo.

It was not Germany that would have initially opposed this course, but Great Britain. Germany would have benefited from a neutral trade that was otherwise denied it. Great Britain, on the other hand, would have been denied the control over neutral trade to which it almost immediately laid claim. Would it have refused to retreat from its early pretensions, even at the risk of a dangerous confrontation with the United States? "We wish in all our conduct of the war," Sir Edward Grey instructed his ambassador in Washington in early September 1914, "to do nothing which will be a cause of complaint or dispute as regards the U.S. Govt. Such a dispute would indeed be a crowning calamity . . . & probably fatal to our chances of success."[24] There is little reason to doubt Grey's postwar testimony that "it was better . . . to carry on the war without blockade, if need be, than to incur a break with the United States."[25]

A Great Britain unwilling to confront a determined America over neutral rights was nevertheless not a Great Britain willing to accept American mediation. The power to compel the observance of neutral rights was not the same as the power to compel acceptance of American mediation. But would compulsion have been necessary to obtain British agreement to peace terms that on almost any reading would have favored Great Britain? A peace based on the prewar status quo was still objectionable if it failed to afford sufficient guarantee for the security of France and the independence of the small states. Provided this could be done, however, the British government might have been receptive to an American-sponsored proposal based on the prewar status quo, and this despite the risk that such a proposal would not be accepted by Britain's allies. Grey indicated as much to House in the winter of 1915 when he asked whether the United States might agree to play an active role in postwar security arrangements, only to receive a negative response. The American government, House declared, could not consider departing from the nation's fixed policy of noninvolvement in European affairs. The president, House went on to state, had no desire or ambition "to become mediator . . . his sole purpose was to serve in the least conspicuous way possible."[26] Wilson had written to the same effect in his commission to House to go to Europe as his personal representative. "Our single object is to be serviceable . . . in bringing about the preliminary willingness to parley which must be the first step toward discussing and determining the conditions of peace. If we can be instrumental in ascertaining for each side . . . what is the real disposition, the real wish, the real purpose of the other with regard to a settlement, your mission and my whole desire in this matter will have been accomplished."[27]

This was Wilson's initial position. It constituted a very cautious first step toward a larger and more ambitious role. Between that first step and the assumption of a larger role was a gap that could be closed only by the abandonment of what House termed the fixed policy of noninvolvement in European affairs. In the first year of the war Wilson remained unwilling to close that gap. Although he increasingly aspired to the role of peacemaker, he did so from a position that clung to the nation's historic separation from Europe. Mediation was itself seen as a means for preserving America's isolation from the old continent. The idea of making a commitment to Great Britain to take an active part in postwar security arrangements was still a considerable step beyond Wilson's purview. Yet that step was an essential prerequisite to any serious consideration of peace proposals by Great Britain.

The case for believing that had Wilson followed a different course, Great Britain might have given serious consideration to American efforts to bring the war to an end is at least plausible. May a plausible case to the same effect be made for Germany? Certainly, it is considerably more difficult to do so. However strict the neutral course Wilson might have followed, it still would have favored Great Britain. A strict neutrality would still not have canceled out the advantages the British enjoyed by virtue of their naval supremacy. However insistent Wilson might have been upon observance of the rules governing contraband

and blockade, the trade Germany could hope to have with the United States would not have approached in volume and kind the trade Great Britain enjoyed.

Even so, it will not do to speculate on how Germany might have responded to a different American course by pointing to how it did in fact respond to Wilson's neutrality. At least it will not do unless it is assumed that Germany's course in the war was all but irrevocably set from the outset and, as such, beyond America's ability to influence. But this assumption is evidently unreasonable. Germany's war leaders were not determined to follow a given course regardless of the consequences to which they might in time come to believe it would lead. Had the German war leaders believed that the use they made of the submarine would not only lead to war with America but seriously compromise their prospects of victory, and quite possibly end in their defeat, presumably they would have forgone such use. Without making the use they did of the submarine, however, they could not have entertained the goal of isolating Great Britain (as Great Britain could not have undertaken the goal of isolating Germany without making the use it did of its vast superiority in surface vessels). Unable to isolate their great adversary, the key to Britain's defeat, Germany might have been receptive to American mediation proposals.

This is the strongest form in which the case may be put. It assumes that the United States would have kept open the channels of trade with Germany in noncontraband goods, that Germany would have had access to foodstuffs as well as to a range of raw materials not designated as contraband either by past practice or by the Declaration of London. And it further assumes that the United States would have been ready to enforce its neutrality against a serious and persistent challenge to it. In practice, such a challenge could only have come from Germany, it being difficult to imagine circumstances in which an Anglo-American confrontation would have arisen. Germany was another matter, and a resolute neutrality had to be backed by arms and a readiness to use them. But until the sinking of the *Lusitania,* Wilson was resistant to the proposition that the defense of neutrality was inseparable from measures of national defense.

In the fall of 1914 the first and only opportunity arose to fashion a neutrality that would have been responsive both to American interests and to the interests of the belligerent states as well. American interests did not require the defeat of Germany; they only required that Great Britain not be defeated and that Britain emerge from the war still dominant at sea. A brief war that ended in a deadlock and, in consequence, a restoration of the prewar status quo would have been, as Wilson stated, the happiest outcome.

If an early end to the war was indispensable for achieving a satisfactory peace, a war conducted with restraint was indispensable for bringing it to an early end. A war conducted with restraint was almost by definition one conducted according to the rules of maritime warfare. The commonplace view that these rules, being a nineteenth-century inheritance, were no longer workable given the social, political, and technological changes that had occurred in the generation preceding the war expresses only a partial truth. These changes did not make inevitable the warfare that soon emerged, though it is true that by making this warfare far easier they made it much harder to avoid. Still, the methods and measures employed by the belligerents were decreed above all by their unlimited ends, ends that as time went by would brook few limits on means.

Given Wilson's objectives, his neutrality policy should have been one of bending all efforts to keep the conflict at sea limited, for in the limitation of means lay the only hope that the war might be brought to an early end through mediation. But that policy could have held out promise only if he had been willing to take measures he turned away from in the first six months of the war. At a time when activism and a clear sense of direction were imperative, Wilson was instead passive and without a clear direction. On more than one occasion in the fall of 1914, House complained that the president seemed not to appreciate the importance of the European crisis.[28] In the far-reaching concessions he made to Great Britain, in his apparent lack of concern over the possible German reaction to these concessions, and in his resistance to any suggestion that measures of preparedness be given serious consideration, Wilson gave the impression of a statesman unable or unwilling to perceive the logic of his actions and how much in conflict they were with his objectives.

At the same time, it must be acknowledged that the prospects for mediating an early end to the war were limited, even had Wilson followed a strict neutrality and supported this course by measures of preparedness. Interest alone precluded any American government from endorsing a peace proposal that did not restore the principal features of the prewar status quo. To this, both sides in the war were opposed—the Allies because a return to the prewar status quo would leave them without greater security against a German renewal of the war, Germany because a return to the prewar status quo meant Britain's continued dominance at sea. And while the United States might conceivably have addressed Britain's concern by promising to take an active part in post-war security arrangements, it could scarcely have addressed German aspirations, intent as they were on changing the prewar status quo. These aspirations might have been altered, perhaps even abandoned, by a radical change in Germany's political-military power structure. This was evidently Wilson's persuasion in declaring that the government of Germany "must be profoundly changed" as a result of the war. But such change would presumably be the consequence of a war in which Germany would be defeated, not a war that would be brought to an early end through mediation. At a time when Germany's military fortunes still seemed promising, as they did during most of the first year of war, it would have been feckless to base a policy of mediation on an outcome that could be expected only in the event of Germany's defeat.

However modest the prospects of bringing the war to an early end through mediation, they presupposed a course that Wilson did not take. The course he did take was one almost perfectly fashioned for America's intervention in the war. By acquiescing in fact in the Allied blockade and by opposing the only active response the Central powers could have made to the blockade, Wilson abandoned the impartiality required of a neutral. Once he had done so, there was but one possible outcome: war with Germany. That he nevertheless managed to stave off this outcome for almost two years after the crisis occasioned by the sinking of the *Lusitania* is rightly pointed to as evidence of the depth of his desire to keep America out of the war. Still, the measure of neutrality—it cannot be repeated too often—is the depth and sincerity not of desire but of action. By the latter test, Wilson was unneutral from the outset, and he remained so until events finally left him with no alternative but war.

Judged by the standard Wilson himself had set, his neutrality ended in failure. Yet the failure went much deeper than he allowed. Wilson judged his course a failure because it eventuated in war. We must judge it a failure because it eventuated in a war too late. Compared with a successful mediation, intervention was clearly a case of *faute de mieux,* above all in Wilson's eyes. But America's early intervention in the war could have been expected to enhance the prospects of at least one of Wilson's objectives, a just and lasting peace. It could have been expected to do so by sparing Europe the destructiveness of a conflict that dragged on for years and that made a satisfactory peace virtually unobtainable. Given this prospect, an early intervention should have been the next best course to one that ended in a mediated peace based on the prewar status quo. By the summer of 1915, however, what modest chances there might once have been for such a peace had all but disappeared.

This being so, the values that might once have been preserved through mediation could be preserved, ironically, only through intervention.

Is this little more than the wisdom of hindsight? Not quite. There were some who possessed this wisdom at the time, even some who were close to Wilson. By the summer of 1915 House had come to the view that America's intervention in the conflict was not only inevitable, given the collision course on which America and Germany were then moving, but desirable. "I need not tell you," he wrote to the president in mid-June, "that if the Allies fail to win it must necessarily mean a reversal of our entire policy." But the Allies were so failing, and House, with his eye on the *Lusitania* crisis, declared: "I think we will find ourselves drifting into war with Germany. . . . Regrettable as this would be, there would be compensations. The war would be more speedily ended and we would be in a strong position to aid the other great democracies in turning the world into the right paths. It is something that we have to face with fortitude being consoled by the thought that no matter what sacrifices we make, the end will justify them."[29] But the man to whom House's letter was addressed could find little consolation in these words.

4

German Submarines and the Long-Distance Blockade

Wilson's early partiality to the Allied cause is a matter of record. To House he was quite open in voicing his pro-Allied feelings. But House, after all, was his confidant. Wilson's remarks to the British ambassador were another matter. "Everything that I love most in the world is at stake," Spring Rice reported the president as saying in early September 1914. If the Germans were to succeed, Wilson went on to tell the ambassador, "we shall be forced to take such measures of defense here as would be fatal to our form of Government and American ideals." These statements, though scarcely conforming to Wilson's "neutrality in thought," were perhaps still less significant than Spring Rice's summary to Grey of the president's remarks: "Officially, he would do all that he could to maintain absolute neutrality, and would bear in mind that a dispute between our two nations would be the crowning calamity."[1] The significance of Wilson's remark was that a serious dispute would be a crowning calamity for *both* countries. Which would it be—the maintenance of "absolute neutrality" or the avoidance of a "crowning calamity"? Wilson's formula, typically enough, encompassed both and thereby assumed that a need to choose between the two would not arise. Events were soon to show this assumption to be much too sanguine. When they did, it was "absolute neutrality" that the president would sacrifice, as Spring Rice had correctly predicted. Several days following his conversation with the president, the ambassador wrote again to Grey: "I am sure we can at the right moment depend on an understanding heart here."[2]

Wilson's understanding heart has often been contrasted with his understanding head, that is, with his awareness that whatever his personal sympathies, the nation's neutral course imposed a duty of absolute impartiality. If the heart was sympathetic and partial to the Allied cause in the beginning, the head was always impartial. But the contrast drawn between Wilson's personal disposition and his official disposition can be taken only so far. The partiality the president betrayed in the opening stages of the war did not respond simply to ties of language, culture, and common institutions. It reflected as well a view of interest that would be jeopardized by a German, though not by an Allied, victory. Although the idea of a peace without victory can be found in his thought almost from the beginning stages of the war, so too may the view that a British defeat would adversely affect American interests. But the converse did not hold. And while he did not regard an Allied victory as an ideal solution—which House did, provided the victory was moderate—he also did not see, as he told a journalist in December 1914, "that it would hurt greatly the interests of the United States if either France or Russia or Great Britain should finally dictate the settlement."[3] Wilson's suspicions of Allied motives and aspirations steadily deepened as the period of neutrality progressed. Still, save in rare moments, this did not blind him from seeing that American interests would suffer were the Allies to lose the war.

In the opening period of the war the expectations of Allied defeat were ever present. The aura of invincibility that attended the progress of German armies through Belgium and France lasted until the end of September 1914, when the results of the battle of the Marne put an end to German prospects for a swift victory. Wilson's expressions of sympathy for the Allies occurred for the most part during this period, as did his expressions of concern over the consequences held out for America by a German victory. Whereas on August 30 House recorded in his diary that he had found the president "as unsympathetic with the German attitude as is the balance of America" and of the opinion "that if Germany won it would change the course of our civilization and make the United States a military nation," on November 4 the colonel depicted a president who had regained his equanimity and his air of detachment. In rejecting House's advocacy of a reserve army, Wilson declared "that no matter how the great war ended, there would be complete exhaustion, and, even if Germany won, she would not be in a condition to seriously menace our country for many years to come."[4] But Wilson no longer appeared to believe, as he had earlier, that Germany might well win the war. Although in a December 1914 interview he spoke of the relative desirability of the war's ending in a deadlock rather than in an Allied victory,[5] he no longer considered the consequences a German victory might hold out. Fears of a German victory had not disappeared, but they had markedly receded. The Wilson of late summer, given to personal expressions of sympathy for the Allies and to private condemnation of Germany for having begun hostilities as well as for its conduct toward Belgium, was succeeded by the more circumspect Wilson of early winter.

American acceptance of the British maritime system in the fall of 1914 owed to an interest in ensuring that the Allies did not lose the war at sea. The avoidance of serious conflict with Great Britain, which dictated acceptance of the British measures to control trade in contraband, was necessitated by and inseparable from this interest. It will not do to admit the one interest, the avoidance of conflict, yet deny the other, the prevention of defeat. Even if the specter of 1812 did haunt Wilson, his actions cannot simply be seen as a response to a badly strained historical parallel.

The president's partiality to the Allied cause was not without limits, but until the spring of 1915 those limits went untested. This simple fact, the result of the way in which the war developed, is of great importance. The sequence of events was such that Wilson was not squarely confronted with the need to choose between a course of strict neutrality and a course that was partial to one side. The contradiction between the desire to remain a nonparticipant and the desire to avoid conflict with Great Britain went unresolved. It might have been faced and resolved had the price that one day might have to be paid for its nonresolution been clearly demonstrated at an early date. But there was no demonstration or even the hint of one until early February 1915, when the German government issued its declaration on submarine warfare, and by then Wilson was quite firmly committed to a pro-Allied course. Even in February the price was not really apparent, and it would not become so until the events of the spring and early summer.

The question of timing was critical, particularly for a president not given to ordering interests or to anticipating events. ("The fact is, I have never had any patience with 'ifs' and conjectural cases. My mind insists always upon waiting until something actually does happen."[6]) America's initial difficulties as a neutral were with Great Britain, not with Germany. Out of these difficulties emerged a definitive position toward the British system of contraband control. Had the outset of the war been marked by serious differences with Germany as well, Wilson might well have reacted quite differently to the development of the Allied blockade. He would have seen—at the very least, he would have been in a far better position to see—the price that might have to be paid for accepting the blockade. Instead, that price was largely obscured to him until he had become committed to a position from which he could withdraw only with great difficulty.

If the sequence of events enabled Wilson to avoid facing up to the predicament his actions were leading to, so too did the American position. That position, it was earlier observed, posed a dilemma. Because of the nation's size and industrial power, America was from the outset, as Baker insisted, the potential arbiter of the war. Whatever course it might take in the war would have an important and perhaps determinative effect on the fortunes of the belligerents. That fact expressed a dilemma, for it virtually ensured that America's neutrality would be the object of never-ending contention on the part of the belligerents, thus adding greatly to the usual problems attending neutral status. But the American position also could be seen to hold out a solution to the dilemma it posed, and during the initial period of neutrality Wilson appears to have seen that position in this light. It encouraged him to believe what in any event he wanted to believe, that by virtue of America's great advantages it might exercise a determining influence on the conduct of the war at sea without becoming a participant in the war. America would determine how the war at sea would be fought but remain outside the conflict. America would not arm. It would not abandon its historic policy of isolation. It would continue to enjoy the benefits of isolation, while also enjoying the fruits of intervention. Only in April and May of 1915 did the light suddenly dawn.

The German government had observed in silence the developments marking the Anglo-American relationship during the first six months of the war. It had made no response to the outcome of the fall negotiations between Washington and London. It had not remonstrated with the American government over the latter's passivity before the British mining of the North Sea in early November. The munitions trade with the Allies had yet to evoke adverse reaction on an official level (indeed in December this trade had been acknowledged by the German ambassador as affording no cause for complaint). In general, the course of German-American relations had been free of controversy. The disappearance of Germany's seaborne trade once hostilities began had virtually ensured the absence of the kinds of disputes that had arisen between the United States and Great Britain.

Yet appearances were deceiving. In the case of Great Britain, controversy over neutral rights overlaid a remarkable measure of agreement. In the case of Germany, the absence of controversy over these rights obscured a growing estrangement. By mid-fall 1914 the operation of American neutrality left no doubt about which side would be strongly favored. Opposition to the Wilson administration's neutrality policy soon found expression among pro-German elements of the American population. Proposals to embargo trade in munitions largely reflected this opposition. So did threats of electoral punishment, threats that provoked Wilson's ire. From the outset the president was far more sensitive to criticism, let alone to threats, from Germany and its supporters in the United States than he was to criticism from Great Britain and its more vocal domestic champions. No doubt one reason for this disparity was the extraordinary heavy-handedness of the Germans and their sympathizers in the United States. But style can take one only so far. Much more important was the built-in bias on the part of a vast majority of the American population in favor of the Allied cause. In this respect, Wilson was quite representative of the nation.

Opposition to Wilson's neutrality policies among pro-German groups in the fall of 1914 was the prelude to rising resentment of those policies in Germany. By January 1915 the American ambassador in Berlin, James Gerard, was reporting on a German public that showed an ever-deepening hostility to the United States primarily because of the trade in munitions with the Allies. "I do not think that people in America realize," Gerard wrote to Bryan, "how excited the Germans have become on the question of the selling of munitions of war by Americans to the Allies. A veritable campaign of hate has been commenced against America and Americans."[7] This trade, together with what the German government saw as American complicity in the Allied blockade, would soon give point and plausibility to Lansing's memorandum of February 15, with its conclusion that Berlin might no longer calculate the disadvantages of war with the United States as outweighing the advantages.[8] Lansing's conclusion was premature. Almost two years would pass before the German government acted on the rough logic of his memorandum. In late January 1915 Berlin had no thought of war with the United States, and it would not have set out on the course that it did had it correctly anticipated the reaction of neutrals, above all the United States.

Germany had begun to consider the submarine as a commerce destroyer in the early fall of 1914.[9] The immobilization of the surface fleet had left Germany with no means to wage the war at sea save the submarine. After almost discounting the submarine at the outset of hostilities, the German government began to take seriously the prospects it held out in September, when the offensive capabilities of the craft were demonstrated by the sinking of several British cruisers with the torpedoes of a single submarine. Once the U-boat's potential as a commerce destroyer was appreciated, its use became all but irresistible. Standing in the way of its employment were legal and political rather than technical military considerations. The submarine could conform to the long-established rules governing cruiser warfare only with great difficulty, if indeed at all. While enemy warships might be sunk at sight, belligerent merchant ships could not be made the object of attack as long as they did not resist visit, search, and seizure. In certain defined

circumstances a belligerent was permitted to destroy rather than conduct captured enemy merchant vessels into port for adjudication by a
prize court. Even in those circumstances, however, destruction was permitted only after passengers and crew had been removed to a place of
safety (an obligation that was not considered fulfilled merely by allowing passengers and crew to take to the ship's boats, unless the safety of
the latter was assured). The same rules applied to neutral merchant vessels seized for carriage of contraband, breach of blockade, or the performance of unneutral services, though the circumstances in which
destruction was permitted were yet more strict.

At the outbreak of World War I these rules went unquestioned; the
fundamental distinction between combatants and noncombatants rested
largely on their observance. Proposals by the German navy to use the
submarine without regard for these rules were accordingly resisted by
German government officials and by the kaiser, Germany's supreme
warlord. But this resistance was short lived, for it soon became apparent
that in less than ideal conditions the submarine could not be effectively
employed were it to conform to the rules of cruiser warfare. It could
conduct visit and search only in favorable weather conditions, and then
only if assured that enemy warships were not in the vicinity. It could not,
save in unusual circumstances, provide for the safety of passengers and
crew of merchantmen. Later, the submarine's vulnerability to attack by
armed merchantmen would further complicate the issues attending its
use, though in the beginning there were few British merchant ships that
carried arms.

The decision to proclaim a war zone around the British Isles was
taken by the German government on February 4, 1915, and immediately announced to the world. Initial opposition to the measure had
steadily eroded in Germany, partly as it became more widely recognized
that the submarine could not be effectively employed save by abandoning the rules of cruiser warfare, partly as the long-term threat held out
by the Allied blockade became increasingly apparent, and partly as
public enthusiasm mounted for using the submarine to fullest advantage. Throughout this period the chief of the admiralty staff, Admiral
Hugo von Pohl, had campaigned unrelentingly for unrestricted submarine warfare. Britain's mining of the North Sea and its declaration that
the North Sea constituted a war zone gave Pohl unexpected support.
The German government might now justify unrestricted submarine
warfare as a measure of reprisal taken in response to the action of Great
Britain. In January the German navy's case for unleashing the submarine was further strengthened by the argument that English food sup-

plies being low, the time to strike had come. A reluctant kaiser grudg-ingly gave his consent. A yet more reluctant chancellor, Theobald von Bethmann Hollweg, did so as well on the condition that the move would not provoke strong neutral reaction. It was the beginning of the long struggle between Bethmann Hollweg and the navy over use of the submarine.

The German admiralty's declaration of February 4 announced that after February 18, enemy merchant ships within a broad zone sur-rounding the British Isles would be subject to attack without warning. Neutral ships were cautioned that as a consequence of Britain's misuse of neutral flags, they might be mistaken for enemy ships and advised to avoid the war zone.[10] On February 7, Berlin explained its action. The declaration was justified as a reprisal, taken in response to Great Britain's alleged violations of international law, which had paralyzed legitimate neutral commerce and which were designed to destroy the German na-tion by starvation. Neutrals, the German memorandum charged, had generally acquiesced in these unlawful measures. Against the British plea of vital interests, neutrals had been content with theoretical pro-tests. Germany was now forced to appeal to these same vital interests. In doing so, it hoped and expected that neutral nations would show no less consideration for the vital interests of Germany than they had shown for those of England and would keep their citizens and property from the area declared a war zone.[11]

Germany's expectation proved vain. All of the neutral states strongly protested. It was the American reaction that mattered most to Berlin, however, for it was largely on the calculation of this nation's passivity that the Germans had acted. In retrospect, that calculation has been seen as a prime example of the political and moral obtuseness that in the end proved so fatal to Germany's fortunes. Yet, considered from Berlin's perspective, at the time the decision to use the submarine in the only way it could be used effectively was not an unreasonable one. The need to make some response to the noose then tightening about Germany's neck was increasingly apparent. Although the Allied block-ade had yet to effect any shortages, food or otherwise, the outlook should the war be prolonged was clear. It was true that the Germans had decided upon a course of action without the military means to support it. The submarine fleet was still much too small to constitute a credible military threat to the Allies. But in the interim period prior to its possi-bly becoming such a challenge, the hope was that it might serve as a weapon of terror that would bring neutral traffic to a halt. The great unknown, of course, was America's reaction. Given the U.S. government's acquiescence in the Allied blockade, though, the assumption of America's passivity in the face of the war-zone declaration was not an unreasonable one.

Wilson's response to the German declaration was to prove as important as any action he took during the years of neutrality. Yet much remains unknown about this critical episode. We do know that the declaration came as a great surprise to the president and his secretary of state, though why it did so is itself rather surprising. Sooner or later, the Germans had to make *some* response to the British blockade. The means at Germany's disposal were limited, a consideration that as time went by increasingly pointed to the submarine. Still, when the declaration did come, it was received with shock and incredulity by Wilson and Bryan. Only in Lansing's case are there reasons for believing that shock and moral outrage were partly feigned.

In a period of six days the fateful reply to Germany was prepared and sent. In Bryan's absence, Lansing had written a draft response after several consultations with Wilson. No sooner had the counselor done so, however, than he had entertained doubts about the advisability of sending a strong protest, or, for that matter, any reply at all. What changed his mind momentarily was the German explanatory memorandum of February 7. Lansing wrote the president that the memorandum "impresses me as a strong presentation of the German case and removes some of the objectionable features of the declaration, if it is read without explanatory statements."[12] It is curious that the German statement should have had this effect on Lansing, for it condemned almost everything he had defended in preceding months. But he recovered quickly enough, perhaps because the memorandum failed to alter Wilson's attitude. Within three days of its receipt, a reply was sent to Germany that flatly rejected the memorandum's major contentions. The note of February 10 was a slightly more moderate version of Lansing's earlier draft. In its final form it bore the president's distinctive imprint.

The severity of the note and the warning it held out were striking. It sharply reminded Berlin of the inviolability of the rules governing visit and search of merchant ships; it dismissed the contention that suspicion of enemy misuse of neutral flags justified departure from visit and search; it denied that the United States had consented to or acquiesced in any belligerent measures in restraint of the lawful trade of neutrals; it declared that if German vessels of war were to destroy an American ship or the lives of American citizens, such an act would be viewed as an "indefensible violation" of neutral rights "very hard indeed to reconcile with friendly relations"; and it warned that "if such a deplorable situation should arise . . . the United States would be constrained to hold the Imperial German Government to a strict accountability for such acts of their naval authorities and to take any steps it might be necessary to take to safeguard American lives and property and to secure to American citizens the full enjoyment of their acknowledged rights on the high seas." Only in closing did the note slightly soften an otherwise hard message by informing the German government that the United States had also protested to Great Britain over the "unwarranted use of the American flag for the protection of British ships."[13]

The full meaning of the February 10 note would only become clear in time, but it was immediately apparent that the note was a very strong one. The *New York Times* wrote of it that "the language of diplomacy could hardly go further."[14] To the same effect, the *Wall Street Journal* declared that the note "had said the last word first."[15] Why had Wilson responded so quickly and so strongly? Why had he said the last word first? Did he quite appreciate the gravity of the commitment he had undertaken? The note had in effect threatened Germany with war if it acted on its declaration and, in doing so, destroyed American vessels or the lives of American citizens. The commitment to take "any steps" necessary to safeguard American lives and property and to secure to American citizens their rights on the high seas could seem to have no other meaning. Was Wilson prepared to carry out this threat?

The record is less than revealing in providing answers to these questions. An exchange between Wilson and Lansing, however, does throw light on why Wilson chose to respond immediately and strongly to the German war-zone declaration. A former secretary of war, Jacob Dickinson, had written to Lansing advising him that with nations, as with individuals, "a clear and firm declaration in advance generally tends to obviate such extreme action as will force a collision, while on the other hand a failure so to do often brings about the very thing we most desire to avoid." Lansing had, of course, shown the letter to the president, and Wilson had returned the letter to Lansing with the comment that such letters "are so exactly in line with the facts and the right way of dealing with them."[16]

The "right way" of dealing with Berlin was a "clear and firm declaration in advance" of any German action. Berlin must be warned, quickly and decisively, that its announced course might well result in a dangerous confrontation with the United States. Wilson's evident hope and expectation was that a strong note would deter the German government from acting on the war-zone declaration. It was a diplomatic method he had resorted to before in dealing with Mexico, and particularly with Victoriano Huerta. Then, he had threatened to employ force against Huerta if the general refused to comply with his demand to relinquish power. When Huerta proved recalcitrant, Wilson was stuck with his threat, one he for a time shrank from carrying out. The resulting erosion of prestige and credibility, though, in the end left him with little choice but to employ force. Wilson would trace essentially the same course again with Germany. But since Germany was not Mexico, this time the course would prove to be much longer and more tortuous. Its consequences would also be immeasurably greater.

Wilson's decision to send the note of February 10 was reinforced by Lansing. And Lansing must have persuaded the president, as he seems to have persuaded himself, that in addressing a note to Great Britain at the time, protesting the use the British were making of the American flag, the United States was demonstrating its impartiality. In fact, there was little balance between the two notes, which, after all, addressed very different belligerent measures. The note to Great Britain, which was mild in tone, held that country to a "measure of responsibility," whereas the note to Germany held the Germans to "strict accountability."[17] Even the northern neutrals sent stronger notes to London protesting the use made of their flags.

Other considerations prompted Wilson's response, not least his sensitivity to criticism the administration had taken for its silence over Belgium and his desire to avoid giving further cause to his critics. By February 1915 Belgium had become a constant theme not only of Republican criticism of Wilson's neutrality but of Allied criticism as well. Certainly Wilson could not have been indifferent to the use critics might be expected to make of a weak response to Germany. And if the German government were then to act upon the declaration, he would be charged with having brought on the result by the weakness of his response.

Wilson saw the German declaration as an assault upon the most basic rule governing war's conduct, which of course it was. At the same time, the declaration was not the first assault upon the rule distinguishing between combatants and noncombatants: the Allied blockade enjoyed this distinction. Yet neither Wilson nor his advisers had expressed any qualms over the moral implications of the blockade. It was only in mid-February that Bryan did so, ostensibly in response to the British refusal to allow the *Wilhelmina*, a ship chartered by German sympathizers in the United States and loaded with food, to proceed to a German port. The episode coincided with the emergence of the submarine as a threat, and it was very likely this development that led the secretary of state to observe that a policy "which seeks to keep food from non-combatants, from the civil population of a whole nation, will create a very unfavorable impression throughout the world."[18]

Bryan's moral sensitivity over the purposes of the blockade, purposes as well known to him as they were to Wilson, was officially aroused only when the German countermeasures raised the possibility of involving the United States in the war. Even so, they still did not appear to have aroused the president. At the time, Wilson was expressing, as he had to State Department special assistant Chandler Anderson in January, "his agreement in principle" with Britain's conduct of the war at sea. That agreement, it should be recalled, included the mining of the North Sea in early November 1914, an action that rendered dangerous and thereby effectively closed off a vast area of the high seas to neutral shipping save as controlled by the British navy. The American government had met the British action with silence. When Norway proposed that the United States join in a neutral protest against the mining, Bryan refused.[19]

Despite these considerations, Wilson's moral condemnation of the use to which the German government intended to put the submarine was not simply a case of interest dressed up as moral principle. This was the view taken by revisionist historians, and it is one that still finds expression today. "The real difference between blockade and submarine in Wilson's view," John Coogan has written, "was not that the former took property and the latter took lives, but that the former was British and the latter was German."[20] This may come close to a fair characterization of Lansing and House, but it falls short of doing justice to Wilson. Lansing believed, whatever his public pose, that necessity in war knew no law, legal or moral. His private memoranda written in the spring of 1915 are fervent disquisitions on this theme.[21]

Wilson was a different case. The view that necessity knew no law would have been alien to him. Then, too, Wilson differed from Lansing (and House) in seeing only what he wanted to see. What he saw was not the prospective long-term consequences of the blockade but the immediate effects of the submarine. In his view, the German government was intent on pursuing a method of warfare at sea that was indiscriminate, while the British government, however one judged the legality of its maritime system, was not. Although interest evidently influenced this conclusion, it was not simply interest that led Wilson to embrace the distinction Britain's foreign minister drew in March 1915 between the Allied effort to shut off all supplies of any kind going to or from German ports and the German attempt to institute a complete blockade of

British ports: "The difference between the two policies is that while our object is the same as that of Germany we propose to attain it without sacrificing neutral ships or non-combatant lives or inflicting upon neutrals the damage that must be entailed when a vessel or its cargo are sunk without notice, examination or trial."[22] While Grey's distinction scarcely disposed of the moral issues the two systems raised, Wilson was nevertheless to voice it time and again in exchanges with the German government over the following two years.

The reasons that prompted Wilson to respond as he did to the war-zone declaration over the following two years, his response, once made, was to take on a life of its own. Events would soon show that it was a life Wilson had not anticipated. A careful reading of the February 10 note allowed, if it did not compel, the conclusion that the American government had asserted the right to determine the use Germany might make of the submarine, whether against neutral or enemy ships. The protest warned not only against attacking American ships but against taking "any actions" injurious to "American lives and property." The absence of any qualification to the warning could be understood as a guarantee by the U.S. government of the safety of its citizens regardless of the ship on which they traveled. The United States could be seen as asserting the right to enforce the rules governing visit and search, not merely as those rules applied to its own vessels, but as they applied to all vessels on which American citizens might be found.

A momentous step had thus been taken. Or had it? At the time, the length and significance of that step remained unclear. The February 10 note could be read to support the position that protection from attack by German submarines had been extended to belligerent ships carrying American citizens, yet it did not have to be read in this way. Lansing acknowledged as much at the time in replying to an acquaintance who raised the question whether the note had omitted holding Germany to account for American lives lost on belligerent vessels. If his correspondent would read the note again, Lansing wrote, he would find "that it is open to interpretation so far as American lives are concerned."[23] This it certainly was. But "open to interpretation" was little more than a euphemism for admitting that the American protest might be read in more then one way. The wording of the note was less than explicit. It was this consideration, together with the unusual nature of the American claim—there being no real precedent for a neutral's contention of a right to protect belligerent ships because they had on board citizens of the neutral—that gave rise to a measure of ambiguity and a resulting uncertainty. While the *New York Times* could write that the note had served notice on Germany that strict accountability would attend the "destruction of American ships or American lives under the conditions covered in her declaration," the *New Republic* could write that "American citizens who sail under the British flag after the German warning do so at their own risk."[24]

Aware as he undoubtedly was that his response to the German declaration was of great importance, why had Wilson permitted the ambiguity and uncertainty that marked the February 10 note? According to an account by a participant in the deliberations, Chandler Anderson, the president had done so because the State Department was anxious to avoid the appearance of partiality. Lansing presumably had persuaded the president that if his government explicitly claimed the right to protect American citizens on board belligerent ships, a note could not be sent to Great Britain protesting the use of the American flag on British ships. Instead, America would have had to approve of the British practice in order to give notice that American citizens were on board. But this would have prevented establishing U.S. impartiality by sending a protest note to Great Britain at the same time that it sent the protest note to Germany. Thus, according to Chandler Anderson, the ambiguity as to the scope of the acts for which Germany was to be held to a strict accountability.[25]

That so important an issue was decided on the grounds Anderson reported is difficult to credit. If true, it would testify to an altogether remarkable incompetence. The protest against the British use of the American flag had no bearing on whether the U.S. government had a right to demand of the German government that the lives of American citizens not be placed in jeopardy regardless of the ship on which they traveled. If that right was firmly grounded, it could not otherwise be ignored by Berlin. No ambiguity was needed in stating it. A more plausible explanation of the ambiguity is simply that Wilson wanted to deter the German government from acting on its declaration without committing the United States to a clear course in the event that Germany refused to be deterred. The emphasis of the note was on deterrence, not on the consequences following a failure to deter. Failure raised the prospect of war, a prospect that in February was still far removed from Wilson's purview.

The German war-zone declaration initiated the cycle of belligerent reprisals, which were destined to persist for the duration of the war. Within days of the German announcement the British government decided to take reprisal measures of its own. On March 1, 1915, the Allied governments announced their intention to prevent goods of any kind from reaching or leaving Germany.[26] Although Great Britain had by this time shut off by far the greater part of Germany's commerce with the world, the Germans had nevertheless managed to sustain a small import and export trade, principally through adjacent neutral countries. To effect the complete economic isolation of Germany by means of the then existing system of contraband control was not possible. The practical limits to that system had been reached; in the process, the law of contraband had been strained to a breaking point.

There was, of course, the belligerent right of blockade, but a traditional blockade of Germany appeared all but impossible. The British did not control the Baltic Sea. More important still, the stationing of ships in close proximity to North Sea ports was considered too dangerous, given the new weapons of naval warfare. If Germany's remaining trade was to be cut off, it could only be done by means that clearly went beyond what was sanctioned by the law governing contraband and blockade. The German war-zone declaration provided the justification for Allied reprisal measures designed to achieve that end and for this reason was welcomed by London. While the then minuscule German submarine force was not considered to hold out a serious threat to Allied shipping, the war-zone declaration was seen to open the way to measures the British government was in any event determined to take.

The British "long-distance" blockade of Germany, so called because it was enforced principally by a cruiser squadron in the North Atlantic operating about one thousand miles from German ports, rested on an order in council issued March 11, 1915.[27] By its terms, no merchant vessel was to be permitted to proceed to or from Germany carrying goods destined to or laden in the ports of the enemy. Intercepted vessels were subject to compulsory deviation to a British or Allied port and required to discharge cargo having an enemy origin or destination. In addition, merchant vessels proceeding to or from neutral ports could be intercepted and required to discharge such goods as were found to be of enemy origin, ownership, or destination. The disposition made of goods discharged in British or Allied ports varied, but in all instances not involving contraband (which was in any case liable to condemnation) it fell short of condemnation. Once the order was put in practice, it soon became apparent that the British intended to compensate neutrals for cargoes that were detained.

The text of the March 11 order in council characterized the measures provided for in the order as based on Great Britain's "unquestionable right of retaliation." The term *blockade* was nowhere to be found.

In Grey's note explaining the order, however, reference was made to "measures of blockade." Even more, the British note assured the U.S. government that those charged with carrying out the order would be impressed with the duty to show such consideration for neutrals as might be compatible with the object of the order, "which is, succinctly stated, to establish a blockade to prevent vessels from carrying goods for or coming from Germany." Evidently, the British government, though relying primarily on a right of reprisal, was not averse to a fallback position of reliance on a right of blockade as well.

As a retaliatory measure, the British order need not have given rise to controversy over the belligerent right of blockade. But the American government took the view, one consistent with its historic position as a neutral, that reprisals by one belligerent against an enemy for alleged misconduct could not justify encroachment upon a neutral's rights. In responding to the order in council, the American government simply brushed aside the retaliatory character of the order as justification for measures otherwise unlawful. Even if the course pursued by the enemies of Great Britain proved to be "tainted by illegality," the American note of March 30, 1915, declared, "it cannot be supposed, and this government does not for a moment suppose, that His Majesty's Government would wish the same taint to attach to their own actions or would cite such illegal acts as in any sense or degree a justification for similar practices on their part in so far as they affect neutral rights."[28] It was Wilson's distinctive way of rejecting precisely what the British were claiming as justification for the order.

As a formal measure of blockade, though, the order appeared no less unsatisfactory. The British warships deployed to enforce the order blocked access not only to German ports but to neutral ports of the Netherlands and the Scandinavian countries as well. At the same time, trade between these neutral ports and Germany, being "inside" the so-called blockade, remained open. Thus the objections to the blockade that it barred access to neutral ports, that it did not bear with equal severity on all neutrals, thereby lacking an impartial character, and that in failing to close off trade between Germany and Scandinavian ports it did not satisfy the degree of effectiveness required of a blockade.

These points were to form the substance of the American reply of March 30 to the British note enclosing the order in council. Judged by the accepted practice of states prior to World War I, there was little basis for disputing the points or for contending that the long-distance blockade of Germany conformed to the rules governing the traditional blockade. Nor did the British government contend otherwise. What it did assert, though only four months later, was that its measures, while admittedly departing from the letter of the rules applicable to traditional blockades, were in substantial conformity with the spirit of these rules and should be regarded as a reasonable adaptation of the latter to the altered circumstances in which the "blockade" of Germany had to be conducted.[29]

The British government set out on its new course with far greater assertiveness then it had shown only a few months earlier. By the late winter of 1915 the war had entered a new, more desperate phase. The sacrifices it imposed upon government and people were apparent in the less tolerant attitude shown toward neutrals, even the neutral on whose support the British remained so critically dependent. The letters to Wilson during this period from the American ambassador in London relate the rising resentment felt toward the many in America who "do not understand the nature of the struggle nor the character of the Germans" and who "are playing, or trying to play into Germans' hands."[30] In taking its measures of reprisal in the face of neutral opposition, the British government responded to a public temper that had been greatly hardened by the imperious demands of an all-consuming conflict.

Still, it is doubtful that these considerations would have carried the day had it not been for an almost unbroken record of concessions by the Wilson administration from October 1914 to March 1915. The practical benefits the British might expect to enjoy from their latest assertion of belligerent control over neutral trade could not prove to be very great given the near-pervasive control they already exercised over this trade by virtue of ever-lengthening contraband lists, ever-expanding definitions of enemy destination, and, perhaps most important, the substitution of diversion and detention for visit and search. These measures did not affect German exports, but the export trade of Germany was by this time quite small.

To risk a serious collision with the United States over these objectives would have made little sense, even for a government whose outlook had greatly hardened. Given the record of American concessions, however, this risk had been largely discounted. By March 1915 a change had taken place in the way London dealt with Washington. In beginning the October negotiations the British government, not knowing what to expect from the American government, particularly from its president, had moved with circumspection. By the beginning of the March negotiations the British government believed that it did know what to expect from America; circumspection had given way to an attitude that bordered on, if not contempt for, then indifference to Washington's reaction. A majority in the British government now questioned whether the reprisal order would provoke even a strong protest from the United States, let alone raise a serious prospect of countermeasures. Instead, the assumption prevailed that the government of Woodrow Wilson would take essentially the same course it had taken in the fall and winter when responding to the developing British system of maritime control. A mild note reserving the U.S. position on the reprisal order in council would likely be attended by the now familiar "case-by-case" position, thus avoiding confrontations between the two countries by transforming political issues into private claims for redress. Predictably, this was the course Page urged at the outset of the March negotiations: "That we content ourselves for the present with a friendly inquiry how the proposed reprisal will be carried out and with giving renewed notice that we hold ourselves free to take up all cases of damage to our commerce and all unlawful acts on their merits as they occur. This will enable us to accomplish all that we can accomplish by any sort of note or protest."[31]

Page's advice reflected his assumption that nothing useful would be served by a protest on Washington's part, which would merely serve to arouse further an already aroused British public opinion, ensuring America's exclusion from any role in the peace settlement. But what Page also assumed was that however misguided an American protest might be, it would not be attended by the threat of serious countermeasures. The British government evidently shared the ambassador's view; it no longer appeared to be terribly concerned, if concerned at all, with the reaction of the American government. A pattern had been established, as the *New Republic* observed at the time. Behind the diplomatic correspondence between Great Britain and the United States, the editors wrote, there were certain realities: "Great Britain will be polite, will administer the blockade as leniently as possible, will treat us with great consideration; but on no essential point will she yield. The United States will be firm, good tempered, and insistent, but on no point will it force the issue. Great Britain has sea power and will use it; we have the power of economic reprisal, but we shall not use it."[32]

The last point was decisive; it underlay Page's contemporaneous observations of the attitude taken by the British government toward its diplomatic exchanges with the Wilson administration. British government officials, Page wrote to Bryan over the reprisals order, received American communications "with courtesy, pay no further attention to them, proceed to settle our shipping disputes with an effort at generosity and quadruple their orders from us of war materials. They care nothing for our definitions [of neutral rights] or general protests but are willing to do us every practical favor and will under no conditions either take our advice or offend us. They regard our writings as addressed either to complaining shippers or to politicians at home."[33]

These were the observations of a dedicated partisan. Even so, they were for the most part well taken. The channels of American trade had been determined by March 1915, and they ran almost entirely in the direction of the Allies. To be sure, there remained the trade between the United States and the European neutrals. It was this trade that formed the principal bone of contention with Great Britain. But in comparison with Allied trade, it was of modest size, the Allied system of contraband control having reduced to a trickle the goods still finding their way to Germany by way of the neutral states. It was with these considerations in mind that Page, defending the reprisals order as a reasonable adaptation of the traditional blockade to novel conditions, pointed out to Bryan that "the only practical difference that the blockade will make will be the shutting out of cotton and food stuffs from Germany. Most food stuffs had already been shut out and the English will buy the cotton they stop."[34] Page's assessment failed to take into account the difficulty stemming from the British claim to the right to seize all goods of German origin. However, economic realities had reduced even this difficulty to modest proportions. As Gerard in Berlin noted at the time, "Germany has placed an embargo on so many goods which America needs and has so discriminated against American goods that it hardly seems worth while to go to war to keep up trade relations with a country that does not seem to wish to trade with us."[35] In refusing to respond with a strong protest against the British order in council, Wilson invoked the same considerations. Page had written that "the American trade with the Allies is increasing rapidly and will grow by leaps and bounds till the war ends." The president echoed the views of his ambassadors in writing to Bryan that "our export trade shows no sign of slackening and . . . there is little left, by the action of Germany herself for us to trade with Germany in."[36]

Economic interest had tied the United States to the Allied cause. It was not the only tie, nor even the most important, but after seven months of war its ever-increasing significance was apparent. The parties to the brief dispute that arose within the administration over how to respond to the Allied reprisal measures were in agreement on this. In opposing the president's position of refusing to enter into a controversy with Great Britain over the lack of conformity of the order in council to the requirements of a formal blockade, Lansing had no thought of jeopardizing America's trade with the Allies. Nor, it would appear, did those who sided with Lansing (the secretary of war, Lindley Garrison, was perhaps an exception).[37] That trade would be jeopardized through sanctions, an embargo on exports being the most severe. But economic sanctions were never seriously proposed by the advocates of a firm response to British pretensions. The idea of countermeasures, which might threaten to go even further, would doubtless have been dismissed out of hand. The British were not to be deterred from undertaking their new programs by an American response that hardly bore even a faint resemblance to the February 10 protest note to Germany. Instead, as Lansing pointed out in a final memorandum on a proposed reply to the British note of March 15: "The idea is to file a *caveat,* to permit their violation under protest deferring settlement until peace has been restored."[38] Lansing's proposal merely repeated what was by then an altogether familiar American policy.

In substance, Wilson yielded in responding to the March order in council. Since the United States would not recognize the lawful status of belligerent reprisals as they affected neutral rights nor consider the threat of countermeasures, what course of action was left? "We are face to face *with something they are going to do,*" Wilson wrote to Bryan in exasperation over Lansing's memoranda, suggestions, and draft notes, "and they are going to do it no matter what representations we make. We cannot convince them or change them, we can only show them very clearly what we mean to be our own attitude and course of action and that we mean to hold them to a strict responsibility for every invasion of our rights as neutrals." If the British chose to label their reprisal measures a blockade, America could only follow them in this (rather than, as Lansing urged, pointing out inconsistencies), while conveying our assumption, and expectation, that in carrying out the order they did not intend to violate the law governing blockade. The British government, Wilson accordingly instructed Bryan, should be told the following:

> You call this a blockade and mean to maintain it as such; but it is obvious that it is unprecedented in almost every respect, but chiefly in this, that it is a blockade of neutral as well as of belligerent coasts and harbors, which no belligerent can claim as a right. We shall expect therefore that the discretion lodged by the Order in Council in the administrative officers and courts of the crown will be exercised to correct what is irregular in this situation and leave the way open to our legitimate trade. If this is not done we shall have to hold you to a strict accountability for every instance of rights vio-

lated and injury done; but we interpret Sir Edward Grey's note to mean that this is exactly what will be done.[39]

The note of March 30 reflected this instruction, though it avoided the phrase *strict accountability*. Instead, it pointed to the "heavy responsibilities" the British government would incur for acts "clearly subversive of the rights of neutral nations on the high seas" and reserved to the American government "the right to enter a protest or demand in each case in which those rights . . . are violated . . . by the authorities of the British Government." Cast in mild terms, the note defined traditional belligerent rights respecting blockade and contraband. Conceding that a close blockade might no longer be practical, it stated that new conditions of war did not relieve a belligerent undertaking a blockade from conforming at least to the "spirit and principles of the established rules of war." In the circumstances, the spirit and principles of the rules gave rise to but modest demands. Although the British were already investing neutral ports, the American note, confident in its expectation that the powers asserted by the order in council would be modified in application, declared that America "takes it for granted that the approach of American merchantmen to neutral ports . . . will not be interfered with when it is known that they do not carry goods which are contraband of war or goods destined to or proceeding from ports within the belligerent territory affected."[40] What the American government took for granted left those applying the blockade with little to complain over or, for that matter, to modify.

5

The *Lusitania*

In the history of American neutrality in World War I, the sinking of the *Lusitania* stands out as the critical event. Its impact was immediate and profound, and although the shock and outrage over the sinking moderated with the passage of time, the effects of the event were to prove lasting. Among the public at large, the sinking confirmed a view that had already taken a firm hold. Nine months earlier, the war had begun with the German invasion of small, neutral Belgium, an act that had also been viewed with shock and outrage by the great majority of Americans. The invasion of Belgium established Germany as an aggressor, contemptuous of the rights of small nations, ready to violate international commitments when interest beckoned. The sinking of the *Lusitania* branded the German government and military leadership as inhumane in the methods by which they were prepared to conduct war.

The emotional response evoked by the sinking resembled a great tide that swept everything before it. The force of the tide may be roughly gauged by the fact that even the acknowledged voices of reason and detachment succumbed to it. The *New Republic* is an instructive example. In response to the sinking, the editors quickly forgot their earlier admonition of February that American citizens "who sail under the British flag after the German warning do so at their own risk." Instead, they declared: "The aim of our policy is to establish the safety of Americans upon the sea. We ask no ceremonials from Germany; we want no legal hair splitting; we desire one thing, and that is the concrete assurance that American citizens on any ship shall be free to go about their business without being murdered."[1] The editors were not unmindful of Germany's case in the great controversy over the allowable role to be given the plea of military necessity. But if Germany had a case, the editors concluded, the sinking of the *Lusitania* had badly compromised if not simply destroyed it. The argument was one that could be understood only on the assumption that no conceivable justification could be made for the German action. It was an assumption that went unchallenged save by Germany's partisans, and even they were for a time silenced.

The opinions of contemporary observers lend support to the view that

Wilson could have taken the nation to war at the time of the *Lusitania,* and if not at once to war, then certainly to the breaking of diplomatic relations. Lansing believed such a break was altogether likely, perhaps even unavoidable, were Wilson to insist upon a position foreshadowed by his note of February 10 and the principle he had set down in the *Falaba* case.[2] And while Lansing did not equate a diplomatic break with war, he acknowledged that war might well be the result.[3] House was, if anything, more inclined than Lansing to think the sinking would result in war with Germany. "I cannot see any way out," he wrote to Wilson from London, "unless Germany promises to cease her policy of making war upon non-combatants."[4]

These were the views, it may be argued, of men who were already disposed to intervention, and if not so disposed, then at least reconciled to that outcome. But there were others who were neither disposed nor reconciled but nevertheless shared the view that Wilson could have taken the nation to war in the period immediately following the sinking. This was, for example, the implicit assumption of former president Taft in a letter written at the time to Wilson. "I presume if you were to call Congress together now," he declared, "it would be difficult to avoid a war; but if you take such a step as I suggest, it might save that necessity for an immediate call."[5] Taft's advice was that Wilson sever diplomatic relations with Germany consequent upon Germany's refusal—which Taft confidently predicted—to disavow the act and to offer reparation. He did not question Wilson's freedom either to move directly on a course that would eventuate in war or to do so indirectly through a reconvened Congress. Nor did many other veteran observers of the political scene.

But the best witness to the president's freedom to take the nation into the European war was the president himself. On the weekend that the *Lusitania* was sunk, Wilson spoke to very few people. One he did speak to was his secretary, Joseph Tumulty, who later wrote of a president who, in the first days following the sinking, took almost for granted his power to lead the nation to war but refrained from doing so because he appreciated that the emotionalism generated by the sinking would sooner or later give way to sober second thoughts. When it did, Tumulty reports Wilson as saying, the people would ask, "Why didn't he try peaceably to settle this question with Germany? Why could he not have waited a little longer?"[6] Although Tumulty may not have used Wilson's exact words, there is little reason to question the substance of the remarks attributed to the president, remarks that clearly assumed the power to use the *Lusitania* catastrophe as a casus belli.

The acute phase of the *Lusitania* crisis lasted roughly one month, from the sinking on May 8 to the sending of the second note to Germany on June 9. It was in this period that the public's reaction to the sinking remained at a high pitch and Wilson's freedom to choose the path of war seemed clear. It was in this period as well that the positions of the two governments remained shifting and uncertain, with the attendant risk that a false step might lead to the breaking of diplomatic relations, which might in turn be the prelude to war. In June the crisis began to ease. The German government, having taken two weeks to respond to the first American note, took a month to respond to the second. Gerard had written House in early June that it was "the German hope to keep the 'Lusitania' matter 'jollied' along until the American papers get excited about baseball or a new scandal and forget."[7] The dilatory tactic seemed to enjoy a measure of success. The controversy did not by any means go away, but it clearly did die down. By late June and early July the press had become less preoccupied with the matter, and this was true of the public as well.

Even the public's leader seemed to feel by July that the crisis of May was no longer the threat it had once been and that although the Germans had not been forthcoming in words, they had become increasingly so in acts. The submarine campaign appeared to have entered a more cautious phase. There had not been a repetition, even on a smaller scale, of the *Lusitania* incident. The president had retired to the New Hampshire hills for a long summer vacation. His letters do not convey the impression of a man oppressed by the prospect of war. To his son-in-law he wrote: "I am faring famously. I have not had such a period of comparative rest and freedom for four years."[8] Wilson had proposed marriage to Edith Galt, whom he had met in the early spring, and she had accepted. A period of loneliness would soon come to an end.

The American government's initial response to the sinking of the *Lusitania* was made on May 13. In every respect it bore the stamp of the president. The note was a sweeping condemnation of Germany's recent conduct of the war at sea. Beginning with the *Falaba* and ending with the *Lusitania,* the indictment included the attack of April 28 on the American vessel *Cushing* by a German airplane and the submarine sinking on May 1 of another American vessel, *Gulflight,* which resulted in the deaths of two American citizens. In its principal points the note of May 13 followed closely the note of February 10, as well as Wilson's suggestions for the outline of a note in the *Falaba* case. The submarine, the note pointedly observed, "cannot be used against merchantmen, as the last few weeks have shown, without an inevitable violation of many sacred rules of justice and humanity"; the note was in effect a call for the abandonment of the use of the submarine against merchantmen. In any event, the American government took for granted that within the practical possibilities of each case, the German government would direct its submarine commanders "to do nothing that would involve the lives of non-combatants or the safety of neutral ships, even at the cost of failing of their object of capture or destruction." For those acts against which the United States was protesting, the German government was expected to disavow them, to make reparation, and to take immediate steps to prevent their recurrence. The note closed with the warning that the German government would not expect the United States "to omit any word or any act necessary to the performance of its sacred duty of maintaining the rights of the United States and its citizens."[9]

The note of May 13 was not the president's only statement in the first week of the crisis. Three days before sending his message to Berlin, Wilson had spoken to a large group of newly naturalized citizens on what it meant to be an American. In an address otherwise uneventful, he had uttered his instantly famous phrase "too proud to fight." The passage in which it occurred reads as follows: "The example of America must be a special example. The example of America must be the example, not merely of peace because it will not fight, but of peace because peace is the healing and elevating influence of the world, and strife is not. There is such a thing as a man too proud to fight. There is such a thing as a nation being so right that it does not need to convince others by force that it is right."[10]

Wilson disavowed the relevance of these words to the crisis at hand almost as soon as they were spoken. At a press conference the following day he said that he had only been "expressing a personal attitude" and "did not regard that [the address in Philadelphia] as a proper occasion to give any intimation of policy on any special matter."[11] The note to Germany appeared amply to bear out his disavowal; it scarcely conveyed the impression of a man too proud to fight or of a nation being so right that it did not need to persuade others by force that it was right. And yet Wilson's statement of May 10 was as significant an indication of his position in the *Lusitania* crisis as his note to Germany of May 13. Both were indicative of his real position, the first because it reflected his profound desire to remain out of the conflict, the second because it registered his determination to vindicate a principle that he believed could not be compromised, let alone abandoned, without the sacrifice of the nation's—and the president's—dignity and prestige. The man and the nation that were too proud to fight were also too proud to relinquish "rights" that in the end could only be vindicated by fighting.

That Wilson's "too proud to fight" statement expressed, as he himself later acknowledged, "a personal attitude" the record makes plain. In that attitude lay the conviction of America as a nation unlike other nations, of a nation that, by virtue of its ideals and institutions, set not merely an example but a "special example" to other nations. This conviction was inseparable from Wilson's justification of America's neutrality in the war, given only three weeks before his May 10 speech.[12]

The spring of 1915 marked the beginning of the struggle in Wilson's mind and spirit between a vision of America as a "special example," exempt from the conflicts that defined the condition of other great powers, and a reluctant though growing perception of America as a state among other states, subject to the same necessities that bound other states. In the spring of 1915 Wilson clearly saw for the first time the dilemma that would confront him for the following two years, a dilemma encompassed by the "too proud to fight" speech of May 10 and the first *Lusitania* note of May 13. Wilson's course in the *Lusitania* crisis was set by an unwillingness to abandon principle and an unwillingness to go to war on behalf of principle.

In the beginning, however, that course remained unclear. The note of May 13 had been well received both at home and abroad. It laid down no explicit ultimatum, held out no express threat. It appealed to Germany's "humane and enlightened attitude . . . in matters of international right and particularly with regard to the freedom of the seas." It found it difficult to credit that the acts of German submarine commanders that were complained of could have been taken with the sanction of the German government.

These considerations notwithstanding, the note contained a hard message. The German government was expected to abandon its practice of war zones and acknowledge that the measures for which war zones were established could have no justification. Even more, it was expected to abandon the use of the submarine altogether as a weapon against the enemy's commerce, given the manifest impossibility of employing the submarine against merchantmen "without an inevitable violation of many, sacred principles of justice and humanity." For those violations already committed, the German government was asked to do what, short of defeat, belligerent great powers had done only on rare occasions: disavow the measures of its military commanders.

It was only Wilson's distinctive way of demanding, even threatening, without appearing to do so that prevented many from seeing the note of May 13 for what it was: a demand for Germany's complete capitulation in the dispute over the submarine. Stripped of its artful camouflage, the note pointed to war if Germany refused to abandon the use of the submarine against merchantmen. That Germany would refuse to do so was at once made clear by Gerard, who reported being told by the German foreign minister on presenting the American note that "he [von Jagow] was sure Germany would never give up this method of submarine warfare." To this Gerard added his own impression, "amounting almost to a certainty . . . that Germany will refuse to abandon present method of submarine warfare."[13]

The note of May 13 was sent under Bryan's signature. "I join in this document with a heavy heart," he wrote to Wilson at the time.[14] Bryan opposed the note for substantially the same reasons that he had opposed making a protest to Berlin over the *Falaba*. Then his unshakable conviction had been that no dispute over neutral rights should be considered an occasion for the use of force. If this meant in the end that neutral rights would have to be compromised, even abandoned, he was ready to accept that outcome. Unlike Wilson and Lansing, he resisted the equation of neutral rights with the nation's dignity and prestige, not because he had no appreciation of these interests but because he feared that their increasing equation with an interpretation of neutral rights that would require Germany either to abandon or to severely curtail its use of the submarine could only result in the sacrifice of what was for him the far greater interest in remaining out of the war. In this, at least, the course of events showed him to have been clear-eyed. What he failed to see was that the sacrifice of prestige consequent upon the sacrifice of neutral interests would destroy what little prospects there were of realizing his dream of America's one day becoming the peacemaker.

Although Bryan too was shocked by the enormity of the *Lusitania* sinking, the event did not alter his earlier position. Instead it reinforced his conviction that Wilson, with Lansing's support, was following a mistaken and perilous course. To the case he had made in the *Falaba* deliberations, he added yet another argument. The cargo carried by the *Lusitania* had been made up almost entirely of contraband goods, including several thousand cases of ammunition. In consequence, Bryan pointed out to Wilson that "Germany has a right to prevent contraband going to the Allies and a ship carrying contraband should not rely upon passengers to protect her from attack—it would be like putting women and children in front of an army."[15]

In the brief period between the first note and his decision to resign, Bryan nourished the hope that he still might somehow persuade the president to accept one or more of the alternative courses he had been urging since mid-April. From the outset of the *Falaba* deliberations, Bryan had favored warning American citizens taking passage on Allied ships traversing the war zone that they did so at their own risk. He continued to urge this course in the *Lusitania* deliberations, but Lansing immediately countered with the argument that Bryan's position, if adopted, would amount to the admission that the American government had been negligent in permitting its citizens to run grave risks without warning them accordingly.[16] Wilson found Lansing's argument "unanswerable." "It is now too late to take it," he wrote to Bryan on May 11. "We defined our position at the outset and cannot alter it—at any rate so far as it affects the past."[17] Wilson's position was definitive for the future as well; a change in position would necessarily open the administration to criticism for the course it had followed from the German declaration in early February to the sinking of the *Lusitania*. Besides, Wilson was as persuaded as Lansing that to warn Americans, even to advise them, not to travel under a belligerent flag was to concede the legitimacy of the German war-zone measure.

Defeated on this course, Bryan sought Wilson's support for the postponement of any final accounting with Germany until after the war. In considering the *Falaba* case, Wilson had presumably supported this position. The note of May 13, however, clearly implied its abandonment. In response to Bryan's wish to make clear to the German government that "strict accountability" did not mean immediate settlement, Wilson agreed to manage a leak to the newspapers to the effect that the administration hoped the *Lusitania* dispute would be dealt with in the "spirit" of the Bryan "cooling off" treaties (Germany had earlier refused to become a party to one). In his enthusiasm, the hapless secretary of state told Lansing and Tumulty of the president's plan. Enlisting the support of other cabinet members, the group prevailed on Wilson to withdraw his support for a measure that, it was argued, would sacrifice any prospect of getting Germany to abandon its use of the submarine.

Bryan was no more successful in the one remaining course he believed would moderate the crisis provoked by the *Lusitania*, a strong note to Great Britain. Not only was Wilson averse to any public move that might convey the impression that he was bargaining with Germany by bringing pressure on Great Britain but he was sensitive to House's view that "our position with the Allies is somewhat different [from America's position with Germany], for we are bound up more or less in their success, and I do not think we should do anything that can possibly be avoided to alienate that good feeling that they now have for us."[18] The loss of British goodwill, House warned, would mean that "we will not be able to figure at all in peace negotiations." In response to Wilson's growing concern over Britain's implementation of the long-distance blockade, House's advice was to rely on methods of unofficial persuasion rather than on a formal note of protest. In the days prior to receiving the German reply to the first *Lusitania* note, this advice seemed all the more cogent inasmuch as House, with Wilson's strong support, was seeking Britain's agreement to an arrangement that would permit foodstuffs to go unchallenged to neutral ports in return for Germany's abandonment of submarine warfare and use of poison gases.

The differences between the president and the secretary had been slowly building since early 1915. Even before then Wilson had expressed to House his unhappiness with Bryan's performance and his hope that Bryan might leave office of his own accord.[19] Still, these differences had been contained prior to the *Lusitania*. It was only then that they became open and unbridgeable, and not because the two men seriously differed in their opposition to American involvement in the war. In this respect Wilson was much closer to Bryan than he was to House and Lansing, whose views he otherwise seemed to share. It is true that Bryan was prepared to pay a much higher price to remain out of the war than was Wilson. But this difference was perhaps less important than the difference in the risks each believed might be run in defending neutral rights without becoming a party to the war. Ironically, Bryan's reputation has always suffered on this score, yet the equations he drew between end (his end of remaining out of war) and means were on balance quite realistic. By contrast, Wilson often seemed unable to order his several ends (of which remaining out of war was but one) and drew equations between ends and means that appeared unrealistic.

Bryan's resignation signaled the final rejection of the position he had championed. What else it pointed to, though, was not apparent. Wilson had set out a position in the first *Lusitania* note that if adhered to carried the likelihood of war. Yet the president had no thought of war. Instead, he appeared to believe that at most the crisis might lead to a break in diplomatic relations with Germany. Even so, he did not accept the view that a break in diplomatic relations would be the prelude to war. Others were less sanguine. Lansing had written the president that although the severance of diplomatic relations "would not necessarily mean war," it might be interpreted as "evidence of a hostile purpose." The counselor had added his own belief that severance of diplomatic ties would be considered by the German government "as unfriendly, if not hostile, and . . . they might consider it to be a practical declaration of war."[20] Wilson's secretary of war, Garrison, had argued to the same effect in the cabinet meeting that considered the first *Lusitania* note.[21]

But Wilson resisted this view, and he would continue to resist it in subsequent crises. Although determined that Germany must be required to abandon a form of warfare that constituted her one means of striking back at the ever more effective Allied blockade, the president remained unwilling seriously to consider, let alone to accept, the consequences his determination, if persisted in, was likely to provoke. It was not until mid-July that he seemed willing to consider these consequences. While drafting the third and final *Lusitania* note, Wilson wrote to House: "They must be made to feel that they must continue in their new way unless they deliberately wish to prove to us that they are unfriendly and wish war."[22] By this time the acute phase of the *Lusitania* crisis had passed. The "new way" of the Germans that Wilson made reference to was the result of decisions made in early June in Berlin that special care was to be taken by submarine commanders to avoid attacks on neutral ships and that no large liners, whether neutral or enemy, were to be sunk. The decision respecting enemy liners was kept secret, however, in deference to the German navy, which had been opposed to making any concessions. The orders issued to submarine commanders had been adhered to; no "overt" act had occurred, although there had been an attack in July on the large Cunard liner *Orduna*. But the torpedo had missed its target, and Wilson chose to ignore the incident. Wilson's words to House about what the Germans "must be made to feel" expressed as much a regained optimism that a way out of the crisis had been found as they did a willingness to accept in July what he had found unacceptable in May and early June. Page, ever intent on American intervention, was close to the mark in writing to House in late July that "the only solution that I see is another *Lusitania* outrage, which would force war."[23]

The *Lusitania* crisis had not resulted in a break with Germany, less because of any moderation in the German position than because Wilson had compromised his initial demands. Although the first *Lusitania* note had not issued in an ultimatum, its evident logic was to lead to one if the demands it made did not receive satisfaction from Berlin. The note had called for abandonment of the use of the submarine against merchantmen and disavowal of the *Lusitania*'s destruction. The German response of May 28 not only failed to meet these demands, it simply ignored them.[24] The German note was careful to distinguish between incidents involving attacks on American ships and those involving attacks on Allied vessels. It did not dispute Germany's responsibility for any attacks on neutral vessels, declaring instead that the "most explicit instructions" had been given to avoid attacking neutral vessels engaged in no hostile act. Germany promised to treat the cases of the *Cushing* and the *Gulflight* accordingly. It had, in fact, already so informed the American government.

The *Lusitania* was another matter. While expressing its "deep regret" over nationals of neutral states that had lost their lives, the German government refused to accept responsibility for the sinking. Instead, it disputed the facts "most directly connected" with the sinking, facts that "may have escaped the attention of the Government of the United States." Until those facts were complete and agreed upon between the two governments, the note implied, further discussion was vain. The remainder of the note was devoted to Berlin's version of the facts attending the *Lusitania* case. The American government was invited to a careful examination of these facts. For the rest, the German note simply brushed aside Wilson's call for the abandonment of the submarine as a weapon employed against enemy merchantmen.

The president had sent a note directing Germany's attention to the fundamental requirements of law, justice, and humanity. In response, he received a note that dismissed the appeal to principle and set out a contentious, largely imaginary statement of the attendant facts, which it recommended to the American government's attention and consideration. Although the unsatisfactory character of the German reply was apparent, Lansing, now acting secretary of state, felt obliged to spell this out for the president. The German note, he wrote Wilson, "does not admit, deny or even discuss these principles which affect the future as well as the past conduct of the German naval authorities. The note reviews the facts . . . [but] the essential issue between the two governments is one of principle and not of fact."[25] There was no point, Lansing argued, in disputing the facts until the parties were in agreement on the principles to which the facts were presumably relevant. In the cabinet, Garrison made much the same point and urged the sending of what amounted to an ultimatum, which, if rejected, presumably would be followed by the breaking of diplomatic relations.[26]

What followed, however, was a response that did little more than reiterate the position set out in the first note. Drafted by Wilson, the second *Lusitania* note, of June 9, replied to Germany's contentions respecting the circumstances of the *Lusitania* by dismissing them as "irrelevant to the question of the legality of the methods used by the

German naval authorities." Wilson had not altered his view, expressed in the first note, that submarines could not be used against commerce without "an inevitable violation of many sacred principles of justice and humanity," but this view did not find direct expression in the second note. Nor did the strong ending of the May 13 note. The note of June 9 concluded by expressing the "expectation" that the German government would adopt the necessary measures to give practical effect to the principles of humanity; it asked for "assurances" that this would be done.[27]

The second note did register one significant change: it altered the circumstances in which merchantmen might become liable to attack. The first note had spoken of the protection that must be accorded "unarmed" merchantmen. Bryan had urged this wording against Lansing's choice of "unresisting" merchantmen, and Wilson, to his later regret, had acceded to Bryan's prompting. The note of June 9 restored Lansing's definition, declaring that "nothing but actual forcible resistance or continued efforts to escape by flight when ordered to stop" could justify measures jeopardizing the lives of a merchantman's passengers or crew. The change marked the beginning of an endless debate over the status of an armed merchantman, a debate that brightly illuminated the irrelevance of rules reflecting the circumstances of an earlier era rather than the reality of twentieth-century warfare.

The German reply, dated July 8, showed no greater willingness to accept Wilson's principles than had the earlier note of May 28. If a diplomatic break was to be avoided, the German government nevertheless had to show itself in some measure responsive to the American position. This it did, though in a way quite different from what Wilson had wanted. The president had wanted and demanded, above all else, an agreement on principle. What he got was the offer of a practical arrangement providing for the safety of American travelers, the terms of which were largely inspired by Gerard. The American ambassador, acting without instructions from Washington, had suggested to the German foreign minister, Jagow, what he, Gerard, considered the least concessions his government would expect. Incorporated in the final draft of the German note, they repeated the assurances already given "that American ships will not be hindered in the prosecution of legitimate shipping and the lives of American citizens on neutral vessels shall not be placed in jeopardy." To exclude any "unforeseen dangers," the note went on to declare, American liners were to be specially marked and their passage given advanced notice. A similar guarantee of safe passage would be extended to a "reasonable number" of neutral steamers flying the American flag. Should this not prove sufficient for the travel of American citizens, the German government was prepared to guarantee safe passage to a limited number of enemy liners operating between England and America. What it was not prepared to do was "admit that American citizens can protect an enemy ship through the mere fact of their presence on board."[28]

The German government had responded to need narrowly interpreted, not to principle. Indeed, its response was an implicit rejection of the principles for which Wilson was contending. In a "war without mercy," the German note declared, Germany had been left with no choice but to embark on the submarine warfare set out in the declaration of February 4, 1915. The German war zone was held up as the necessary retaliatory response to England's making the North Sea a war area, to her effort to starve the German nation, and to her arming British merchantmen and instructing them to ram submarines. The "accidents" suffered by neutrals on enemy ships were no different from the accidents neutrals were exposed to on land when venturing into dangerous areas in spite of previous warning. In both instances, Berlin contended, the German government was without responsibility.

The third American note, of July 21, closed out the exchange and revealed, as perhaps no other note written by Wilson did, the president's understanding of the legal status of neutrality. The view that neutral rights are absolute, not relative, that their observance by one belligerent is in no way conditioned by the behavior of the other belligerent, and that in consequence belligerent acts of retaliation against an enemy cannot in any circumstances operate to deprive neutrals of their acknowledged rights is here given its most striking expression: "If a belligerent cannot retaliate against an enemy without injuring the lives of neutrals, as well as their property, humanity, as well as justice and a due regard for the dignity of neutral powers, should dictate that the practice be discontinued." The United States could not "consent to abate any essential or fundamental right of its people because of a mere alteration of circumstance. The rights of neutrals in time of war are based upon principle, not upon expediency, and the principles are immutable." Belligerents must find a way to adapt the new circumstances to these principles. The failure of the German government to do so, the note concluded, "must be regarded by the Government of the United States, when they affect American citizens, as deliberately unfriendly."[29]

This was the hard side of Wilson's last *Lusitania* note. There was also a soft side, however, which found in the events of the preceding two months a clear indication "that it is possible and practicable to conduct such submarine operations as have characterized the activity of the Imperial German navy within the so-called war zone in substantial accord with the accepted practices of regulated warfare." The submarine was no longer considered illegitimate per se by virtue of its necessary mode of operation. Moreover, the note of July 21 no longer demanded the disavowal *tout court* of the act occasioning the crisis. Instead, it merely expressed "disbelief" that the German government "will longer refrain from disavowing the wanton act of its naval commander in sinking the *Lusitania* or from offering reparation for the American lives lost." Nor was this all that the soft side contained; the promise of German-American cooperation was also held out. The German government was reminded that the two governments were, after all, contending for the same great object. "They are both contending for the freedom of the seas." The United States would continue to contend for that freedom "from whatever quarter violated, without compromise and at any cost." In pursuit of this "great common object," it invited the cooperation of the German government and expressed the hope, as well as the conviction, that freedom of the seas might in some measure be achieved "even before the present war ends."

It was a bravura performance even by Wilsonian standards. "So skillfully had Wilson managed his descent from the high horse," Patrick Devlin rightly observes, "that the great reduction in his demands was not at first appreciated."[30] The Germans, led to believe by Gerard that the American government would accept their proposal for the safe travel of American citizens, were disappointed and angry at the American response. Their failure to appreciate the softer side of the note had its analogue in the British failure as well to appreciate the note's softer side. London was as pleased with the note as Berlin was unhappy. Wilson had rejected the German suggestions, insisting that their acceptance would be a betrayal of principle. He had asserted yet again the unconditioned character of neutral rights. In doing so, he had refused to consider belligerent reprisals as having any possible justification in limiting these rights, and he had warned the German government that the repetition of acts injurious to neutral rights would be considered "when they affect American citizens, as deliberately unfriendly."

It was these features of the note that the Germans fixed upon, just as it was largely the same features that the British chose to single out, as indeed did the American public. Nevertheless, the thrust of the note did not point in one direction but in two. Not only had the submarine been reinstated as a means that might be employed in accordance with the accepted practices of warfare but its previous unlawful use would

not continue to occasion demands for immediate disavowal and reparation. The German government would be encouraged, but no longer
pressed, to atone for past sins. The American government was now
looking to the future rather than remaining fixated on the past, and the
future pointed to the manifest possibility of lifting, in the words of the
note, "the whole practice of submarine attack above the criticism which
it has aroused and remov[ing] the chief causes of offense." Should Germany once realize that possibility, the United States was ready to join
with it in contending for freedom of the seas.

The implication was clear enough, though both the Germans and the
British seem to have missed it. Absent German misbehavior, freedom of
the seas would be threatened only by Great Britain. If the pledge made
in the note had any meaning, it could only be understood as holding
out the prospect to Germany that once it had mended its ways, America was ready to act "without compromise and at any cost" to lift the
Allied blockade that had shut off legitimate neutral trade. Wilson would
have indignantly rejected the view that he was thereby bargaining with
the German government, yet it is difficult to understand his offer in any
other way.

A period of scarcely more than two months separated the first *Lusitania* note from the third, yet the differences between the two were
striking. The president had backed away from a signal part of his initial
response. The hard core of the July 21 note still represented his position, but the soft side did so as well, and it was the soft side that betrayed
the character of the change that had occurred since May, not only in
the demands addressed to the Germans but in the waning of moral pretensions and fervor. The first note excoriated the German government's action as a threat to the lives of noncombatants "whether they
be of neutral citizenship or citizens of one of the nations at war." The
third *Lusitania* note, though still intent on protecting the lives of noncombatants, had a decidedly narrower focus on the rights of neutrals,
and particularly the rights of one neutral. In May, Wilson had appeared
intent above all in the defense of universal moral principle. By late July
a different tone seemed to prevail, one markedly more parochial. From
the defense of humanity in May, Wilson came back to the defense of
Americans in July. From an emphasis on universal values in May, Wilson
came back to the defense of particular values—national dignity and
prestige—in July.

What accounted for the change? Why had Wilson made the demands
he did in his first *Lusitania* note only to back away from a significant

part of them in his third note? The prevailing explanation has emphasized the shift in the public's outlook during the course of the summer. A marked change had taken place. A public disposed to intervention in May had changed by July. With the passage of time, the outrage provoked by the sinking of the *Lusitania* had partly subsided. The newspapers reflected this shift.[31] Among the public, a majority rejected the path leading to the compromise of right. Yet those who did on the whole rejected as well the ultimate means of enforcing right, prompting Wilson's remark to Lansing that the people wanted the controversy with Germany "handled in a way that will bring about a definitive settlement without endless correspondence, and that they will also expect us not to hasten an issue or so conduct the correspondence as to make an unfriendly issue inevitable."[32]

The question persists whether the moderation of the president's position in July was mainly a response to a shift in public outlook or to his own indisposition to press his initial demands, if necessary to the point of war, an indisposition that made him only too ready to seize upon a changed public outlook. Neither in May nor in June had he been prepared to push matters to the point of war with Germany. This much, at least, is clear. At most, he had been prepared to accept a diplomatic break, not war. That a break would have been the likely prelude to war does not alter matters, for Wilson did not see it as such. Nor, for that matter, did many in the German government. Although this was not true of Bethmann Hollweg, others contemplated a diplomatic break with apparent equanimity.

It may of course be argued that in May, when the public would very likely have supported Wilson in almost any course he proposed, the president had been obliged to wait until the German government responded to his first note. Although he had little reason to expect Berlin to accept his demands—others had warned him against harboring any such expectation—he might nevertheless have expected a more compliant response than he got. It seems that he did expect such a response and that he counted on that response as much as he counted on the public support then given him. Indeed, with respect to the latter, he appears to have had mixed feelings. There is the often quoted statement Wilson made in a letter to a friend in late May. Referring to the broad public support his note of May 13 had received, Wilson wrote: "I know . . . that I may have to sacrifice it all any day, if my conscience leads one way and the popular verdict the other."[33] Of the two possible ways of interpreting this statement, one may almost surely be discarded. Wilson was not alluding to a public clinging to peace and a president determined on war, but to a public then disposed to war and a president whose conscience bade him to cling to peace.

Wilson might have chosen to bring matters to a head on receiving the German response to his note of May 13. The beginning of June marked the onset of the change in the public's outlook from a readiness to accept war with Germany to something resembling the pre-*Lusitania* disposition. Still, the reversion did not occur overnight. Wilson would in all likelihood have enjoyed broad support had he elected to present Germany in early June with what would have been an ultimatum or the functional equivalent of one. Urged at the time by some of his advisers to demand that the German government accept or reject the principles set out in the first *Lusitania* note, he refused to follow this course. In the brief period between the note of May 13 and the German response of May 29, his efforts were instead directed to seeing whether House, then in London, could resurrect the American proposal of the preceding February, which had provided that Great Britain allow the unhindered passage of foodstuffs to neutral ports and German use of the submarine according to the rules of cruiser warfare. In February the British had shown no interest in reaching such agreement, the threat then held out by the submarine having been generally discounted. Nor had the Germans shown great interest in the American proposal; they had responded by adding raw materials to foodstuffs, and although this may have been done only for bargaining purposes, it afforded the British ample justification for taking the position they did.[34]

In May, circumstances appeared no more propitious than in February for an agreement between the belligerents on the conduct of the war at sea. While the potential of the submarine as a commerce destroyer had been demonstrated in the intervening period, the demonstration had not been sufficiently persuasive to the British government to entice it to go beyond the essential equation of foodstuffs for submarines. Even this equation never received the approval of the British government as a whole, only of the foreign minister. Grey had indicated to House, following Wilson's first *Lusitania* note, that the government would consider raising the embargo on food if Germany would discontinue its practice of submarine warfare and the use of poison gas.[35] When House duly reported this to Wilson, an enthusiastic president directed his trusted adviser and agent to pursue the matter, though on this occasion not as an American proposal. "It seems to me very important indeed," Wilson warned House, "that we should not even seem to be setting off the one government against the other or trying by any means resembling a bargain to obtain from either of them a concession of our undoubted rights on the high seas."[36] The president was intent on preserving the fiction that the rights America claimed from one belligerent had no connection with the rights it claimed from the other. Nor were they to be considered dependent on the agreements belligerents might strike with one another. The United States, the president insisted, was not pursuing a deal between the belligerents, one that would relieve it of growing difficulties with both sides; it was simply providing "good offices" to the belligerents.[37]

Nothing was to come of this effort, to Wilson's great disappointment. The Germans were not interested in a proposal that offered them no better terms than those held out in February. Gerard reported that Jagow had rejected the proposal, saying that if raw materials were added an agreement could perhaps be arranged. Germany, the foreign minister added, was in no need of food.[38] The denouement was ironic. Wilson had wanted to include in the proposal what Jagow had asked for, that is, raw materials. He had been quite precise with House on this, writing to the colonel to "please make it plain that it is not foodstuffs merely in which we are interested, but in all non-contraband shipments to neutral ports."[39] Wilson evidently wanted the proposed agreement to solve all of his problems as a neutral. And so it might have done had England and Germany accepted it in the form Wilson intended, for it would have put an end not only to Germany's use of the submarine against merchant ships but also to Britain's strategy of shutting off Germany's imports, whether by an elaborate system of contraband control or by the so-called long-distance blockade.

The proposed agreement would thus save Wilson from a confrontation with Great Britain over the implementation of the order in council of March 11. But House ignored Wilson's instructions, convinced that they would make no headway with the British and only jeopardize his relationship with Grey, a relationship on which he had come to set great value. When he relayed the terms of the understanding he had reached with Grey, terms that made no provision for raw materials, Wilson entered no objection but simply instructed Gerard to convey them to the German government.[40] The president's response was inexplicable given his insistence on including "all noncontraband shipments to neutral ports." The episode foreshadowed Wilson's response to the agreement House reached with Grey in the winter of 1916. The House-Grey memorandum outlining the terms of American mediation, and possible intervention, seriously departed from Wilson's instructions, and on that occasion as well Wilson would enter no objection to House's work.

The effort in late May to effect an agreement between Germany and

England over the conduct of the war at sea reflected Wilson's mounting anxiety that war with Germany might well be the outcome of the *Lusitania* controversy. The failure of that effort prompted him to do what he had forsworn doing: bargain with Germany. At the end of May, immediately following the collapse of the proposed modus vivendi, Wilson, apparently without the knowledge of either Lansing or House, informed the German ambassador that he was entertaining the idea of a mediation intended to put an end to the war. If only the *Lusitania* controversy could be settled favorably, he would approach the English government with the objective of dissuading it from continuing its unlawful interference with neutral trade. With the war at sea again being waged in conformity with international law, the United States, at the head of a coalition of the neutral states, would move forward to a peace mediation. The neutral states would be pledged to cut off all trade with those belligerents who refused to participate in the peace conference that the neutrals would call. The peace conditions Wilson held out were the prewar status quo in Europe; freedom of the seas equal to a neutralization of the seas; and adjustments of colonial possessions. The president, Bernstorff wrote to Bethmann Hollweg, "seems to realize that pressure cannot be applied on us, as we are almost completely cut off from foreign supplies in any case. On the other hand, he believes that the above mentioned peace conditions are so favorable to us that we, rather than our enemies, would be inclined to accept them."[41]

Why had Wilson made an overture that was on the surface so favorable to Berlin? Bernstorff wrote that the starting point for the plan was "the assumption that all neutral states, including America, would face economic ruin or, at least, very difficult conditions if the war should continue much longer or even spread to other areas."[42] But this was evidently not true in America's case. While the war had worked considerable hardships on some sectors of the economy, other sectors had benefited greatly from it. On balance, the war had been a great stimulant to an economy in recession at its outset. The motivation of Wilson's peace overture was not economic but political; it was an attempt to turn aside the tide then running strongly toward war with Germany by holding out to that state the prospect of considerable gain if only it would abandon its position on submarine warfare.

In a matter of days the German ambassador had a second meeting with the president. Wilson repeated to Bernstorff his conviction that the only way out of the dangerous impasse in which the two countries found themselves was through "the complete cessation of submarine warfare." "Compared to this final objective," Bernstorff reported the president as saying, "lesser concessions from our side would only be a compromise." If the Germans would give up the submarine, Wilson not only would press the English to end the blockade of foodstuffs but would launch "a peace move in grand style . . . as the head of the neutrals." In Bernstorff's account of his audience with Wilson, the president emphasized that "the point upon which we could unite is that Germany and the United States have always stood for the freedom of the seas."[43] The meaning was unmistakable. A German-American understanding on the submarine would be followed by a German-American effort to restore the Declaration of London as the operative law governing warfare at sea.

The dangers of his position now quite apparent to him, Wilson was evidently intent on regaining a neutrality that had been progressively compromised in the preceding year of war. He wanted nothing less than to start over. If Germany would but abandon the use of the submarine against merchantmen, Wilson would in turn undertake to restore a legal regime that the Allies, with American acquiescence, had largely eviscerated by the spring of 1915. The Germans showed little interest in the president's overtures. Although for the time being moderating their conduct at sea, they continued to insist that their use of the submarine in areas declared war zones was a legitimate reprisal measure. Departures from this position were considered concessions on Berlin's part.

There matters essentially stood throughout June and July. Wilson's determination to find a peaceful resolution of the controversy is apparent and finds expression in his third *Lusitania* note of July 21. The terms of the note reveal how far he had moved from his position of early June, let alone of May 13. In June Bernstorff had been promised a joint German-American effort to restore "freedom of the seas" if Germany would abandon submarine warfare. In the note of July 21 Germany's partnership in contending for freedom of the seas was no longer conditioned on Berlin's abandonment of the submarine (or even the disavowal of the *Lusitania* sinking). Events since the *Lusitania*, the note observed, had "clearly indicated" that it was "possible and practicable" to conduct submarine operations according to the rules governing cruiser warfare. In fact, events had clearly indicated only that Germany's submarine commanders were momentarily observing a greater measure of restraint, much to their growing disaffection. The isolated episode on which Wilson apparently chose to base his changed view did not clearly indicate the practicability of the submarine's conforming to the rules governing cruiser warfare. A British mule transport, the *Armenian,* chartered by the Admiralty, had been shelled by a German submarine after refusing to stop. Ultimately obliged to surrender, the ship's company—the *Armenian* carried no passengers—had been ordered to the boats, following which the vessel had been torpedoed. The loss of life, which included twenty-one American crew members, had resulted from the shelling, not from the ship's company's having to take to the boats.[44] It was this episode that seems to have led Wilson to reach the conclusions he did. Yet its significance was limited, for the circumstances that permitted the submarine commander to act as he did in the case of the *Armenian* could not be duplicated in many, perhaps most, instances without the submarine's incurring grave risk. Wilson was determined to place the best possible interpretation on events. If principle was not to be compromised, yet war was to be avoided, there was no alternative to contending that circumstances had changed.

The result of these considerations was a diplomacy that even now appears baffling. One side of that diplomacy was characterized by the refusal to consider any proposal that might be seen as the least modification of principle. Time and again, Gerard suggested the desirability of agreeing to limited modifications of the principle Washington had set down at the start of the controversy with Germany: the right of American citizens to travel in safety on neutral or belligerent merchant ships. To all such suggestions, Lansing, with Wilson's approval, not only turned a deaf ear but did so in a manner that scarcely hid annoyance with the ambassador.[45]

Wilson's position plainly admitted the compromise of principle. It did so by virtue of his readmission of the submarine as a legitimate instrument of naval warfare. It did so by his backing away from the demand for the immediate disavowal of the *Lusitania* sinking. And it did so by his willingness to hold out the prospect of cooperation with the German government if only it would agree to rein in the submarine. Indeed, it even did so by redefining the right that constituted the heart of the controversy between the United States and Germany. For at the outset of this controversy, if not in February, then in April, the principle on which Wilson had stood was the right of Americans to travel in safety on merchant ships, whether neutral or belligerent, of their choice. No distinction had been drawn between liners, or passenger ships, and freighters. By July, however, this distinction had emerged to the extent that the pledge the American government demanded of Germany was one that appeared to refer only to passenger ships. It is true that Lansing subsequently wrote in his *Memoirs* of a meeting with Bernstorff in late July in which he had told the German ambassador that "unless we received explicit assurances that submarine attacks on private ships would cease, the American government would not be responsible for the consequence."[46] Yet in the *Arabic* crisis, which broke out in mid-August, the government threatened to break relations with Germany over the right of Americans to travel in safety on all passenger ships, large and small, not on passenger ships *and* freighters. In conceding, Germany made no commitment on the treatment of freighters. Lansing then sought to broaden Berlin's commitment to include all merchant vessels (Lansing's "private ships"), observing to Bernstorff that "in the past the practice of the German submarines had been to warn freight vessels and I could not see why an exception should be made in their case as to the general principle, since some of these freighters might have American citizens in their crews." Bernstorff reportedly replied that he would do what he could "to obtain such an extension of the principle which his Government had announced."[47] The scope of the right claimed by the American government had evidently become uncertain, else Lansing would never have spoken as he did.

Wilson's diplomacy in the *Lusitania* crisis was thus by turns unbending in principle and given to the compromise of principle; rigid in one instance, it yielded in the next. It reflected the dilemma of the statesman who having once firmly committed himself to a given course draws back in dismay over what he then sees as the ever more likely consequences of commitment. Wilson had firmly committed himself and the nation at the time of the first *Lusitania* note. In doing so, he had not foreseen war as the outcome. When once he did, a diplomacy of inconstancy was the inevitable result. It was the inevitable result not only because of his deep aversion to American involvement in the war and his growing fear that involvement would be the eventual outcome of the course he had set out on but also because of a mounting unease over what he undoubtedly perceived as the disproportion between the interests at stake in the controversy with Germany and the dangers of involvement. As long as Wilson could identify those interests not simply with national dignity but also with the rights of humanity, the disproportion either was not apparent or, even if apparent, did not seem oppressive. But as the *Lusitania* crisis wore on, the rights of humanity increasingly gave way to the rights of Americans, and the rights of Americans were increasingly reduced to the right of Americans to choose how they should travel across the Atlantic.

What was once a persuasive position to someone of Wilson's outlook seemed in peril of becoming either a trivial or an unreasonable claim. It was merely trivial if seen as little more than a demand to have commodious accommodations—"a stateroom with a bath," as Gerard once put it. It was unreasonable if the result was to safeguard Allied ships carrying munitions of war. Wilson earlier had as much as acknowledged this in responding to a request by Bryan that steps be taken to prevent American citizens from traveling on Allied ships carrying munitions of war. Only the fear that such steps would weaken an impending protest note to Germany, Wilson had responded, prevented him from acting on Bryan's suggestion.[48] And while he did not subsequently act on Bryan's suggestion, he was also uneasy over having failed to do so.

House and Lansing, by contrast, did not share the president's unease. They did not see a disproportion between the issue at stake in the controversy with Germany and the consequences to which the controversy threatened to lead. They did not do so in part because they did not share the president's aversion to war and in larger part because they entertained a quite different view of the interests at stake in the controversy. Given their conviction by the summer of 1915 that the United States would be seriously threatened were Germany to emerge the victor in the war (or, as Lansing put it, even to "break even") and that this eventuality must be prevented, the difference that had arisen with Berlin over the use of the submarine was for them little more than the tip of the iceberg. To House, who had very little interest in the legal issues marking the controversy with Germany, and even to Lansing, who did set considerable store by these issues, the right of American citizens to travel in safety on ships of their choosing was significant primarily as a test of their larger position. But for Wilson this right *was* his larger position in the summer of 1915. Had this not been so, it would be very difficult to account for his course from the first to the third *Lusitania* notes.

To be sure, the public's disposition did change during this period, but the change cannot alone explain Wilson's retreat from the stand he initially took in the *Lusitania* crisis. The view often taken of an otherwise resolute president who followed the course he did largely because of a public that was ever more resistant to intervention is unpersuasive. The public's subsequent indisposition in the *Lusitania* crisis to push the dispute with Germany to the point of war was the president's as well. Similarly, the public's insistence on vindicating what it understood to be the nation's rights as a neutral was the president's as well. Wilson's lament about the public might have been made with equal justice about himself.

By the summer of 1915 the controversy that had arisen between Germany and America could no longer be resolved simply on the basis of a mutually agreeable interpretation of neutral rights. The nature of the war and the course of American neutrality had by then made this virtually impossible. The old order of neutrality had been largely destroyed during the first year of the war. What might take its place, however, remained unclear. A continued appeal to neutrality, to what now lay in shambles, could not answer this question. Only a clear idea of interest and a readiness to pay the price required by interest could do so. Wilson's advisers—House, Lansing, and Page—realized this, whatever one may think of the views they took of interest. But Wilson was a different case; he remained adrift, suspended between a past he could no longer recover and a prospective future he could not yet bring himself to accept.

6

The Maritime Blockade and Submarine Warfare: A Balance Sheet

On August 19, 1915, the British White Star liner *Arabic,* westward bound from Liverpool, was torpedoed without warning by a German submarine. The vessel was unarmed and carried no contraband. Among the forty-four casualties were two American citizens. While the *Arabic* sinking did not by any means provoke the public reaction the *Lusitania* did, the reaction it did provoke was strong enough. Tentative at the outset of the crisis, Wilson soon showed a quite different face. He did so against the background of mounting signs that the German government was deeply alarmed over the prospect of a diplomatic rupture with the United States and would go to considerable length to avoid a break. The *Arabic* pledge stated: "Liners will not be sunk by our [German] submarines without warning and without safety of the lives of noncombatants, provided that the liners do not try to escape or offer resistance."[1] But the American government had insisted above all upon a disavowal by the German government of the *Arabic* sinking, and in the ensuing weeks Wilson was prepared to break diplomatic relations with Germany if Berlin did not disavow the actions of its submarine commander. In the end, the president got the disavowal he demanded as settlement of the *Arabic* crisis.

The last of the great crises provoked by the submarine began on March 24, 1916, with the torpedoing of the *Sussex,* a channel passenger steamer sailing under the French flag. The ship had not sunk and was towed to Boulogne. Among the casualties were four wounded Americans. In Wilson's note of April 18, 1916, to the German government he declared: "Unless the Imperial Government immediately declares that it abandons its present methods of submarine warfare against passenger and freight-carrying vessels, the Government of the United States can have no choice but to sever diplomatic relations with the German Empire." The American government thus wiped away the distinctions drawn in the preceding year and returned to the position initially taken in response to the *Lusitania* sinking. On May 4 the Germans accepted the American note subject to the condition that the Allies as well abide by the "laws of humanity." Wilson replied on May 8 that the United States "cannot for a moment entertain, much less discuss, a suggestion that respect by German naval authorities for the rights of citizens of the United States upon the seas should in any way or in the slightest degree be made contingent upon the conduct of any other government affecting the rights of neutrals and non-combatants. Responsibility in such matters is single, not joint; absolute, not relative."[2]

The period of American neutrality beginning with the *Arabic* crisis in August 1915 and ending with the *Sussex* crisis in May 1916 was dominated throughout by the deepening controversy with Germany over employment of the submarine. That controversy centered on one issue: the right claimed by the American government on behalf of its citizens to travel in safety on Allied merchant ships. Other issues arose between the two governments. None, however, held out the potential for war as did the insistence of the United States that Germany not use the submarine in a manner that endangered American lives. Had it not been for this claim and the intractable controversy to which it led, the course of German-American relations would have been quite different. It may well be the case that the position the American government took toward the submarine would not have been carried to the lengths it was carried had there not been other interests at stake. In his war memoirs, Robert Lansing contended that even had American citizens been kept off belligerent merchantmen, as Bryan urged, the controversy with Germany over use of the submarine "would have gone on just the same, the subject being loss of property instead of loss of life."[3] But the other interests that presumably would have kept the dispute over the submarine both alive and dangerous would have had to find acceptable expression as a justification for threatening war. That they could have done so for Woodrow Wilson seems very doubtful. What did do so was the right claimed for American citizens to travel in safety on Allied merchant ships.

In law that claim was nevertheless open to serious question and had been so from the start. American citizens on the high seas evidently could not be safeguarded unless the ships on which they traveled were also safeguarded. If American citizens had a right, as the American government contended, to travel in safety on any merchant ship of their choosing, the American government was in effect also claiming the right to protect ships, whether neutral or belligerent, on which its citizens took passage. And since German submarine commanders could never be sure of the vessels on which American citizens might be found, the American claim ultimately became indistinguishable from the claim that Germany could not destroy Allied merchant ships, whether liners or freighters, armed or unarmed, without first exercising visit and providing for the safety of passengers and crew. By the *Sussex* pledge, the capstone of Wilson's effort to rein in the submarine, Germany was required to instruct its naval forces to this effect, the sole exception being in the case of a merchant ship that attempted to escape or to resist.[4]

The American contention of a right to insist upon the safety of its citizens who chose to travel on belligerent merchant ships (or, as eventually interpreted, to work as crew) was one no other neutral state ventured to make. In claiming a right to protect American citizens taking passage on Allied merchant ships, the Wilson administration gave a near absolute character to what was a novel position. It did so by contending that there were virtually no qualifications to the right it came to champion against Germany. From the outset of the controversy, the German plea of reprisals was rejected on the grounds that whatever justification measures of reprisal might have when aimed solely against the adversary, they could not serve to justify any infringement of neutral rights.

Even apart from the fact that the German war zone was justified as a reprisal, the administration's case for opposing the measure rested on doubtful grounds. But the defense Germany advanced on behalf of its measure could not simply be dismissed. Despite the abuse to which reprisals so often led, the right of a belligerent to take reprisals against an enemy that persisted in unlawful behavior was well established. The American government could scarcely deny that Germany's enemy had persisted in behavior that departed from the accepted practices of warfare at sea, for it had itself so charged the British government. What it could deny was that it bore any responsibility for Great Britain's actions. This it did by rejecting the German government's accusation of acquiescence in the British blockade measures. In fact, the German accusation had substantial merit. The United States had acquiesced in the British blockade; its protests notwithstanding, it had neither taken nor threatened to take those measures that were within its power and that might have led to Britain's abandonment of the blockade.

Although the American government's case in the controversy with Germany rested on questionable grounds, Wilson remained throughout persuaded that America's position was, to use a favorite term of the president's, unanswerable. One reason he did so was that virtually from the beginning of the controversy the American position was based on grounds that went beyond the narrowly legal. The appeal to law was regularly combined with the appeal to principles of humanity. Given his propensities, Wilson was most at home with a broad moral indictment of Germany's conduct of submarine warfare. "The force of America," he had insisted in the days following the *Lusitania* sinking, "is the force of moral principle."[5] The broader case brought against Germany centered on the charge that submarine warfare struck at the fundamental principle on which civilized warfare was considered to rest: the distinction between combatants and noncombatants. In declaring that enemy merchant vessels found in the waters surrounding Great Britain and Ireland would be sunk without warning, Germany openly abandoned a distinction seen to have no justifiable exceptions. That distinction expressed an inviolate principle of humanity; it defined the essential difference between war and murder, between the permitted and the forbidden taking of human life.

Wilson's shock and moral outrage over Germany's conduct of submarine warfare must not be judged in the light of later developments in twentieth-century warfare.[6] At the time his reaction was altogether understandable. The German war-zone declaration was a direct assault on the principle distinguishing between combatants and noncombatants. Moreover, the problem raised by the submarine went beyond the German threat to employ it as an instrument of reprisal. Given the vulnerability and limited size of the underseas craft, it could not, save in unusual circumstances, conform to the rules regulating the seizure and destruction of enemy merchantmen. The first *Lusitania* note to the German government had stated the simple truth about the submarine: it could not be used as an effective weapon against the enemy's commerce without violating the rules governing cruiser warfare. Even when it did not destroy without warning, it could normally only leave the passengers and crew of merchantmen who took to small boats to the mercy of the sea.

At the same time, the submarine could not be dealt with in isolation from the British blockade. The blockade of Germany also struck at the principle distinguishing between combatants and noncombatants, though it did so in a manner quite different from that of the submarine. While the effects of the submarine were immediate and starkly apparent, the effects of the blockade, at least in the beginning, were removed and speculative. And although the blockade eventually claimed many times the number of noncombatant lives the submarine took, the submarine drew a degree of condemnation the blockade escaped.[7] Even as the war progressed and the effects of the blockade became increasingly apparent, they failed to provoke in Wilson and his assistants anything approaching the reaction that met the German use of the submarine. On occasion, Lansing did point out to the British ambassador that the strategy of starving an enemy nation incurred a moral onus in the eyes of neutrals. In doing so, however, he stressed expediential considerations and otherwise left no doubt with his interlocutor that the American government viewed the British conduct of the war at sea in a light altogether different from the repugnance it felt toward German submarine warfare. House went further in the moral distinctions he drew. During the *Lusitania* negotiations he urged the president not to give an inch on the grounds that "the soul of humanity cries out against the destruction of the lives of innocent noncombatants, it matters not to what country they belong."[8] But he considered it "entirely legitimate," as he recorded in his diary, "for the Allies to starve Germany into peace if they could do so."[9]

Lansing and House distinguished between British and German actions, condoning in the one case and condemning in the other, largely on the basis of their view of the war as a struggle between freedom and tyranny. Their moral judgment of the means employed by the belligerents was usually subordinated to the values the respective belligerents presumably embodied. Wilson's case was more complicated in that he qualified, when he did not simply resist, the view Lansing and House took of the conflict. Accordingly, he might have been expected to view the Allied blockade, if not with the same revulsion with which he viewed Germany's submarine warfare, then at least with some degree of moral disapproval. Yet he seems never to have expressed himself on the morality of a strategy whose principal aim was to starve an entire nation. Wilson's silence may be taken as an indication of his indifference to, if not his approval of, the purpose and methods of the blockade.

Given the advantage of time and distance, the historian may instead conclude that the moral case mounted against Germany's use of the submarine was largely offset by the Allied blockade. The simple fact is that both sides in the great conflict were determined from the outset that respect for the combatant-noncombatant distinction not stand as an obstacle to victory. In consequence, there was always an air of artificiality marking the broader case on which condemnation of the submarine rested, assuming as it did that the distinction in question remained not only valid but also effective in the war at sea. Yet the belligerents began to erode that distinction from almost the first month of the conflict. Great Britain took the initial step by erasing, for all practical purposes, the distinction between absolute and conditional contraband, a distinction that paralleled the distinction between combatants and noncombatants. At the time, the United States offered little more than token resistance to the change. Lansing, the legal defender of the nation's neutral rights, quietly pronounced the distinction between absolute and conditional contraband dead in January 1915.[10]

The abandonment of what had been a mainstay of the law of contraband was only one indication of the breakdown of the combatant-noncombatant distinction in naval warfare. More serious still was the erosion of the distinction between the naval forces of a belligerent and its merchant ships. On the clarity of that distinction rested the very possibility of exempting merchant vessels from the hazards of warfare at sea. The rules that applied to naval warfare the general principles distinguishing between combatants and noncombatants necessarily assumed a reasonably clear separation between the public and private spheres. The course of the war quickly demonstrated that this assumption was vain. Even before the outbreak of hostilities, in 1913, the British government decided upon a policy of arming its merchant vessels in the event of war. When the conflict began, measures were taken to implement that policy more effectively. By the time the *Lusitania* was sunk, in May 1915, some 150 British merchant ships had been armed; by the end of 1915 the number had increased to nearly 800.[11]

The traditional law did not forbid the arming of merchant ships. It assumed, however, that the private owner of a vessel would decide whether or not to arm, would bear the expense of arming, and would determine the circumstances in which the arms would be used. The fact that a ship was armed did not imply that it was incorporated into the military effort of a belligerent or that it acted under the control of the state. In World War I, though, it was the state that decided to arm merchant vessels bearing its flag, just as it was the state that not only provided both the guns and naval personnel to operate the guns but also directed when and how the armament was to be employed.

Arming was but one measure by which merchant ships were integrated into the belligerent's military effort at sea. In the first year of the war, the British government laid down measures by which merchant ship owners might reduce the risk either of seizure or of destruction by German submarines and, at the same time, assist in the military effort to reduce the threat posed by the submarine. Merchant ships were instructed on routes to follow, tactics of evasion and of active resistance (e.g., ramming), the sending of position reports upon sighting enemy submarines, and a host of related matters. These measures, the German government contended in the summer of 1915, gave to enemy merchant ships a combatant status, making them liable to attack and destruction without warning and without provision for the safety of passengers and crew.[12]

It is against the background of these developments that not only the armed-ship controversy but the still larger issue of the general liability of belligerent merchant vessels to attack and destruction must be seen. No question arose over the liability of merchantmen, whether armed or unarmed, that, when summoned by an enemy warship, attempted to escape by flight or offered forcible resistance to visit and seizure. Controversy did arise over the effect that the carrying of armament had on the immunity from attack normally granted merchant vessels. The German government took the position that the act of arming itself sufficed to deprive a belligerent merchant vessel of immunity from attack. To this contention was added the novel circumstances in which the war was being waged, above all the vulnerability of the submarine in relation to armed British merchant ships instructed to use their arms against any attempt at visit and seizure by an enemy submarine.

In opposition to the German position, the British government invoked its long-held view that the arming of merchant vessels for defensive purposes was sanctioned by customary law. So long as these vessels restricted the use of their armament to measures of self-defense, they could not be lawfully deprived of their noncombatant status. The British position raised serious questions even as an appeal to customary law. But its real difficulty lay in the consideration that even if it was taken to conform to the customary law, it was applied during World War I in a manner as well as in circumstances that bore little relation to the circumstances and manner of employment characteristic of an earlier period.

The ancient rule allowing belligerent merchant vessels to arm in self-defense was an anomaly by 1914. Its continued retention, along with the immunity granted to merchant vessels if they refrained from measures of resistance, was to be explained by the disparity in power that had grown up between warship and merchant vessel over the course of the nineteenth century. In retrospect, it is clear that one of the principal reasons for the growing immunity accorded merchant vessels in the nineteenth century was this disparity in power. But in the case of submarines the disparity became negligible, provided the merchant ship was armed and the submarine was required to observe the rules applicable to surface warships. In these circumstances, the submarine was very likely to encounter active resistance if it attempted to conform to the traditional law. In the case of British armed merchantmen instructed to attack enemy submarines on sight, the line between defensive and offensive action, never very clear, became altogether blurred. This being so, it was not apparent why belligerent merchant vessels could be armed for the sole purpose of attacking enemy submarines on sight, while submarines were considered to have no right to take "defensive" measures by attacking armed merchant vessels on sight. And since the submarine could seldom be certain that an enemy merchant vessel did not carry arms, the fact that some were armed inevitably came to mean that all were liable to attack.

The strength of the British position was not to be found in the contention that the defensive arming of merchant vessels was sanctioned by customary law, but in the argument that the effective use of the submarine was, in the great majority of instances, incompatible with the observance of the rules distinguishing between combatant and noncombatants, that Germany had not observed these rules in conducting submarine warfare, and that the arming of merchant vessels was the only effective means of countering the submarine. Yet the fact remained that the initial British decision to arm merchant vessels had been taken prior to World War I and any thought of the submarine. More important still were the circumstances in which merchant vessels were armed and directed to use their arms, circumstances that scarcely supported the assumption that those vessels retained a private, peaceful, and thus noncombatant status. The immunity granted merchant ships by the traditional law could be observed only under the conditions that in terms of their armament they did not present a serious threat to enemy warships and they were in no way integrated into the military effort of a belligerent. These conditions did not obtain in World War I, and thus warships, whether submarines or surface vessels, could not be expected to refrain from attacking enemy merchant vessels.

Yet this was the expectation that, save for a brief period, informed President Wilson's policy toward the submarine. The second *Lusitania* note, of June 9, 1915, had articulated it in these words: "Nothing but actual forcible resistance or continued efforts to escape by flight when ordered to stop for the purpose of visit on the part of the merchantmen has ever been held to forfeit the lives of her passengers or crew."[13] Not only did the American position ignore the conditions characterizing the conflict at sea in 1915 but the constraints it placed on warships went beyond the practice even of an earlier period. Surface vessels were no longer the only warships. Merchant ships no longer operated independently of the state. "Actual forcible resistance" no longer encompassed, if indeed it had ever encompassed, the range of acts that legitimately constituted resistance to visit and search.

If the force of America was ultimately the force of moral principle, as Wilson insisted, the force of principle the president appealed to in the controversy with Germany seemed no less questionable than the appeal to more narrowly legal considerations. The applicability, if not the relevance, of principles of justice and humanity was no more apparent than principles of law. In fact, on closer examination the two turned out to be not very different. The appeal to principles of justice and humanity was more often than not simply an appeal to what Wilson considered the spirit rather than the letter of the law, the spirit as expressed by general principles—of which the combatant-noncombatant distinction was one—rather than, as he might say, in "special circumstances of detail."[14] But in the controversy with Germany the devil was in the details. At least this was so in the absence of a clear view of interest that at once transcended issues of neutrality and provided guidance for their application.

In the absence of such a view, issues of neutrality had to be considered and decided on other grounds. Wilson believed that these other grounds were neither more nor less than the merits of the case as determined by law (and, of course, by the higher moral principles this law embodied). Even granting that this belief may once have had merit, after a year of war it no longer represented a possible basis for resolving the differences that had arisen between Germany and the United States. The right of American citizens to travel in safety on Allied merchantmen could not be separated from the right of Germany to take reprisals against an enemy that had flouted, with American acquiescence, the law of neutrality. Similarly, German submarine warfare could not be considered apart from measures Great Britain had taken to integrate its merchant ships into the military effort at sea. By the summer of 1915 the war had reached a point that threw most traditional distinctions, along with the rules that had grown from them, into eclipse.

By the late summer of 1915 America had been brought close to war. However blind he may once have been to the ultimate destination of the course he had taken, Wilson could no longer have had much doubt over where his neutrality policy was leading. His search for a way out of the labyrinth in which he found himself turned first to the immediate source of his predicament. But such change in neutrality policy as Wilson might have made without considerable risk and effort would not have enabled him to escape his plight; only a radical shift might have done so. In its absence, his hope of making a new beginning, of starting over as a neutral with both Germany and Great Britain, would remain vain.

In the case of Germany, the president had in fact momentarily backed away from a significant part of his initial position taken in the *Lusitania* crisis. Not only had he readmitted the submarine as a commerce destroyer but he had indicated a willingness not to press for immediate settlement of the *Lusitania* case. Where he would not and could not compromise was on the right of American citizens to travel in safety on Allied merchant ships of their choice. Having made repeated claim to this right, having solemnly committed the nation to its defense, and having rejected the German proposal that would have restricted safe passenger traffic to specially designated neutral and belligerent ships, Wilson could further yield his position only by jeopardizing prestige and credibility abroad and leadership at home. When the *Arabic* crisis broke out in late August 1915, House quickly reminded the president of this. "If by any word or act you should hurt our pride of nationality," House wrote to Wilson, "you would lose your commanding position overnight."[15] Although displeased by his adviser's warning—"It is not of how I will stand that I am thinking," he complained at the time to Edith Galt, "but of what it is right to do"[16]—Wilson did not dissent from it.

In the case of Great Britain, in the summer of 1915 the American government made clear its opposition to the blockade measures London had imposed in implementing the March order in council. In October, Washington sent its most vigorous protest yet to the British government. Had the protest been attended by the threat of strong action, it might even have led to the abandonment of the order in council. But it was not so attended. Nor is it apparent that abandonment of the order in council would have meant abandonment of the substance of the blockade. For the principal effects of the blockade might almost as well have been based on the system of contraband control the British had set in place prior to the March order in council. It was this system, after all, that in the first six months of the war had effectively shut off Germany's import trade and that the British government could have fallen back on in case of necessity. The system had largely been invested with legitimacy by the American government in the initial period of the war, and the possibility of effectively opposing it in the fall of 1915 had been all but foreclosed by a record of past acquiescence as well as by an economic interest that had by then grown to considerable proportions.

These circumstances broadly defined the nature of Wilson's predicament after a year of war. They accounted for his growing realization and fear that his neutrality policy might not afford a way out of the labyrinth that was leading him ever nearer to active participation in the war. Yet his response was to deepen his predicament. The pattern of neutral-belligerent relations set in the first year of the war was reaffirmed and even strengthened. While toleration of the Allied blockade persisted, the moderated position that marked the *Lusitania* negotiations in the summer of 1915 came to an end. America's neutral course from the *Arabic* crisis on was characterized by the expansion of the claims of principle against Germany's conduct of submarine warfare. By the spring of 1916 Wilson had virtually reverted to his position taken at the outset of the *Lusitania* crisis. In the *Sussex* crisis, which extended from late March to early May 1916, a break in diplomatic relations with Berlin was averted only by Germany's acceptance of terms that wiped out the distinctions so laboriously constructed during the preceding year. While employment of the submarine was not in principle forbidden, the constraints placed on its use would have led to very nearly this result had Germany only adhered to them.

The middle period of American neutrality raises a central question: Why did Wilson pursue the course he did toward the submarine, aware as he then was that this course held out the strong prospect of war with Germany? Why did he persist on a path that made ever more likely the outcome he so dreaded? The question does not arise for the initial period of neutrality. Until the sinking of the *Lusitania,* Wilson did not clearly see where his course was taking him. In the wake of that crucial event, however, he evidently did see the fate toward which he was being increasingly drawn. And while he was no longer free simply to abandon the position he had initially taken in response to the *Lusitania* sinking, he was still free, as his actions in the summer of 1915 demonstrated, to temporize and moderate that position. Yet in the period from the *Arabic* to the *Sussex* crisis his position steadily hardened. The bounds within which Germany might employ the submarine without incurring the risk of war with America progressively narrowed. In the *Sussex* crisis that risk was avoided only by Germany's pledge that its submarines would thereafter strictly conform to the rules governing cruiser warfare. The pledge extended to all Allied merchantmen, whether liners or freighters, armed or unarmed, carrying American citizens. Its faithful observance would have gone a long way toward effectively depriving Germany of its one means of responding to the ever more stringent Allied blockade.

The question put here may be made still more pointed by recalling that Wilson's overriding aim in the summer of 1915 was to restore a then badly eroded neutrality to something resembling what it had been at the outbreak of war. The president had made this clear in his secret talks with Bernstorff in the first week of June 1915. In the third and last *Lusitania* note, of July 21, he had all but spelled out his objective publicly. Wilson promised that if Germany would only act "in substantial accord with the accepted practices of regulated warfare," the two governments might once again stand together in "contending for the freedom of the seas."[17] A Germany that abandoned its conduct of submarine warfare might join the United States in opposing the pretensions of British sea power.

Wilson's aim was to go unrealized. Although the right claimed by the American government on behalf of its citizens—to travel in safety on Allied merchant ships—was the only issue of diplomatic consequence to arise between Germany and the United States, it led America to the point of war with Germany. In contrast, the rights Great Britain was charged with violating, while making up the core of the rights of trade traditionally claimed by neutrals, never held out a similar prospect. In the spring of 1916, House summed up the matter in remarking to Bernstorff that U.S. relations with Great Britain "are quite different from our relations with Germany; that war with Germany would be possible, whereas, war with Great Britain was more or less out of the question."[18]

In his war address a year later, the president reiterated the by then familiar explanation for the American government's different responses to the belligerents' respective violations of neutral rights. "Property can be paid for," Wilson declared, "the lives of peaceful and innocent people cannot be."[19] Allied measures of blockade affected only property; German submarine warfare took the lives of noncombatants. The former was reparable, while the latter were not. Thus the resort to diplomatic protests, to prize courts, and to postwar claims commissions in response to Allied blockade measures and to the threat of war in response to German submarine measures. The explanation has persisted among historians. Arthur Link expressed it in these terms: "It is inconceivable that Wilson could have thought of going to war with the British over issues of search and seizure or of blockade. It is equally inconceivable that he would not have been willing to think about going to war with a government that instructed its naval commanders wantonly to slaughter American citizens on the high seas."[20]

Certainly Wilson saw himself at the time as having had no choice in responding to Germany's submarine warfare but to take the path he did. In his eyes, that path had been dictated by the imperative requirements of law and humanity. Not to have followed it, he came to believe, would have been incompatible with the nation's dignity and honor. He also believed that in defending these interests he had been too patient with Germany. "My chief puzzle," the president wrote to House during the *Arabic* crisis, "is to determine where patience ceases to be a virtue."[21] This assessment of his behavior has also been followed by historians. In Ernest May's depiction of Wilson's neutrality diplomacy, patience is put on a par with firmness; aggressive advisers are contrasted with a president found to insist throughout on patience in dealing with Germany.[22]

Wilson was patient with Germany in the sense that "he offered the Germans opportunity and ample time to meet his contentions."[23] His patience was manifest throughout the several crises that occurred in the middle period of the nation's neutrality. At the same time, his was a patience put in the service of a position that for all the questions it might have raised went largely unquestioned. Although Wilson did retreat from his initial demand in the first *Lusitania* note, that Germany abandon use of the submarine against merchant ships, he would not compromise on the position that made readmission of the submarine largely meaningless: that the underseas vessel strictly conform to the rules of cruiser warfare. It was the insistence on this condition that led him to reject the German proposal to extend special protection not only to American liners and to a reasonable number of other neutral liners flying the American flag but also, if necessary, to a small number of enemy liners also flying the American flag. The German offer would have met the needs of American travelers, but Wilson dismissed it out of hand on the grounds that it "would, by implication, subject other vessels to illegal attack and would be a curtailment and therefore an abandonment of the principles for which this government contends."[24] Acceptance of the German offer would also have amounted to the admission that American citizens did not have the right to travel in safety on Allied merchant vessels of their choice. This was the right that Wilson would not allow to be compromised.

The president's necessity, then, was one of principle—a principle he came to equate with the nation's dignity and honor. On almost any traditional calculus of national interest the principle seemed altogether insufficient as a reason for threatening war. Even so, in the middle period of neutrality Wilson still might have remained reasonably faithful to principle while following a course quite different from the course he did follow. He might not have pushed Germany as hard as he did. He might have refrained from so deepening his commitment to principle that almost any compromise with Germany over the submarine became impossible. And he might have applied greater pressure on Great Britain, not to abandon but to moderate its blockade.

Wilson did none of these things. He did none of these things despite his dread of becoming an active participant in the war and despite his belief that in the restoration of a position of strict impartiality lay the only real prospect of remaining out of the conflict. Instead, he followed a course that seemed almost designed to bring Germany to heel whatever the risk run in doing so. Yet it was no preconceived design and no necessity that led to this course but a series of striking diplomatic triumphs that encouraged the view that Germany could be forced either to employ the submarine in strict conformity with the rules of cruiser warfare or to abandon it altogether as a weapon of commercial warfare.

In the period beginning with the *Arabic* crisis Germany gave way in each confrontation with the United States. It did so, moreover, in the absence of any compensation by way of concessions exacted from Great Britain. Not surprisingly, Wilson came to see in German submission not only the effectiveness of the threat of war but the vindication of principle as well. Success reinforced his conviction that principle could not and need not be compromised, a position he gave extreme expression to in his February 1916 letter to the chairman of the Senate Committee on Foreign Relations. The stage was thus set for the *Sussex* crisis, Wilson's greatest triumph over Germany in the submarine controversy. But the *Sussex* proved to be one success too many. In its wake Wilson realized that it was a success to be repeated only at the price of war. Yet the commitment to principle was now complete and beyond the possibility of change.

7

The House-Grey Memorandum

In the late winter of 1915–16, mediation took on a new significance for Wilson. While he had never dismissed the prospects of mediating an end to the war, throughout the first year of the conflict he had never placed much faith in these prospects. He had rejected Bryan's repeated urging that he put himself forward as mediator for what would have been in effect a peace without victory, contending that any role greater than one of transmitting such messages as the belligerents might want to communicate privately to one another would be futile and might even prove offensive to them. A modest conception of America's role as mediator reflected Wilson's belief that anything more ambitious might alienate the Allied powers, with the result that America would lose any influence it might otherwise have to shape the postwar international order. But it also reflected his continued commitment to the traditional policy of noninvolvement in Europe's politics. A nascent commitment to world order thus appeared alongside a more than century-old tradition of remaining aloof from participation in European order.

The significance Wilson eventually came to give mediation must be seen in the context of a neutrality that had brought the nation to the verge of war. That a faltering neutrality was the great and compelling reason for the vital role the president ultimately gave to mediation became unmistakably clear only in the wake of the *Sussex* crisis. No one appreciated more than Wilson that the victory gained in the *Sussex* crisis could not be safely repeated, that another such crisis would almost certainly result in war between the two countries. Committed more than ever by the spring of 1916 to oppose any use of the submarine that departed from the traditional law governing cruiser warfare, yet determined as well to avoid war, Wilson could look only to mediation for deliverance.

In the spring of 1916 Wilson came to appreciate, as he had not before quite appreciated, that his neutrality policy, which was leading him to war, was the principal obstacle to mediation, which held out the one prospect of avoiding war. House had long appreciated this and, as opposed to the president, was prepared to employ mediation to the same ends he had employed neutrality. The plan he proposed to Wilson in early October 1915 was one of mediation in name only. As partial to the Allies as the neutrality policy that had largely occasioned it, House's proposal pointed to intervention on the Allied side. It outlined a way to bring America into the war other than through the controversy with Germany over the submarine. "I thought we had lost our opportunity to break with Germany," he recorded in his diary only days following the settlement of the *Arabic* crisis, "and it looked as if she had a better chance than ever of winning, and if she did win, our turn would come next, and we were not only unprepared but there would be no one to help us stand the first shock. Therefore, we should do something now— something that would either end the war in a way to abolish militarism or that would bring us in with the Allies to help them do it."[1]

House proposed that the American government, in the name of all the suffering neutrals, demand of the belligerents that they cease hostilities and initiate peace talks on the basis of mutual disarmament. Germany would be led to believe that the American demand was made without prior consultation with the Allies and without prejudice to the interests of either side. In fact, it would be preceded by secret talks with the Allies in order that they might understand the American purpose and that, so informed, they might unofficially signal the American government when it would be agreeable to them for the U.S. government to make its demand. Should the Central powers also acquiesce to the American demand, House noted, "we would then have accomplished a master stroke of diplomacy." But given Germany's favorable military position at the time, this eventuality was recognized as highly improbable. Should the Central powers refuse the demand for a peace conference, the diary reads, "we could then push our insistence to a point where diplomatic relations would first be broken off, and later the whole force of our Government . . . might be brought against them." The president "startled by this plan . . . seemed to acquiesce by silence."[2]

Thus began the story that for House would end in momentary disappointment with the Allies and for Wilson would end in lasting suspicion of Allied intentions and purposes. House viewed his plan primarily as a way to get into the war. He had considered America's intervention on the Allied side as inevitable since the sinking of the *Lusitania*. Although quite prepared to intervene if necessary over the issue of the submarine, House had come to favor intervention for reasons he believed would better justify to the American people the assumption of a new role for the nation in the postwar world. The plan he proposed to Wilson was conceived with this possibility in mind. It foreshadowed intervention from, in House's words, "the highest human motives."[3]

The origins of the House plan go back to House's discussions with Sir Edward Grey in early February 1915, on the occasion of House's first wartime trip to Europe. "There was one thing Grey was fairly insistent upon," House reported to Wilson, "and that was we should come into some guarantee for world wide peace."[4] House had resisted the idea, contending instead for a new Hague convention laying down rules of civilized warfare. Grey did not accept this as America's "full duty," and they passed on to other things. The following day the discussion took a similar turn. This time House was more direct, telling Grey that "it was not only the unwritten law of our country but also our fixed policy not to become involved in European affairs."[5]

But Grey would not let go of the need for American participation in some general guarantee for world peace. "The more I consider this war," he wrote to House shortly before the latter left England, "the more I feel that your government must take a hand in the larger aspects of the peace, if human ideals are to get and keep the ascendancy over material militarism and political ambition."[6] In letters written to House over the summer, Grey returned to this theme. His words found a willing listener.

By August, House had already begun to doubt Wilson's willingness to enter the war over the *Lusitania*. Moreover, as that dispute wore on, he began to question the wisdom of making it the occasion for war. For a brief period in late August and then again in late September, the *Arabic* case seemed to hold out the prospect of a break in relations. When a break did not occur, House came forth with his plan. He was presumably encouraged to do so by a remark Wilson had made to him two weeks earlier. "Much to my surprise," House's diary reads, "he said he had never been sure that we ought not to take part in the conflict and if it seemed evident that Germany and her militaristic ideas were to win, the obligation upon us was greater than ever."[7]

Wilson had made his remark at the height of the *Arabic* crisis, when a diplomatic break with Germany appeared imminent. If it came, the president already sought a justification that went beyond neutrality. Hence, in all likelihood, his ruminations to House. With the recession of the prospect of a break, Wilson's natural propensity to remain at peace would reassert itself. The president at bottom did not share his adviser's outlook. He did not believe that America's intervention was inevitable. While determined to vindicate his version of neutral rights against Germany, he was also determined to remain out of the war. If these goals could not in the end be reconciled, an eventuality Wilson never really confronted until March 1917, the status of belligerent would only be accepted, as the president later declared in his war address, because the German government had left him no choice. The plan House proposed in the fall of 1915 did not fit this condition of necessity; it quite clearly posed a choice.

Despite this marked difference in outlook, Wilson does not appear to have discouraged House from pursuing his plan. It may be that from the start the president had a different understanding of the plan, that the "force of our Government," which would be brought against the Germans if they "refused to acquiesce," carried a different meaning for Wilson. But this seems doubtful if House's diary entry is accurate. Once diplomatic relations were broken off, the meaning of the phrase "whole force of our Government" would seem clear. Still, House had not used the term *war*. Then too, the president had remained silent, and though House took this as acquiescence, it might have meant something quite different.

In the days following their discussion, Wilson could have made his position clear to House, if not by the spoken then by the written word. He did not do so. House proceeded on his way. He got the apparent support of Lansing for his plan.[8] On his next trip to Washington he noted in his diary: "I was pleased to find the President cordially acquiescing in my views regarding intervention in Europe, and that it was only a question as to when and how it should be done. I now have the matter in my own hands and it will probably be left to my judgment as to when and how to act."[9] House had received a letter from Grey, written on September 22, responding to an earlier inquiry about the possibility of the president's making peace proposals to the belligerents based on the "elimination of militarism and navalism and a return, as nearly as possible, to the status quo."[10] Grey's answer dealt instead with the framework for eliminating arms. He was still intent on getting the United States to enter into a general guarantee for world peace. "How much are the United States prepared to do in this direction? " he asked. "Would the President propose that there should be a League of Nations binding themselves to side against any Power which broke a treaty; which broke certain rules of warfare . . . or which refused, in case of disputes, to adopt some other method of settlement than that of war?"[11] Only in some such agreement did he see a prospect of diminishing armies and navies, and only the government of the United States, he was sure, could make such a proposal with effect. As for House's immediate question, Grey would have to consult with the cabinet and Britain's allies, though he felt that neither side was ready to consider peace.

It was not the answer House had sought. Even so, it could be seen as a beginning. House showed it to the president, who said that "it gave much ground for hope" and assented to House's suggestion that he prepare a draft response for Wilson's criticism and approval.[12] On returning to New York, House immediately prepared a response, which he described as "one of the most important letters I ever wrote."[13] "It has occurred to me," the letter began, "that the time may soon come when this Government should intervene between the belligerents and demand that peace parlays begin upon the broad basis of the elimination of militarism and navalism." House would not want to suggest this to the president until he knew that it would meet with Allied approval. He warned against the "world wide calamity" of continuing the war "to a point where the Allies could not, with the aid of the United States, bring about a peace along the lines you and I have so often discussed." What he wanted Grey to know was that whenever Grey considered it propitious, House would propose intervention to the president, who might then desire him to go to Europe in order to effect a "more intimate understanding." This followed the same outline of the plan House had earlier suggested to Wilson, with the admonition to the Allies against the "danger of postponing action too long. If the Allies should be unsuccessful and become unable to do their full share, it would be increasingly difficult, if not impossible, for us to intervene." The letter closed with the "understanding" that for the time being the discussion was entirely between Grey and House.[14]

The president approved the letter, adding the word *probably* in qualification of the pledge "to join the Allies and force the issue" should the Central powers prove obdurate about accepting the American proposal. "I do not want to make it inevitable quite that we should take part to force terms on Germany, because the exact circumstances of such a crisis are impossible to determine," Wilson wrote to House.[15] House considered the change "quite important," presumably as qualification of the commitment.[16] This it certainly was. At the same time, Wilson's statement indicates that there was no misunderstanding between himself and House over the meaning of the letter.

Grey had asked whether the United States would join a league of nations to guarantee peace. House had replied with a proposal that the U.S. government should intervene either to stop the war or to bring it to a victorious end. On what basis? Grey wanted to know. Was the proposal for eliminating militarism and navalism that proposed by Grey in his letter of September 22, in which Grey had posed the issue of American participation? Sending Grey's cable on to the president, House urged Wilson to respond affirmatively. "It seems to me that we must throw the influence of this nation in behalf of a plan by which international obligations must be kept, and in behalf of some plan by which the peace of the world may be maintained. We should do this not only for the sake of civilization, but for our own welfare, for who may say when we may be involved in such a holocaust as is now devastating Europe." And he ended his entreaty by declaring: "This is the part I think you are destined to play in this world tragedy, and it is the noblest part that has ever come to a son of man. This country will follow you along such a path, no matter what the cost may be."[17]

Wilson approved, and his approval is seen as a milestone on the way to the abandonment of an isolationist policy. How significant a milestone was it? The day after he gave House the go-ahead to send a positive reply, the president wrote to his counselor: "I am sure that you understand the telegram I sent you about your message to Grey. I think the paragraph quoted from his letter of September twenty second contains the *necessary* program."[18] America might join a league of nations, but she would not participate in the territorial settlement of the war. On November 19, in a conversation with Bernstorff, House emphasized that the president "believes that he must not interfere in questions involving . . . territorial changes, indemnity etc. Such matters are of no concern to the Americans."[19] Isolation was to be given up for the general conditions of peace but retained for the specific conditions. This partial abandonment of isolation would persist with Wilson until the eve of America's entrance into the war. However untenable, it was given striking expression in Wilson's historic address of May 27, 1916, to the League to Enforce Peace. Declaring that we would henceforth be "partners" with the world, the president nevertheless refused to end the U.S. separation from Europe by affirming America's interest in the terms of peace that would end Europe's greatest war.[20]

A letter from Grey revealed the extent to which House had gotten ahead of the British foreign secretary. Writing before House's response to his cable reached him, Grey did not see how the Allies or the cabinet could commit themselves "without knowing exactly what it [i.e., the proposal to eliminate militarism and navalism] was, and knowing that the United States of America were prepared to intervene and make it good if they accepted it." He wished House were in England so they could talk things over, "but the situation at the moment and the feelings here and among the Allies, and in Germany as far as I know, do not justify me in urging you to come on the ground that your presence would have any practical result at the moment."[21] A frustrated and disappointed House observed that "the British are in many ways dull, or they would better realize what this country has done and is willing to do toward bringing about a proper settlement of the war."[22]

Still, House was not to be deterred. Grey had complained bitterly in his letter about America's attitude toward the blockade, writing that "it looks as if the United States might now strike the weapon of sea power out of our hands, and thereby insure a German victory."[23] The next time House saw Lansing, he "tried to impress upon him the necessity of the United States making it clear to the Allies that we considered their cause our cause, and that we had no intention of permitting a military autocracy [to] dominate the world if our strength could prevent it." Since cordial relations with Germany were now impossible to maintain, "unless we did have a complete and satisfactory understanding with the Allies, we would be wholly without friends when the war was ended and our position would be not only perilous, but might become hurtful from an economic standpoint." Lansing agreed to this, House reported, and the two discussed the best means of reaching an understanding. The talk was apparently limited to personnel, although House undoubtedly had policy in mind as well. They agreed that Spring Rice should be recalled and that a man such as Lord Bryce should replace him. (Whereas Spring Rice was the intimate of Roosevelt and particularly of Lodge, Bryce was not. A former ambassador to the United States and a shrewd commentator on matters American, Bryce was considered an ideal choice to replace Spring Rice.) Once this was done, Lansing thought, "an understanding could be reached in Washington." House suggested that he might outline to Grey the impossibility of dealing through Spring Rice. The passage in the diary concludes that "it was understood between us that we should go at it this way provided the President consented." House urged Lansing to send as many Germans and Austrians home as he reasonably could and, if at all possible, to use the *Ancona* to break off relations with Austria. His idea was to hold on to Bernstorff—"the best of the lot"—as long as possible, while making that connection "as slender as possible . . . so Germany will be careful not to commit any other overt act. I have a feeling now that they do not want to sever relations with us and will become less inclined as the war goes on."[24]

That same day, November 28, House reported to Wilson what he had said to Lansing. Although the president felt that the United States should let the Allies know "how our minds are running," he did not think it could be done by changing ambassadors, necessary as that change was. Nor did Wilson favor "putting our thoughts and intentions into writing"; he wanted them conveyed by word of mouth. House agreed: "I feel, myself, that it could not properly be done excepting in this way. . . . We are now in the most delicate situation that has yet arisen and such negotiations as we have under advisement need the best that we all have in us. It means the reversal of the foreign policy of this Government and no man can foresee the consequences."[25] House offered to go to Europe. No decision was made as to when, or even if, the colonel should go, but the president was strongly disposed to House's making the trip.

Up to this point House could be excused for believing the president agreed with him. Certainly he had not disagreed. At the time House thought that Wilson treated him "as if I were a partner with an interest equal to his own."[26] Acting as a partner, House wrote to Page in London: "It would be well for you to call to the attention of our friends in England the fact that the lower their fortunes seem the more ready we are able to help."[27] To Grey he wrote that British sea power was the "one reassuring potential element in the war" and that what was needed was a better understanding between Washington and London. The existing machinery was not "altogether satisfactory." Perhaps for this as well as for other reasons it would be necessary for House to see Grey in person. It was almost as near as House would come to asking for a change of ambassadors.[28]

Early December found House persuaded that America was "drifting slowly but surely into war" and afraid that the president would not "move with celerity, thereby bringing upon himself merited reproach."[29] The *Ancona* and *Lusitania* cases were unresolved. Lansing had decided to send the German military and naval attachés home.[30] On December 15, House went to Washington at the president's request. "I found the President not quite as belligerent as he was the last time we were together. He seemed to think we would be able to keep out of the war. His general idea is that if the Allies were not able to defeat Germany alone, they could scarcely do so with the help of the United States because it would take too long for us to get in a state of preparedness. It would therefore be a useless sacrifice on our part to go in." House called Wilson's attention to the necessity of having the Allies on America's side if America did not wish to undertake the task alone when Germany was ready to deal with her. "He admits this, and yet I cannot get him up to the point where he is willing to take action. By action, I mean not to declare war, but to let the Allies know we are definitely on their side and that it is not our intention to permit Germany to win if the strength of this country can prevent [it]. The last time we talked he was quite ready to take this stand, but he has visibly weakened."[31]

What had happened to change Wilson's disposition, if indeed it had changed? House wondered whether he had been influenced by congressmen and senators. The Congress had met, and its antiwar mood was apparent. Wilson was not impervious to that mood or to its anti-British undertones. Still, it doubtfully played the role that House would have assigned it. In taking the position he did, Wilson was simply returning to his true self. He had strayed from that self during the fall when he had said to House that he had never been sure that the United States ought not to take part in the conflict. He had departed from that self again in acquiescing in House's ideas regarding intervention in Europe (assuming, of course, that House's reporting of his views was accurate). Rather than ask what had led Wilson to take the position he did with House on December 15, one might more profitably ask what had led Wilson away from his original position. Now, at any rate, he was reaffirming that position.

Nevertheless, the president was insistent that House should go immediately to Europe. "His reasoning is that Great Britain is so inadequately represented here that it is essential that we get in better communication with them, and he does not believe this can be arranged unless I go in person." House too thought something must be done to improve communications with London, yet he was at the time reluctant to undertake the trip. Not only was the immediate task Wilson charged him with uncongenial—"I do not like to handle this disagreeable matter, for my personal relations with the Ambassador are of the most cordial character"—but the trip meant a disruption of personal plans. Lansing, who had joined the meeting, thought the United States had come to an impasse with Austria and Germany (over the *Ancona* and *Lusitania*) that might well lead to a break in diplomatic relations, "in which event, questions with the Allies will become automatically settled." But Wilson was unmoved by Lansing's argument. "He is evidently not satisfied with existing conditions," wrote House, "particularly in regard to our relations with the Allies, and he thinks I may materially strengthen our position by this trip."[32]

House's diary entry on the meeting of December 15 carried not a word on his plan of intervention in the war. On December 22 House wrote the president of the invitation he had received from Germany to go to Berlin to discuss peace based upon the general terms of military and naval disarmament. The German government wanted him to come directly to Berlin. Bernstorff understood that this was impossible and would so inform his government. House related to Wilson that he had told Bernstorff that "if they would consent to a plan which embraced general disarmament, you would be willing to throw the weight of this

Government into the scales, and demand that the war cease." America had no concern with territorial questions and indemnity, only with the larger questions involving not only the belligerents but the neutrals as well. House believed America should move with circumspection lest the Germans place her in "a disagreeable position with the Allies." He was "always suspicious of their diplomacy." The letter closed with a specific request from House. "Will you not write me immediately upon receipt of this your impressions as to what to say in London and what to say in Berlin and how far I shall go."[33] Wilson responded:

> Sir Cecil is certainly a most puzzling and incalculable person. It is very important that some less childish man should take his place.
>
> I do not know that Bernstorff is much more satisfactory. I feel, with you, that it is necessary to get corroboration of his representations from the other side before we can act with confidence on them. What you tell me of your latest conversation with him about peace is, nevertheless, most interesting. It makes me feel, as you evidently do, that it is possible that we are on the eve of some real opportunity. I pray it may turn out to be so! At any rate, it is the more clear that you are starting on your present errand at just the right juncture.
>
> You ask for instructions as to what attitude and tone you are to take at the several capitals. I feel that you do not need any. Your own letters . . . exactly echo my own views and purposes. I agree with you that we have nothing to do with local settlements,— territorial questions, indemnities, and the like,—but are concerned only in the future peace of the world and the guarantees to be given for that. The only possible guarantees, that is, the only guarantees that any rational man could accept are (a) military and naval disarmament and (b) a league of nations to secure each nation against aggression and maintain the absolute freedom of the seas. If either party to the present war will let us say to the other that they are willing to discuss peace on such terms, it will clearly be our duty to use our utmost moral force to oblige the other to parley, and I do not see how they could stand in the opinion of the world if they refused.
>
> The errand upon which you are primarily bound you understand as fully and intimately as I do, and the demand in the Senate for further, immediate, and imperative pressure on England and her allies makes the necessity for it the more pressing. About the possibilities in the direction of peace you need no further intimation

than that given above. If any particular question arises I know that you will cable me fully, and I shall of course reply at the earliest possible moment.[34]

The letter confirmed House's December 15 conversation with Wilson. The president had pulled away from his flirtation with the House plan, being prepared to use "moral force" only. Even then he had taken the plan and recast it in a form that was entirely neutral regarding the two sides. And he had called House's attention to the errand upon which he was "primarily bound," namely, representation in Washington that would prove more responsive to U.S. complaints about the blockade. House noted in his diary the day he received Wilson's reply: "He clearly places the whole responsibility back on my shoulders where I would gladly have it, for if I am to act, I wish to act with a free hand."[35] And on the following day he wrote the president: "I think we agree entirely."[36]

On January 6, 1916, in London, the errand upon which House was "primarily bound" was almost immediately abandoned. "I touched lightly upon the British Ambassador at Washington and of his temperamental unfitness for the position he occupies," the colonel recorded after his first meeting with Sir Edward Grey. "I did not push this further but will perhaps take it up later."[37] It was never pushed further, House being alerted to the affection and esteem Grey had for Spring Rice.[38] Nor did Wilson ever admonish House to press the case against the British ambassador.

House lost no time in acquainting Grey with the "real purpose" of his visit. "I outlined the suggestion I made by letter regarding the United States' intervention," he wrote in his diary the day of his arrival, "based upon a demand for freedom of the seas and the curtailment of militarism." House gave his views on freedom of the seas and what it meant for Great Britain. "It was gratifying to have Sir Edward meet me halfway," which could not have meant much more than that Grey listened politely. Grey was pleased to hear House declare that public opinion in the United States would now support the nation's entrance into "some world agreement having for its object the maintenance of peace if a workable plan could be devised." House thought it far better for the democracies to unite on a plan that would enable the United States to intervene in the war rather than drifting into war by breaking diplomatic relations with the Central powers over the issue of submarine warfare. He confessed to Grey that he had advised the president against a break with Germany in the hope that an agreement with Great Britain along the lines now contemplated could be reached. The president was sympathetic to this view, House told Grey, although Lansing was insistent upon a diplomatic break with Germany on the grounds that if the Central powers won, the United States would have to reckon with them later. "While I felt the weight of this argument," House admitted, "still I believe the plan we have in mind will give better results."[39]

That House assumed Grey's support in principle for his plan was critical. The assumption was only partially correct, however. Of course Grey did want American participation in the postwar order. Pleading that his colleagues were doubtful that Wilson intended to pursue a vigorous foreign policy, he even had House cable the president asking for "some assurance of your willingness to cooperate in a policy seeking to bring about and maintain permanent peace among civilized nations."[40] (Wilson answered that he would be "willing and glad" to do so "when the opportunity comes."[41]) Beyond this, Grey was willing to talk and to listen but not, as it turned out, to act.

Grey had asked House in their first meeting which members of the cabinet House would like to meet in order to discuss his plan. They had agreed upon Arthur Balfour, head of the British Admiralty, "but could not think beyond him of anyone who would be in sympathy with our purposes."[42] On the fourth day following House's arrival the three men met for lunch to talk the matter out. House found Balfour "not very constructive, but analytical and argumentative" and wondering whether the president would be able to carry out such an agreement. House hastened to assure them. "[America] had a President more powerful during his term in office than any sovereign in Europe," he asserted, adding that "it would be easier for me to persuade the President to accede to what I would be willing to agree to, than it would be for them to succeed with their colleagues." And he repeated what he had already told Grey alone, that he had been "largely responsible" for Wilson's not sending Bernstorff home and breaking off diplomatic relations with Germany, actions that, House now explained, would have made the plan he was proposing "impossible of success, and we would be merely in the ruck of the war along with the balance of them, and with no hope of a satisfactory solution unless militarism was completely crushed by force of arms." Grey and Balfour were described as "full of suppressed excitement at the proposal," an unlikely reaction given House's assessment of its effects.[43]

All this House reserved for his diary. In a letter to the president he gave the general line of his argument. Although the United States could still safely lead an "isolated life of our own," he reported Wilson as believing that "in order to fully justify our existence as a great nation, it might be necessary to bring to bear all our power in behalf of peace and the maintenance of it." Grey and Balfour wanted to know how far Wilson would be willing to enter into an agreement concerning European affairs. House thought the president would not be willing to do this at all. He would be willing to come to an agreement with the civilized world only upon the broad questions touching the interest and future of every nation, for example, the elimination of militarism and navalism. Balfour remarked that he would see what concessions his colleagues might make to American opinion. House took exception to this, remarking that it was America that was making the sacrifice, for she was willing to consider some means by which to save civilization, even if it entailed the sacrifice of her traditional policy.

"They are so confident of ultimate success," House wrote to Wilson, "that I endeavored to shake it somewhat, and I think I did." House pointed out to Grey and Balfour that they were running the risks that Germany would make a separate peace with Russia and France. It was a theme to which he would return more than once in the days ahead. Germany had but one antagonist, and before going under she would do her best to detach Britain's two major allies. If she succeeded, British sea power "would not last three months, not because it might be defeated at sea, but because all nations would protest against the restrictions of trade."[44]

Although nothing was resolved at the meeting, House described it in a cable to Wilson as "entirely satisfactory." The three men agreed to meet again and continue the discussion. "My plan is to come to a tentative agreement with them before going to the Continent on the twentieth, [of January]," House informed Wilson, "and let them bring their colleagues into line before I return. They have agreed to undertake this."[45]

What did Wilson think of House's cable? The only indication we have is his brief reply: "It now looks as if our several difficulties with Germany would be presently adjusted. So soon as they are the demand here especially from the Senate will be imperative that we force England to make at least equal concessions to our unanswerable claims of right. . . . I send this for your information and guidance."[46] The president apparently was concerned more with addressing shipping problems resulting from the blockade than with House's grand plan. After all, he had sent House to Europe with the understanding that the Colonel would pursue those problems. This was implicit in his emphasis on the inadequacy of Spring Rice. His letter of December 24 to House had closed with the distinction between "the errand upon which you are primarily bound" and "the possibilities in the direction of peace."[47]

House soon discovered that the British were immovable on the issue of the blockade. At a dinner party given by Page in House's honor, attended by Austen Chamberlain, the colonial secretary, Reginald McKenna, the chancellor of the exchequer, David Lloyd George, the minister of munitions, and Lord Chief Justice Reading, Page remarked that he had been asked "what the United States wished Great Britain to do." House replied that "the United States would like Great Britain to do those things which would enable the United States to help Great Britain win the war." The reply brought "general approval," House's diary reads, "and then came the discussion as to what Great Britain must do to help the United States help her. I went into our shipping troubles at some length and told them of the burden their restrictions placed upon the President."[48] When House repeated the phrase the following day at lunch, for the benefit of Sir Edward Grey and Lord Robert Cecil, the newly appointed minister of blockade, along with conveying to them the president's cable, Cecil told him that if he acceded to Wilson's request, "his resignation would be demanded at once," and that he did not believe in "half way measures." The blockade had "to be rigid, or not at all."[49]

House had not asked the British to moderate the blockade and did not want them to. He drew a distinction between the substance of the blockade and the way it was carried out; in his view, it was the latter that should be altered. But the British could not readily distinguish substance from form in the operation of the blockade. In their view, what House would have them concede to ease the president's problems went to the heart of the controls exercised over neutral shipping. Thus their resistance to any suggestion that the blockade be altered. It was soon apparent to House that a choice, if one could call it that, would have to be made between pressing issues of neutral right and concentrating on his grand plan. House had not come to Europe primarily to press issues of neutral right; it was his plan that held him in thrall.

But the plan did not appear to progress, momentary signs to the contrary. One such sign had been a dinner meeting with Lloyd George and Reading on January 14. Lloyd George did not know the "real purpose" of House's visit or, apparently, that House had talked with Grey and Balfour. He delighted House by endowing the president with an all-encompassing power. "We agreed that the war could only be ended by your intervention," House wrote to Wilson. "[Lloyd] George thought intervention should not come until around the 1st of September, therefore we settled tentatively upon that date." By then the great battles of the summer would have been fought and the Allies would have more than offset the advantage Germany held at the time. The British were already planning for the summer offensive along the Somme and would have, according to Lloyd George, "four million men fully equipped and trained and with guns larger than any now in use." The belligerent countries being unable to make peace by themselves, public opinion "would force the governments to accept your [Wilson's] mediation."

The two men discussed the terms of peace. Lloyd George thought the president could demand the evacuation of Belgium and France and the restoration of Alsace-Lorraine to France and have Russia consent to an independent Poland. Militarism would also go at Wilson's demand. Turkey must be eliminated, and Germany and Russia must take over parts of it. Although at first insistent that England would never consent even to discuss freedom of the seas, after a short argument with House he admitted that it was debatable and might be done. The main thing was "that this peace should be a peace to make friends and not enemies." House was enthused. "I hope and pray you will not let anything interfere with this plan. It can be done, but only by making it paramount and not allowing the lesser things to confuse it."[50] On the same day that House wrote the letter, he sent a cable to Wilson that read: "I have something of importance to communicate by letter. . . . Would suggest not sending any note to England concerning shipping troubles until it arrives. It is equally *utmost importance* to continue relations with Germany and Austria until then. There seems to be some daylight ahead if fortune favors us."[51]

Fortune did not seem to favor House. The following day, he told Grey and Balfour of his meeting with Lloyd George and of Lloyd George's "division of the world . . . and of the extraordinary part he would have the President play." House asked whether they had discussed the matter with him. They had not. Both looked upon Lloyd George as "brilliant and unstable," jumping to conclusions quickly but as quickly forming another. The meeting did not go well. In addition to the many objections Balfour still had to House's plan, neither Balfour nor Grey considered it prudent to discuss these questions with their colleagues, let alone with their allies. Even if they could do both, the people could not be told. House noted in his diary: "We parted with the understanding that they should think the matter over and discuss it with the Prime Minister and Lloyd George and take it up with me when I returned from the Continent."[52]

So instead of House's reaching agreement on the plan with Grey and

Balfour before leaving for the Continent—House's initial expectation—the three men had only been able to agree on whom to include within the secret circle. On January 16 a disappointed House wrote to the president. His advice was to play a waiting game. Time would favor America's position—"Our power is increasing in double ratio," House wrote—if we were but patient.[53]

But what he found in Berlin in late January caused the colonel to modify his views. Talks with Chancellor Bethmann Hollweg, Foreign Minister Jagow, and Arthur Zimmermann, undersecretary at the foreign office, made plain to House that the German terms of peace were impossible. More important were the signs of a struggle over submarine policy, pitting Bethmann Hollweg and the foreign office against the navy and an army increasingly in favor of an aggressive underseas campaign. "I do not believe the Chancellor will be able to hold the first place long," House wrote on February 3 from Paris, on his way back to London, "particularly if we do not take measures against the Allies, which, indeed, it would be impossible for us to take in a manner that would satisfy Germany." House continued:

> When they find this cannot be brought about, and when the pinch of the blockade becomes greater than even now, a revulsion of feeling will probably take place and a sentiment will develop for any measure that promises relief.
>
> The Navy crowd are telling the people that an unrestricted undersea warfare will isolate England. I look, therefore, in any event for troublesome times with Germany during the next few months and I am afraid that my suggestion that we remain aloof until the time becomes more propitious for you to intervene and lead them out, is not promising.
>
> The reason I am so anxious that you do not break with Germany over the Lusitania is that any delay may make it possible to carry out the original plan in regard to intervention. And if that cannot be done because of Germany's undersea warfare, then we will be forced in a way that will give us the advantage.[54]

House had not given up on his plan. What he had learned in Germany had led him to think in terms of greater urgency. In Paris on February 2 he saw Jules Cambon, the then acting director of the French foreign office, and talked to him, the diary reports, "very frankly." On the *Lusitania,* House recorded saying that he was doing all he could to avert a break over an incident then months old and practically forgotten by the public. In his opinion, Germany would give America another opportunity if she desired one. House sought to impress upon Cambon the gamble the war represented for both Great Britain and France. He pictured the danger in Germany's attempt to make a separate peace with Russia. He urged that France use all her influence with Great Britain to modify the illegal features of the blockade. And he informed Cambon of his discussion with the German leaders regarding peace terms.[55]

To the president he wrote largely in the same vein, adding, "I cannot begin to tell you by letter how critical the situation is everywhere, not only as between themselves, but with us as well. In my opinion, hell will break loose in Europe this spring and summer as never before and I see no way to stop it for the moment. I am as sure as I ever am of anything that by the end of the summer you can intervene."[56] On what House based this confidence in the prospects for American intervention remains obscure. Perhaps it harked back to his conversation with Lloyd George and to Lloyd George's view that by fall public opinion in the belligerent countries would force the governments to accept Wilson's mediation.

A French memorandum of the talk, made by Cambon, was at variance with what House reported. According to Cambon, House had emphasized that the initiatives the Allies took that might affect neutrals must be "manifestly guided by military necessity." America would accept all measures that met a military need. Anything in excess would stir up complaints and resentments. But if that stricture were adhered to, Cambon quoted House as saying, "inevitably America will enter the war, *before the end of the year,* and will align herself on the side of the Allies. However, for that to happen, it would be necessary for an incident to occur that would cause all the American people to rally behind the President." An astonished Cambon had had House repeat the statement, which Cambon had taken down and read back to House. House had responded, "Exactly." To Cambon's question as to what kind of incident might precipitate American entry into the war, the Germans apparently being willing to grant everything America demanded, House had replied that the Germans would not acknowledge the illegality of their attack on the *Lusitania.* "As a result, any settlement that might be reached in this matter, if one could be reached, will only postpone the conflict, not prevent it."[57] House had concluded this part of the conversation by telling Cambon of his conviction, based on his trip to Germany, that sooner or later the Germans, in response to England's tightening of the blockade and confident in the effectiveness of their mines and submarines, would commit the act that must force America's hand.

Several days later, on February 7, House had a final meeting with Aristede Briand, premier and acting foreign minister, and Cambon. The colonel's diary entry for the day describes it as "an important meeting—perhaps the most important I have had during this visit to Europe."[58] Until then, he wrote to Wilson, "I have been confidential with the British Government alone, and have left to them the bringing into line their Allies." Impressed as never before by the "slowness and lack of initiative" of the British, he had concluded that "we had best take the risk and talk plainly to the French. The result was surprisingly satisfactory."[59]

One can only wonder why he thought so. What House related to Wilson was mainly what he had told the French, not what the French had told him. He had outlined "with care" the risks the French were facing and how deeply concerned America was for the future of democratic government. "It was finally understood," House went on, "that in the event the Allies had some notable victories during the spring or summer, you would intervene, and in the event the tide of war went against them, or remained stationary you would intervene."[60] In the diary an apparently different formulation is given: "In the event the Allies are successful during the next few months I promised the President would not intervene. In the event they were losing ground, I promised the President would intervene."[61] And the French account of this part of the conversation reads: "Also, you can be assured, Colonel House added, that if the Allies should have a little success, this spring or summer, the United States will intervene in favor of peace, but if they have a setback, the United States will intervene militarily and take part in the war against Germany."[62]

The French version must be considered the most accurate account of what House said, having been recorded on the spot by Cambon and read back to House for his approval. A comparison of House's letter to Wilson with what Cambon recorded indicates either that House was being quite careless with words or that he wanted to convey different meanings to the different parties. We know that House employed the term *intervention* in both a nonmilitary and a military sense. Even so, this cannot account for the different formulation given in the letter to the president. It may be that House meant in the letter (and, for that matter, in the diary as well) no more and no less than that, as the French version stated, if the Allies had a little success, the United States would intervene in favor of peace, presumably along the lines set out by Wilson in his letter of December 24 to House, and if the Allies had a setback, the United States would intervene militarily. If this was his intent, it was not clearly or adequately expressed in his letter to Wilson. The letter to Wilson went on to state: "Briand and Cambon know and seem to agree to the advice I gave you concerning the settlement of the Lusitania matter. It is impossible for any unprejudiced person to believe that it would be wise for America to take part in this war unless it comes about by intervention based upon the highest human motives. We are the only nation left on earth with sufficient power to lead them out, and with us once in, the war would have to go on to a finish with all its appalling consequences. It is better for the Central Powers and it is better for the Allies, as indeed, it is better for us to act in this way, and I have not hesitated to say this to the British and French Governments and have intimated it to Germany."[63]

But had House spoken in this manner to Briand and Cambon? Not if the Cambon version is credited. For that version has House taking an Allied offensive in the spring or summer for granted and telling his interlocutors that "the lower will be the situation of France, the stronger will be the friendship of America." The prospect of peaceful intervention was put off to the fall. Even then it was dependent on Allied success in the field. House had promised American military intervention in the event that the Allies were not successful—"the war would have to go on to a finish with all its appalling consequences."

The French asked House his view of Alsace-Lorraine. It would have to be restored to France, replied the colonel, but in return Germany would have to get compensation, for example, in Asia Minor. In any event, Turkey must disappear. In the eyes of the colonel, the French account reads, "England and France should act in concert, in a broad and liberal spirit, concerning the conditions of peace that they think possible when the right occasion comes. The United States would support them in their proposals and would enter the conflict if Germany did not accept their terms." To all this, Cambon and Briand responded "that the moment for such propositions had not arrived."[64]

"Events are moving rapidly," House wired Wilson on February 10, the day after he returned to London, "and if nothing is done in Washington to disturb the situation I am hopeful that soon after my arrival home you will be able to initiate the great movement we have in mind."[65] House had met with Grey that morning and given him an account of his visit to Germany. The two men discussed the *Lusitania* controversy, then nearing resolution, and the successive phases of Germany's underseas warfare. Grey, the diary records, took the ground that it would be "best for us to enter the war. . . . His argument was that if we were in the war we could at anytime say to the Allies we were ready to make a separate peace with Germany, naming conditions upon which we would treat." House thought this "impracticable" and that once in, "we would have to remain until all sides were exhausted, or a decisive defeat had been brought about."[66]

House reported to Wilson that he had brought Grey quickly around on the *Lusitania* controversy. But there was another development that threatened to "disturb the situation," the modus vivendi. In a letter to Wilson of January 7, 1916, Lansing had made the following proposal. In exchange for an undertaking by the Central powers not to torpedo enemy merchant vessels without first putting the people on board in safety, the Entente powers would not permit their merchant vessels to carry armament. The president had found the proposal "reasonable and thoroughly worth trying."[67] The British had taken a different view. Page had already warned House of Grey's reaction to the modus vivendi. While there is no mention of it either in the diary or in House's letter to Wilson of the same date, Grey almost certainly raised the matter. Not only that but, as Patrick Devlin has argued, Grey "must have told House that America must drop either the *modus vivendi* or the House plan."[68] If so, it is plausible to assume that House took it upon himself to assure Grey that the modus vivendi would be dropped.

House took away from the conference with Grey the conviction that Grey had agreed to the president's calling a peace conference, free of conditions, within a very short time, perhaps soon after House returned. "The Allies will agree to the conference," he wrote Wilson, "and if Germany does not, I have promised for you that we will throw all our weight to bring her to terms." The timetable for American intervention had apparently been shortened. In Paris, House had assured Wilson that he could intervene by the fall. In London, the following week, he said that he could intervene much sooner. "You will see that we have progressed pretty far since I left Paris—further than I had any idea that it was possible to do."[69] In neither case did the assurance correspond with reality. Briand and Cambon had rejected the call for a peace conference. In the case of Grey, House recorded in his diary that "we finally agreed it was best for the President not to set any conditions whatever, but merely to demand that war cease, and a conference be held."[70] Even if this does represent a faithful account of what the two agreed to, it says nothing about the time. But House was determined to let nothing stand in the way of his optimism.

On February 10 an agreement on how to proceed was reached. "I am to meet the Prime Minister, Balfour and Grey tomorrow at lunch to acquaint them with our discussion and to endeavor to get their approval. If this is done there will be a dinner on which I have requested that Page be present. At this dinner there will be the Prime Minister, Grey, Balfour, Lloyd George and the Lord Chief Justice. There will be no others taken in at any later conference, but what is determined there will be a finality and I can bring you home definite news."[71]

Although the February 11 luncheon meeting did not go as well as House had expected, it did not shake his confidence about the final result. "They were not as amenable to the plan as Grey," he reported to Wilson, "but adopted it tentatively and I have but little doubt now that when I leave we will have an absolute understanding that you are to propose a peace conference and act as mediator when the time is propitious."[72] Grey outlined the discussion he had had with House the previous day, taking the position that Great Britain could do nothing until one of her allies was ready to discuss peace. House warned that this could prove dangerous; if the British waited for that, they would run the risk of making U.S. intervention impossible because of having delayed too long. To avoid this risk, while also avoiding the charge of double-dealing by allies, House suggested sending Grey coded cables at regular intervals offering intervention. Sir Edward could ignore the messages until the time was propitious, then bring them to the attention of the Allies as coming from the United States rather than from Great Britain. Balfour, who seemed "less argumentative than I have seen him," put the question "what assurance did I wish to take back to the President." House replied that "I wished a definite understanding whether it would be agreeable to the British Government in the circumstances outlined, to have the United States propose cessation of war and a conference to discuss peace terms. If I could take back a favorable reply to the President, we would then know what to work to." He cautioned them again about allowing the matter to run too far. If they made the mistake of waiting until Germany had a decisive victory, or nearly so, they need not expect any help from the United States. In that event, America would withdraw altogether from European affairs.[73]

That afternoon (February 11) Page told House that he thought it best not to take part in any peace talks House had with the cabinet. Page had been particularly critical of American policy in the winter of 1916. When the British had moved to tighten the blockade in late January, Page had sent a memorandum to Lansing asking whether the United States was going to oppose the move. What was it that America wanted, a draw or a German defeat? The perils of a draw and the advantages of a peace dependent on Anglo-American cooperation were elaborated.[74] The ambassador railed against the course he saw the *Lusitania* negotiations taking, and he found the modus vivendi the height of folly. When, on returning from the Continent, House explained his plan to Page, it met with a dismal reception. The "fatal moral weakness of House's plan," Page observed in his diary, "is that we should plunge into the war, not on the merits of the cause, but by a carefully sprung trick. . . . Of course such a morally weak indirect scheme is doomed to failure—is wrong, in fact."[75] Now House was asking him to play a role in such a scheme. Page refused. "I did not argue with him," House noted, "because it served my purpose to have him remain out of the conference, since in his frame of mind he is a hindrance rather than a help."[76]

On the evening of February 14 the dinner meeting regarded by House as determinative for his plan took place. House set the stage by promising that the president would go to The Hague, if invited, and remain as long as necessary. He then asked the others what they thought would happen if the conference were held at The Hague and the president presided over it. Lloyd George outlined what he thought the peace conference might do, and the rest commented upon the different phases of the questions as they arose. The "nationalization of Poland was discussed at great length," along with the difficulties this would pose for Russia and France. "We all cheerfully divided up Turkey, both in Asia and Europe." The fate of Constantinople, however, produced a division over whether or not to give it into the hands of Russia.

As it was growing late, House brought them back to the point of the meeting, "that is, when should the United States demand that the war should cease and a conference be held." Although Lloyd George seemed "thoroughly committed . . . to the idea that the President should act in this capacity," he was "rather chary of naming a definite time." Grey, on the other hand, "was evidently leaning toward an immediate venture in this direction."

The discussion turned to how the Allies could be approached and what might be done about them. Prime Minister Herbert Asquith put the question of the proper time. House thought that "if the Allies could make an impression on the German lines of sufficient importance to discourage Germany, that would be the psychological moment." The drawback would be that a heartened public in the Allied countries would then be resistant to peace proposals. While Asquith thought this would not be the case unless the success of the Allies was greater than he now considered possible, Lloyd George and Balfour were inclined to take the risk and to postpone action.

"While the conference was not conclusive," House summed up, "there was at least a common agreement reached in regard to the essential feature, that is, the President should at some time to be later agreed upon, call a halt and demand a conference. I did not expect to go beyond that and I was quite content." But House did go beyond that. He affirmed that the peace would have to conform to Wilsonian standards of justice:

> Asquith again asked what the President would do in the event he presided at the peace conference, and the Allies proposed a settlement he considered unjust. I replied that he would probably withdraw from the conference and leave them to their own devices. On the other hand, he wished to know what the President would do in the event Germany proposed something totally unfair, and against the interest of civilization and humanity. In these circumstances, I thought the President would throw the weight of the United States on the side of the Allies. In other words, he would throw the weight of the United States on the side of those wanting a just settlement—a settlement which would make another such war impossible, and which would look to the advancement of civilization and the comity of nations.[77]

The following day, February 15, House met with Grey, who was, House records, "visibly pleased" with the results. "He said he knew it would be unpopular in England—so unpopular indeed, that he would expect to have the windows of his house broken by angry mobs, nevertheless, he is ready to face it because he feels he is right."[78] Grey thought it necessary to put the proposal before the entire cabinet, but not until House had left England. He promised to write a memorandum of understanding, which House would take with him. He did not consider it necessary to have a further meeting for general discussion. With all this, House agreed.

On February 17 House met with Grey again to draft the memorandum. Before doing so, Grey showed House the French memorandum of the second conversation House had had with Briand and Cambon. "They reported me as saying that no matter how low the fortunes of France got, that when they said the word, we would intervene." House asked Grey to correct this impression. If the Allies "put off calling for our assistance to a time when our intervention cannot serve them, then we will not make the attempt." The diary goes on to note: "I am trying to force early action by making both the English and the French feel that they run the risk of losing our support entirely unless they act quickly."[79]

On February 22 House and Grey drew up the memorandum, which was written by Grey. It read as follows:

Colonel House told me that President Wilson was ready, on hearing from France and England that the moment was opportune, to propose that a conference should be summoned to put an end to the war. Should the Allies accept this proposal, and should Germany refuse it, the United States would probably enter the war against Germany.

Colonel House expressed the opinion that, if such a conference met, it would secure peace on terms not unfavorable to the Allies; and, if it failed to secure peace, the United States would leave the Conference as a belligerent on the side of the Allies, if Germany was unreasonable. Colonel House expressed an opinion decidedly favorable to the restoration of Belgium, the transfer of Alsace and Lorraine to France, and the acquisition by Russia of an outlet to the sea, though he thought that the loss of territory incurred by Germany in one place would have to be compensated by concessions to her in other places outside Europe. If the Allies delayed accepting the offer of President Wilson, and if, later on, the course of the war was so unfavorable to them that the intervention of the United States would not be effective, the United States would probably disinterest themselves in Europe and look to their own protection in their own way.

I said I felt the statement, coming from the President of the United States, to be a matter of such importance that I must inform the Prime Minister and my colleagues; but that I could say nothing until it received their consideration. The British Government could, under no circumstances, accept or make any proposal except in consultation and agreement with the Allies. I thought that the Cabinet would probably feel that the present situation would not justify them in approaching their Allies on this subject at the present moment; but, as Colonel House had had an intimate conversation with M. Briand and M. Jules Cambon in Paris, I should think it right to tell M. Briand privately, through the French Ambassador in London, what Colonel House had said to us; and I should, of course, whenever there was an opportunity, be ready to talk the matter over with M. Briand, if he desired it.[80]

House described the memorandum as "covering what I actually said, not only in Paris, but at the meeting the other night at Lord Reading's." Grey was to show the memorandum to the French ambassador and to give House a copy so there would be "no mistake as to how far I committed the President and upon what line."

The memorandum written, the conversation returned to the issue uppermost in the colonel's mind, namely, the importance of acting quickly. "We both think there is more to gain for Great Britain by the President's intervention now, than there would be if the Allies won a complete victory a year from now." House pointed to the dangers of a complete victory, that Britain's allies would make demands and do things that Great Britain would not approve and that would not be in the interest of permanent peace. He called Grey's attention to the gambles taken by postponing action, of the possible death of Wilson and of the uncertainty of the president's reelection. "Grey said with much feeling, 'history will lay a great charge against those of us who refuse to accept your proffered services at this time.'"[81]

House saw Grey again on February 21. They took up the issue of the best time for acting on the president's proposal. "Grey thought it depended upon the military leaders of the Allies. If they considered the situation warranted waiting a few months for military success, it would be necessary to yield to this opinion. He understands, however, that the president and I desire to act as soon as possible." The following day, Lord Chief Justice Reading called on House to tell him of a talk he had had with the prime minister, who had spoken "much more strongly in favor of the agreement than he had at the conference." Reading had also seen Lloyd George, who had also been cordial in support of the understanding. In order to expedite affairs, it was the intention to push militarily in the west at the "earliest possible moment."[82]

Although House left Great Britain confident that he had succeeded, he worried on the voyage home that the president and Lansing had interfered with his efforts by their ill-timed proposal on armed merchantmen. "If they had held the situation quiescent as I urged them to do, I am sure my plan for intervention by the United States to end the war would have gone through without trouble. I am deeply disappointed but I hope matters can be ironed out in a way to yet make the plan possible." Upon arriving in Washington on March 6, he found an apparently receptive president. "I showed him the memorandum which Sir Edward Grey and I had agreed was the substance of my understanding with France and Great Britain. The President accepted it *in toto* only suggesting that the word 'probably' be inserted in the ninth line after the word 'would' and before the word 'leave.'"[83] Wilson was effusive in his praise of House.

The following day Wilson wrote a telegram to Grey, which House signed and sent. It read as follows: "I reported to the President the general conclusions of our conference of the fourteenth of February and in the light of those conclusions he authorizes me to say that, so far as he can speak for the future actions of the Untied States, he agrees to the memorandum with which you have furnished me with only this correction that the word probably be added at the end of line nine."[84] In fact, the word *probably* was added to the memorandum in not one but two places, the second dealing with the peace terms to be secured. Thus the amended sentence stated: "Colonel House expressed the opinion that, if such a conference met, it would probably secure peace on terms not unfavorable to the Allies; and, if it failed to secure peace, the United States would probably leave the Conference as a belligerent on the side of the Allies, if Germany was unreasonable."

Did the addition alter the character of the proposal? The question has been debated since the memorandum first became public. Charles Seymour, House's early biographer, thought not. "The value of the offer was in no way lessened by the use of the word 'probably', which was a conventional covering expression in diplomatic documents. Since the power to declare war resides in Congress and since the President shares with the Senate the control of foreign policy, it would have been impossible for Wilson to give a categorical guarantee of the future action of the United States. As a matter of practice, however, the President can determine the question of peace and war, and the expression of his intention appears here in the strongest possible form."[85]

In a review of Seymour's work, written in 1926, Walter Lippmann took issue with this interpretation: "The President did not say categorically; 'I will recommend to Congress that the United States enter the war,' as he might have done if that was what he was intending to do. The use of the word 'probably' reserved liberty of action for Wilson, and so the Allies must have understood it. . . . Once you reject Mr. Seymour's explanation and take the Wilson amendment as meaning what it appears to say, you arrive at this result: *House* proposed a conference which would either obtain moderate terms for the Allies or American assistance in the war; *Wilson*, on the other hand, proposed a conference to end the war with no commitment that he would even try to enter the war if the conference failed."[86]

Wilson had not once intervened in the course of House's negotiations. He had in fact indicated approval of the course the negotiations were taking. "I have not replied to your messages," he wired House on February 12, "merely because they seemed to need no comment. . . . What you have done seems admirable and gives me lively hope of a development of events that may bring peace."[87] Then, too, there is his acceptance of the memorandum and his warm praise of House's efforts. But Seymour's interpretation would require us to say that the president, in Lippmann's words, "offered in secret to commit this country to enter a war in order to achieve a certain diplomatic settlement in Europe."[88] In turn, this would require the assumption that Wilson's indisposition to entering the war unless forced to by Germany's use of the submarine was only a public pose, to be abandoned at the first opportunity. For the language of the memorandum was clear, as was the conflict between it and Wilson's public commitment. Wilson had only recently reiterated that commitment to Senator William J. Stone, a democrat from Missouri, chairman of the Committee on Foreign Relations, writing, "You are right to assume I shall do everything in my power to keep the United States out of war."[89] Yet the House-Grey memorandum stipulated that the United States would probably enter the war on the side of the Allies should Germany either refuse to attend a conference "summoned to put an end to the war" or, attending such a conference, prove "unreasonable" in accepting "terms not unfavorable to the Allies."

Unless it is assumed that President Wilson was insincere in his desire to stay out of the war, we are driven to accept Lippmann's interpretation and the conclusions he draws from it about Wilson's intentions. "I think Wilson wished above all to avoid war. I think he would have been willing to have almost any peace in Europe if he could keep America out of war. I think he saw that if once he could induce the belligerents to begin talking that they never could resume fighting. He was willing to try any device, including the House negotiations, that might bring on a conference, *provided* it did not commit him to entering the war."[90] House was scarcely in a position to question the president's reservation even if he discerned its real purpose.[91] Quite apart from his subordinate position, he had exceeded his instructions in drawing up the memorandum. At best, he could only wait to see what use the president would make of it.

The use the president would make of the memorandum depended upon a prior decision of the Allies. It was France and England who had first "to propose that a Conference be summoned to put an end to the war." But the British and French were not disposed to take any action. The French had made clear from the start their opposition to House's plan. By the last week of February the battle for Verdun had begun, and as time went on, French confidence in a victorious outcome rose. Intent on achieving military victory, they were not interested in the prospects of a negotiated peace. Given a copy of the memorandum by Grey, the French government never subsequently brought it up with their ally.

The British were more circumspect, but the end result was very nearly the same. When the memorandum was considered by the War Committee, an inner group of the cabinet, once Wilson's acceptance became known, the decision was to leave the initiative to the French. To urge a conference on the French before they desired it, Grey wrote to House on March 24, "would lead them to suppose that we were not prepared to support them when they wished to go on. To give such an impression would be most repugnant to our views or feelings, besides having a disastrous political effect." Grey proposed therefore "(1st) to let M. Briand know that since you left I have heard if France and England were willing, President Wilson would on his initiative summon a conference to end the war on the terms and in the spirit indicated by you at Paris and London . . . (2) that we could not put the matter before any of the other Allies unless after consultation with and in concert with the French Government and do not therefore propose to mention this subject at the Conference of Allies in Paris this week. (3) That if M. Briand has any views to express on the subject he will no doubt let me know them either himself or through M. Jules Cambon, while we are in Paris. . . . Of course there is nothing in this to prevent your making any communication to the French you think opportune."[92]

On April 7 Grey wrote again to House. He had sent to Briand the message proposed, but at the conference of Allies neither Briand nor Cambon had mentioned the subject and "it was very clear from the whole feeling at Paris that the French Government could not take up the idea of a conference then." Grey felt "bound to say" that the feeling in London was the same as in Paris. "Everybody feels that there must be more German failure and some Allied success before anything but an inconclusive peace can be obtained." Meanwhile, the *Sussex* case had arisen, and it, along with the torpedoing of other neutral ships, "created a dilemma. If the United States Government takes a strong line about these acts, it must, I suppose, become more difficult for it to propose a conference to Germany; if on the other hand, it passes them over, the Allies will not believe that the United States Government will at the conference take a line strong enough to ensure more than a patched up and insecure peace."[93]

Although the House-Grey memorandum continued to disturb the relations of the Allies with the United States, it had in effect died by the end of March 1916. Why did the Allies—the British, in particular— treat it as they did? In Walter Lippmann's view, they had no promise from Wilson that "really counted." In a conference the Allied divergence of aims would have become apparent. The secret treaties would have damaged their moral standing.[94] The Allied coalition might have broken up. "Finally and above all they knew that if they maintained their blockade, Germany would either starve or resume submarine warfare. If Germany starved, Wilson's restraining influence would be eliminated in the peace conference; if Germany resumed warfare, Wilson would be driven to enter the war without conditions." Lippmann concluded that the negotiations failed "because Wilson had nothing to negotiate with: he would promise nothing and he would threaten nothing. He would not promise to go to war with Germany and he would not threaten to enforce American rights against the Allies. The offer inspired neither hope nor fear."[95]

Certainly the offer did not inspire much hope. But would any offer that fell short of joining the Allies have done so? In the winter and early spring of 1916 Wilson's standing was very low in Allied countries. Page had uttered the simple truth in telling House that the British "no longer have confidence in the President."[96] Even had the president left the House-Grey memorandum unaltered, this lack of confidence alone probably would have served to vitiate the understanding. But the principal reason for the bleak view taken of the memorandum was that it held out the promise only of a partial victory, and the British, like the French, were interested in a complete victory.[97] Grey had concluded the agreement with House largely because House had insisted. He looked upon it as an insurance policy of sorts, to be resorted to in the event the war went badly. As he wrote to the British ambassador to France, a severe critic of the Americans who thought the House mission a stunt for the president's reelection: "As long as the military and naval authorities of the Allies say they can beat the Germans there need be no talk of mediation; but if the war gets to a stalemate the question to be asked will not be whether mediation is good electioneering for President Wilson but whether it will secure better terms for the Allies than can be secured without it."[98]

Nor did the offer inspire fear so long as it left the blockade intact. House was intent on assuring the British of virtually unconditional U.S. support of the blockade. The "threat" he held out was one of running the risk that America would not intervene if the Allies waited too long in calling for a peace conference. Since the Allies could not be sure that America would intervene in any event, this alone could not have moved them much.

8

The "Great Utterance"

The *Sussex* crisis sharpened Wilson's determination to mediate an end to the war. The president was keenly aware of how close he had come to breaking relations with Germany. He knew that another such crisis would all too likely result in America's participation in the war. Apart from his detestation of the war, he believed that once America was in, there would be no one left to lead the belligerents out. The war would go on until the Central powers gave in through exhaustion, an unlikely setting for achieving a satisfactory organization of the peace. And a satisfactory organization of the peace was becoming ever more Wilson's objective in the spring of 1916, as the shortcomings of neutrality became increasingly apparent to him. Then, too, the political appeal of a successful effort at mediation could not have escaped Wilson's attention. It was an election year, and a successful peace move would ensure the president's reelection. House encouraged Wilson's peacemaking propensities. "I have been urging the President from time to time today not to allow the war to continue beyond the autumn," the colonel wrote in his diary on May 3, 1916. "I am certain he can end it whether the belligerents desire it or not." The Germans having faltered at Verdun, it was not likely that the Allies would be any more successful in making a dent in the German lines. Wilson could so word a demand for a conference "that the people of each nation will compel their governments to consent."[1]

The *Sussex* crisis had no sooner been resolved than Wilson decided to try again with Sir Edward Grey. On May 10 House sent a cable to Grey telling him of an "increasingly insistent demand here that the President take some action toward bringing the war to a close." The impression was growing, he warned, that the Allies were more determined to punish Germany than to exact a just peace, and the feeling would increase if Germany discontinued her illegal submarine activities. House then came to the heart of the matter: "I believe the President would now be willing to publicly commit the United States to joining with the other powers in a convention looking to the maintenance of peace after the war, provided he announced at the same time that if the war continued much longer, he purposed calling a conference to discuss peace." The convention would follow along the lines Grey had expressed in his letter of September 22, 1915, binding the signatory powers "to side against any nation refusing in case of dispute to adopt some other method of settlement than that of war." Requesting an answer by cable from Grey, House said in closing, "If it is not done now the opportunity may be forever lost."[2]

The day before, House had suggested that Wilson reconsider the invitation he had earlier turned down to address the League to Enforce Peace, meeting in Washington May 26–27. An organization dedicated to international reform, the League to Enforce Peace had proposed an agreement to submit all differences arising among the signatory powers not settled by negotiation to a judicial tribunal or to a council of conciliation. In the event that a government failed to comply with this provision, the other parties to the agreement were to unite in compelling it to do so by the exercise of economic and military force. Presided over by former president Taft, the league included in its membership a number of prominent Americans. "Is not this the occasion?" House asked.[3] On hearing from the president that it was, House sent the cable to Grey. It was followed by a letter House had earlier written saying that America's entrance into the war would not be a good thing for England, leading as it probably would to the "complete crushing" of Germany; that the *Sussex* settlement had shown that the "wearing down" of Germany now made it "certain that at a peace conference she would yield again and again rather than appeal to the sword"; and that from House's cable Grey "will see how far the president has gone within the year." The letter closed on the admonitory note that "England should be immediately responsive to our call. Her statesmen will take a great responsibility upon themselves if they hesitate or delay, and in the event of failure because they refuse to act quickly, history will bring a grave indictment against them."[4]

The cable brought a quick response from Grey. "The President's suggestion of summoning a peace conference without any indication of a basis on which peace might be made would be construed as instigated by Germany to secure peace on terms unfavorable to the Allies while her existing military situation is still satisfactory to her."[5] In sending the cable, House, it may be assumed, had in mind the terms of the memorandum he had earlier concluded with Grey. But did Wilson? In any event, Grey's point was a fair one. Despite the setbacks she had recently suffered at Verdun, Germany enjoyed a favorable military situation overall. At a peace conference the Allies would have little with which to bargain.

House was disappointed that Grey "does not rise to the occasion. For two years he has been telling me that the solution of the international well being depended upon the United States being willing to take her part in world affairs. Now that we indicate a willingness to do so, he halts, stammers and questions."[6] To Wilson he wrote that he saw "evidence of the Allies regaining their self-assurance and not being as yielding to our desires as they were when they were in so much trouble. We have given them everything and they ever demand more."[7] House could foresee trouble with the Allies in the event of their military success. They might even change their views on militarism and navalism. Wilson's reaction to Grey's letter was more pointed. In a letter to House he wrote:

> I have been giving some very careful thought to your question, how we should deal with Sir Edward and his Government at this turning point,—for it really is that.
>
> It seems to me that we should get down to hard pan.
>
> The situation has altered altogether since you had your conferences in London and Paris. The at least temporary removal of the acute German question has concentrated attention on the altogether indefensible course Great Britain is pursuing with regard to trade to and from neutral ports and her quite intolerable interception of mails on the high seas carried by neutral ships. Recently there has been added the great shock public opinion in this country has received from the course of the British Government toward some of the Irish rebels. We are plainly face to face with this alternative, therefore. The United States must either make a decided move for peace (upon some basis that promises to be permanent) or, if she postpones that, must insist to the limit upon her rights of trade and upon such freedom of the seas as international law already justifies her in insisting on as against Great Britain, with the same plain speaking and firmness that she has used against Germany. And the choice must be made immediately. Which does Great Britain prefer? She cannot escape both. To do nothing is now, for us, impossible.
>
> If we move for peace, it will be along these lines. 1) Such a settlement with regard to their own immediate interests as the belligerents may be able to agree upon. We have nothing material of any kind to ask for ourselves and are quite aware that we are in no sense or degree parties to the quarrel. Our interest is only in peace and its guarantees; 2) a universal alliance to maintain freedom of the

seas and to prevent any war begun either a) contrary to treaty covenants or b) without warning and full inquiry,—a virtual guarantee of territorial integrity and political independence.

It seems to me to be of imperative and pressing importance that Sir Edward should understand all this and that the crisis cannot be postponed and it can be done with the most evident spirit of friendliness through you. Will you not prepare a full cable putting the whole thing plainly to him? We must act, and act at once, in the one direction or the other.[8]

The letter was indeed one of the most important Wilson ever wrote to House.[9] It revealed the president's full awareness of his plight. To do nothing was impossible for him if he wished to avoid war. This had been Bethmann Hollweg's warning, made both publicly and privately. Wilson credited it privately even while rejecting it publicly. Neither alternative could prove attractive to Great Britain. Insistence on America's full "rights of trade" portended a season of rising controversy, foreshadowed by the note of October 21, 1915.[10] To "move for peace" along the lines Wilson indicated held out a prospect potentially much worse than that spelled out in the House-Grey memorandum. The memorandum had specified territorial terms not unfavorable to the Allies. In his letter to House, Wilson returned to his original view of having "nothing to do with local settlements,—territorial questions, indemnities and the like."[11] Grey's objection to summoning a peace conference without any indication of a basis on which peace might be made would surely hold here.

The cable House prepared did not have quite the bite of Wilson's letter, nor did it have the clarity. Still, it was plain enough. Explaining that his recent cables and letters "have not been sent with any desire to force the hands of the Allies or to urge upon them something for which they were not ready," House quickly got to the point. "America has reached the crossroads," he warned, "and if we cannot soon inaugurate some sort of peace discussion there will come a demand from our people in which all neutrals will probably join, that we assert our undeniable rights against the Allies with the same insistence we have used towards the Central Powers." Once the insistent assertion of rights was taken up, "friction is certain to arise and our people will not sustain the President in doing those things that they would now welcome." America was ready to join England in the cause of freeing the nations of the earth from the shadow of autocracy and the specter of war. "If we are to link shields in this mighty cause, then England must recognize the conditions under which this alone can become possible and which we are unable to ignore." House sought to reassure Grey that the Germans had made no overtures looking at a peace conference but, on the contrary, had indicated that "German public opinion would not at present tolerate the President as a mediator." It was "not the President's thought that a peace conference could be immediately called and the Allies would have ample time to demonstrate whether or not Germany is indeed in a sinking condition and the deadlock can be broken." The cable closed by suggesting that Grey talk with those of his colleagues "with whom we have discussed these matters for it is something that will not bear delay."[12]

Wilson found House's cable "admirable," making no changes to it but observing: "It is deeply discouraging to think what the effect will be upon the minds of the men who will confer about it. They have been blindly stupid in the policy they have pursued on the seas, and must now take the consequences."[13] What the consequences were is not made clear, though the president's remark was apparently in response to House's statement in his covering letter of the previous day that "I am now convinced that it is your duty to press for a peace conference with all the power at your command, for whether they like it or not, I believe you can bring it about."[14] In his diary entry of May 17 House expressed some doubt about the course he and Wilson were following. "The President and I are getting into deep waters, and I am not sure we are coming out as we desire. If he will play our hand with all the strength within our power, I believe we can make them do as we wish. But if he does not, we will lose some prestige and perhaps the good will of the Allies." The following day Wilson approved the cable and House's apprehension receded. "I feel sure if he will follow our present plans all the way through, history will give him one of the highest places among the statesmen of the world."[15]

What exactly did following "our present plans all the way through" mean? Did it mean no more than a determination to confront Great Britain with the alternatives spelled out by Wilson in his letter of May 16 to House, either a "decided move for peace" or insisting to the "limit upon our rights of trade"? This was apparently the only plan the two men had discussed. To House, however, it would appear that only the first alternative was intended; following their present plan all the way through meant insisting on the move for peace. The colonel had never seriously considered breaking the blockade as a policy option. He looked upon the blockade as a given. Although he believed it might be made more palatable in application, he had come to realize that even here there were strict limits. When Bernstorff went to House following the *Sussex* crisis and told him of his government's insistence that something be done about the blockade, House reports in his diary that he had told the ambassador to "let it alone . . . that it was a situation we could not force, and at best, could do but little."[16] He could not, of course, say the same to Wilson on being confronted with the president's alternatives. But he may have thought, and probably did think, that the threat to "assert our undeniable rights against the Allies with the same insistence we have used towards the Central Powers" would work to "inaugurate some sort of peace discussion." This would then account for his remark in the diary about getting into "deep waters" and the need for the president to "play our hand with all the strength within our power" in order to make them do as America wished.

The president took the alternative of breaking the blockade more seriously. To be sure, for Wilson as well the threat to assert America's "undeniable rights" was intended to "inaugurate some sort of peace discussion." That was implicit in the very act of juxtaposition. But for the president the assertion of America's "undeniable rights" was also intended to reestablish her position as a neutral in the event that a move for peace failed. Whatever the shortcomings of neutrality, it was still preferable to war. In the late summer and fall of 1916 Wilson would make his greatest effort to give expression to this preference.

At the same time, it was clearly the alternative of moving toward peace that commanded the attention of the president and his adviser. On May 18 Wilson wrote House that he had been thinking a "great deal about the speech I am to make on the twenty seventh because I realize that it may be the most important I shall ever be called upon to make, and I greatly value your suggestion about the navy programme."[17] House had suggested to Wilson the desirability of coming out again for a strong navy. "If we are to join with other great powers in a world movement to maintain peace, we ought to immediately inaugurate a big naval programme."[18] The effects would be far-reaching.

Wilson had another purpose in writing: "Would you do me the favour to formulate what you would say, in my place, if you were seeking to make the proposal as nearly what you deem Grey and his colleagues to have agreed upon in principle as it is possible to make it when concretely formulated as a proposal? Your recollection of your conferences is so much more accurate than mine that I would not trust myself to state the proposition without advice from you, though it may be wise to strengthen and heighten the terms a little."[19]

The president wanted something that did not exist, an oral agreement between House and Grey on the postwar league. There is no evidence of House and Grey having agreed on the outlines of the league idea. What Grey had agreed upon was something altogether different. To refresh his memory, Wilson had only to reread the House-Grey memorandum. The president apparently had not kept a copy of the memorandum, or he would have seen that its terms were incompatible with the direction he was taking. The memorandum spelled out quite specific terms, favorable to the Allies, that the United States would support at the risk of war should Germany prove to be "unreasonable." But Wilson had since returned, as his "hard pan" letter of May 16 indicates, to his earlier position of having nothing to do with "local settlements"—or, what is more likely, he had never really departed from that position.

House did not respond directly to the president's request. In sending his thoughts on the speech Wilson was to give, the colonel merely noted: "I do not believe I would make the calling of the conference any more definite," a reference to House's statement that "this war has been caused by a hideous misunderstanding and what is necessary is for some friend to bring about a reconciliation—a reconciliation that will be lasting."[20] The speech was already beginning to change in focus. It would change still more as a result of a conversation French Ambassador Jusserand had with Frank Polk, counselor of the State Department. Jusserand spoke of rumors in the press of the president's taking steps toward peace. "He referred to the construction put on one of your recent speeches," Polk reported to Wilson, "and said he sincerely hoped that nothing would be said at present which would indicate an intention on the part of this Government to offer mediation or an intention to take any other steps toward bringing about peace." France had wanted peace before the war but now could not consider peace until it could be assured that it was a real peace and not merely a breathing spell for Germany. In closing, the ambassador observed that "anyone suggesting peace now would be considered by his people a friend of Germany."[21]

House and Wilson met at House's apartment on May 24, the president having gone to New York to attend the wedding of his physician, Cary Grayson. They discussed the European situation and the futility of trying to please the different belligerents. "It is evident," House concluded, "that unless the United States is willing to sacrifice hundreds of thousands of lives and billions of treasure we are not to be on good terms with the Allies." House records the two men coming to an important decision. "We agreed it would be wise in the circumstances to greatly modify the speech. . . . He is to treat the subject as we have outlined it with the exception that he is not to do more than hint at peace."[22] House would soon become reconciled to the change. Wilson, however, would prove to be a more difficult case.

In preparing his speech, Wilson took freely from the rough draft House had sent him. While almost all of the major themes of the address may be found in the House draft, they were for the most part Wilson's ideas as well. Lansing had no role in the preparation, but he did send Wilson a letter giving his views on the program of the League to Enforce Peace. Whereas House had considered the league's program impractical at the time, believing that the first thing was to get the various governments to "stand together for the things you have so admirably outlined,"[23] Lansing was opposed in principle to the program. "I do not believe that we should put ourselves in the position of being compelled to send our armed forces to Europe or Asia or, in the alternative, of repudiating our treaty obligation," he wrote to the president. "Neither our sovereignty nor our interests would accord with such a proposition, and I am convinced that popular opinion as well as the Senate would reject a treaty along such lines." Instead, Lansing favored "outlawing" the delinquent nation, cutting off all economic and moral ties with it. "No nation today can live unto itself," he noted confidently.[24] These intimations of a great debate to come were at the time brushed aside by Wilson.

The nation's popular press gave the speech a mixed review.[25] A favorable response was balanced by criticism that the way had been opened for entangling alliances, with a subsequent weakening of the Monroe Doctrine. The *New Republic,* however, saw the address as inaugurating a new period in American and world history. "No utterance since the war began compares with it in overwhelming significance to the future of mankind," the liberal journal declared. "For us in America it literally marks the opening of a new period of history and the ending of our deepest tradition."[26] When measured against the historical record, this view was plainly wrong. Wilson's program failed. Isolation returned and remained more or less intact for another generation.

Yet in an important sense it is right to see the address as the abandonment of isolation. Wilson was intent on acknowledging a condition. "We are participants, whether we would or not, in the life of the world. The interests of all nations are our own also. We are partners with the rest. What affects mankind is inevitably our affair as well as the affair of Europe and of Asia." The experience of the war had shown him that American neutrality was no longer a viable policy in a war involving the great powers. That condition pointed to the passing relevance of a policy of isolation. But a newly found partnership with the world did not herald a willingness to participate in the conflict then rending the world. Wilson's historic statement also registered a determination to remain out of the war and the territorial settlement that followed the war.

Wilson did have one observation to make on the causes of the war. Had the belligerents been able to foresee just what would happen if they took the steps they did, "those who brought the great contest on would have been glad to substitute conference for force." The lesson of this experience was clear: "the peace of the world must henceforth depend upon a new and more wholesome diplomacy. Only when the great nations of the world have reached some sort of agreement as to what they hold to be fundamental to their common interest, and as to some feasible method of acting in concert when any nation or group of nations seeks to disturb those fundamental things, can we feel that civilization is at last in a way of justifying its existence and claiming to be finally established. It is clear that nations must in the future be governed by the same high code of honor that we demand of individuals."

A new diplomacy was made the precondition of America's involvement with the world. The essence of the new diplomacy came to this: "that the principle of public right must henceforth take precedence over the individual interests of particular nations, and that the nations of the world must in some way band themselves together to see that right prevails as against any sort of selfish aggression; that henceforth alliance must not be set up against alliance, understanding against understanding, but there must be a common agreement for a common object, and that at the heart of that common object must lie the inviolable rights of peoples and of mankind."

What were those inviolable rights that would make the world safe for American participation? Wilson's answer was to be repeated in varying form in all of his subsequent major addresses: "First, that every people has a right to choose the sovereignty under which they shall live. . . . Second, that the small states of the world have a right to enjoy the same respect for their sovereignty and for their territorial integrity that great and powerful nations expect and insist upon. And, third, that the world has a right to be free from every disturbance of its peace that has its origin in aggression and disregard of the right of peoples and nations."

The United States was willing, the president pledged, to become a partner in any feasible association of nations formed in order to realize these objects. Should it ever become America's privilege to initiate a movement for peace, it would be along these lines: "First, such a settlement with regard to their own immediate interests as the belligerents may agree upon. We have nothing material of any kind to ask for ourselves, and are quite aware that we are in no sense or degree parties to the present quarrel. Our interest is only in peace and its future guarantees. Second, an universal association of the nations to maintain the inviolate security of the highway of the seas for the common and unhindered use of all the nations of the world, and to prevent any war begun either contrary to treaty covenants or without warning and full submission of the causes to the opinion of the world—a virtual guarantee of territorial integrity and political independence."[27]

Thus did Wilson abandon isolation. The abandonment of isolation was not seen to imply the abandonment of neutrality. On the contrary, the immediate purpose of the speech was to reenforce a waning neutrality. The apparent contradiction between becoming a partner with the world yet remaining neutral in its greatest conflict was reconciled by the need of a disinterested party that could speak on behalf of a suffering humanity and lead the way out. Even so, the relative ease with which Wilson abandoned isolation, as compared with his difficulty in abandoning neutrality, reflected more than the difference between a decision that did not entail an immediate and painful price and one that did. It also reflected his refusal to equate the abandonment of isolation with the acceptance of the prospects—alliances and war—that such an abandonment would normally be considered to hold out.

Wilson's challenge, then and in the future, was to reconcile the abandonment of isolation with the avoidance of those consequences that abandonment could normally be expected to lead. The war had shown the inadequacies, even the risks, of persisting in a policy of isolation. An isolated America would have little, if any, voice in the postwar international system. Moreover, an isolated America confronted by a reconstituted old order might have to sustain a level of arms that could prove a threat to its domestic institutions. Yet as against these risks were those incurred in abandoning isolation, if abandonment meant participation in the system that had led to the catastrophe of the world war. Wilson's address was his response to the old dilemma of how to make the world safe, or at least safer, for American participation.

The response to Wilson's speech in the United States contrasted with its reception by the Allies, who took its unconcern with the "causes and objects" of the war as a refusal to draw a moral distinction between the belligerents. It was true that America had had no part in starting the war. It did not follow, however, that she had no interest in what was being settled. Wilson obviously thought that nothing of consequence was being settled. A quarrel had simply arisen among the nations of Europe. They had, as was their wont, gone to war. But the war had not only engulfed them; it had gravely affected the rest of the world. Hence the interest of the rest of the world in the "arrangements which would ensue in the world at large." Hence also the absence of interest in the peace settlement among the parties.

Not only did the Allies resent the implication that there was little to choose between the two sides but their suspicions were aroused by Wilson's emphasis on maintaining freedom of the seas as a task coequal with that of preventing aggression. In the context of the war, freedom of the seas was for the most part a demand addressed to Great Britain by neutrals wishing to trade with Germany. It had no place in a call for a league of nations to prevent aggression. The two aspirations were in principle contradictory. The demand for freedom of the seas was applicable, for all practical purposes, only in time of war, the seas being free in time of peace. But in time of war freedom of the seas was inseparable from the institution of neutrality. That institution was in turn based on the assumption of the unlimited right of sovereign states to resort to war. To the extent that war is no longer a prerogative of the sovereign state, neutrality, with its demand for freedom of the seas, must correspondingly be limited. Yet here was Wilson calling for a universal association of the nations to maintain freedom of the seas. It was only natural to assume that the call was made to placate Germany. The assumption was privately confirmed by Wilson's remark to House, who had congratulated him on the speech: "I was handling a critical matter and was trying to put it in a way that it would be hard for the Allies to reject, as well as for Germany."[28]

The "critical matter" was of course the movement for peace. While not calling for a conference in his address, Wilson had been clear that he needed only an invitation to initiate action. But an invitation was not forthcoming. On the German side, the response to his speech in the Reichstag and the press had been negative. True, there were the reassuring words of German Foreign Minister Jagow to Gerard. "He said that he hoped President and you," Gerard wrote Lansing, "would not be affected by what was said in the Reichstag against the peace mediation of the President . . . that I know the position of Government here."[29] However, in the late spring of 1916 the German government was still opposed to asking for American mediation. The prospect that the war would issue in a favorable outcome had by no means been given up. Bernstorff was instructed by Jagow on June 7 that "as soon as Mr. Wilson's mediation plans threaten to assume a more concrete form and an inclination on the part of England to meet him begins to manifest itself, it will be the duty of your Excellency to prevent President Wilson from approaching us with a positive proposal to mediate."[30] It was only over the months of the summer that the German government's attitude toward an American mediation would clearly change. Even then it remained tied to impossible goals.

A hostile reception in Germany was one thing, a hostile reception in Great Britain something else. The move for peace had the House-Grey memorandum as its guide. It was to Great Britain that Wilson's speech had been primarily directed, yet the reaction in England was almost as negative as it had been in Germany. Wilson's indifference to the "causes and objects" of the war appeared to the public and officialdom alike to disqualify him from playing a great role in securing future peace, as Grey would later tell Page.[31] The British were in principle no more disposed to accept American mediation than were the Germans.

Grey made this clear in his reply to House's cables of May 10 and 19. Sent two days after Wilson's address—"Here is a cable from Sir Edward," House wrote in sending it on to the president. "Like most of his countrymen he travels by freight"[32]—Grey's reply advised the president that if he did not wish to approach all of the Allies, he should "take the French Government at any rate into his confidence as directly as he has taken us." The messages House had sent raised two closely related questions: the territorial terms of peace and the means for securing a lasting peace. Mindful of the impossibility of separate negotiations, Grey pointed out that this much could be said with respect to the terms of peace: if they were satisfactory to Germany, militarism would remain the dominant force there and would render ineffective any convention for maintaining future peace. They had to be "sufficiently favorable to the Allies to make the German people feel that aggressive militarism is a failure."

On the means for securing a lasting peace, Grey had this to say:

> The best chance for the great scheme is the President's willingness that it should be proposed by the United States in convention a peace favourable to the Allies obtainable with American aid. The worst chance would be that it should be proposed in connection with an inconclusive or disastrous peace accompanied, perhaps promoted, by diplomatic friction by [between] the Allies and the United States over maritime affairs.
>
> Between these two extremes there are endless interminable possibilities. But evidently a premature announcement of intervention

by the President might be dangerous to the cause he and we have at heart because it would be interpreted as meaning that he desired peace on a basis favorable to Germany and for the reasons above stated. No such peace could secure a reliable and enduring international organization of the kind he contemplates.[33]

House saw the French ambassador on June 1, with the predictable result. Jusserand told him, he wrote to Wilson, "that any peace talk at this time will have a tendency to encourage her [France's] enemies and break the spirit of her people. He thinks the thing for us to do now is to encourage her to fight on for the present."[34] And to Grey, House wrote on June 8 that Jusserand "thinks France will not consider peace proposals of any sort at this time no matter how far we might be willing to go toward preventing aggressive wars in the future." France felt that never again could she have as strong a combination fighting with her, and she desired to defeat Germany decisively. In his letter to Grey, House questioned once again the optimism of the Allies. Even in the unlikely event of an Allied victory, House observed, England might find herself in a worse position later. He wondered, as well, whether the Allies fully realized that their position might materially change after November. The letter ended on a note of resignation: "As far as I can see there is nothing to add or to do for the moment and if the Allies are willing to take the gamble which the future may hold, we must rest content."[35]

House remained puzzled by the Allied response. He had held out to them the prospect of American intervention in the war in the event that Germany was recalcitrant in accepting Wilson's terms. As he wrote to Grey on May 27: "There is one thing to which I wish to call your attention, and that is the German Chancellor's statement that Germany would make peace on the basis of the map as it stands today. This cannot mean anything except a victorious peace for Germany. If England and France, under our invitation, should go into a peace conference now, it would probably lead either to Germany's abandonment of this position or war with us."[36] A month later he wrote in his diary that the Allies were "prolonging the war unnecessarily. It is stupid to refuse our proferred intervention on terms I proposed in Paris and London. I made it clear to both governments that in the event of intervention we would not countenance a peace that did not bring with it a plan which would make for permanent peace, as far as humans could do so. If Germany refused to acquiesce in such a settlement, I promised we would take the part of the Allies and try to force it."[37]

But the Allies had refused. In House's view there was nothing to add or to do but to "rest content." Perhaps the Allies would change their minds if their military fortunes again declined. In any event, there was little to do for one who wanted a moderate Allied victory. House might rail at the Allies, but it was impossible to satisfy them, he declared to an English friend. "It is always something more."[38] In the end, though, he was always to be found on the side of the Allies.

The president was another story. He was not prepared to rest content, for he wanted desperately to stay out of the war. "To do nothing is now, for us, impossible," he had declared to House. It was impossible for the reason that it was leading America to war. Disappointed by the Allied response to his proposed call for a peace conference, Wilson had hoped that his speech of May 27 would elicit a positive reply. When it failed to do so, his mind turned to the alternative of independent action. In a letter of June 22 to House he wrote: "The letters and glimpses of opinion (official opinion) from the other side of the water are not encouraging, to say the least, and indicate a constantly narrowing, instead of a broad and comprehending, view of the situation. They are in danger of forgetting the rest of the world, and of waking up some surprising morning to discover that it has a positive right to be heard about the peace of the world. I conclude that it will be up to us to judge for ourselves when the time has arrived for us to make an imperative suggestion. I mean a suggestion which they will have no choice but to heed, because the opinion of the non-official world and the desire of all peoples will be behind it."[39]

The "imperative suggestion" was not made until December 1916, but in the late spring of 1916 Wilson concluded that America had come too close to the Allies, who merely wanted to use her for their purposes. He would not become the unwitting instrument of Allied aims. Their purposes were not America's purposes. America, he resolved, would have to move back from the too intimate relationship it had been drawn into with one group of belligerents. Mediation could play no favorites and must be so seen by all of the belligerents.

9

Woodrow Wilson's War Address

On April 2, 1917, the president of the United States addressed a joint session of Congress and "advised" it to declare "the recent course of the Imperial German Government to be nothing less than war against the Government and people of the United States."[1] The end of the long period of American neutrality in the Great War had come very painfully to Woodrow Wilson. From his reelection in November 1916 to the German declaration of unrestricted submarine warfare on January 30, 1917, he had nourished the hope, at times bordering on expectation, that he might mediate an end to the war. If Germany would only confide in him, he had plaintively written to his closest counselor when his efforts appeared on the verge of failure, he could yet show her the way out.[2] It was an astonishing thought in the light of all that had passed in the preceding two and a half years between Washington and Berlin, yet Wilson had never been more sincere. By the end of 1916 the president had come close to, perhaps even achieved, the neutrality in thought he had urged upon his fellow citizens at the outset of the war. In Berlin, however, there were only skeptics left.

Given the depth of Wilson's desire to avoid American participation in the war and the intensity that marked his last and greatest effort to mediate an end to the conflict, he seemed utterly unprepared for the denouement. The day following the German declaration, Colonel House wrote in his diary that Wilson had said "he felt as if the world had suddenly reversed itself; that after going from east to west it had begun to go from west to east and that he could not get his balance."[3]

The reversal of the president's world did not at once impel him to conclude that the nation's neutrality was at an end. Although Berlin's announced new course rudely repudiated the pledge it had given Washington the preceding May, to conduct submarine warfare within the constraints laid down by customary international law, Wilson refused to accept that the end had finally come. A year earlier the president had solemnly stated that he could not "consent to any abridgement of the rights of American citizens in any respect," that such abridgement involved the nation's "honor and self respect," and that while America coveted peace, she would "preserve it at any cost but the loss of honor."[4] The German declaration was a direct and sweeping challenge to the nation's rights and thus to its honor and self-respect. It left Wilson with no alternative but to break diplomatic relations. In doing so, he nevertheless took care to indicate that he did not consider this step as merely a prelude to hostilities; and he did not so consider it because he could not believe that the Germans would act upon their declaration. Announcing to the Congress on February 3, 1917, the severance of diplomatic relations with Berlin, he insisted that "only overt acts on their part can make me believe it even now."[5]

Thus began Woodrow Wilson's last stand against America's involvement in World War I. If it had its pathetic side, it also had an undeniably heroic character. While refusing to acknowledge to others, and probably to himself as well, that the end had come, he provided little reason for others to believe that America's intervention in the war might still somehow be avoided. Although the desultory diplomatic efforts of February were barren of results,[6] Wilson clung desperately to convictions that the course of the war had suddenly and rudely shaken. Unwilling to abandon the views and the hopes of earlier months, he remained for a time unwilling to accept the measures a new reality demanded. It was a position that could not be sustained. "He does not mean to go to war," Henry Cabot Lodge wrote at the time to his friend Theodore Roosevelt, "but I think he is in the grip of events."[7]

The president was indeed in the grip of events. Unlike in previous crises that had arisen between the United States and Germany, on this occasion the government in Berlin showed no disposition to conciliate Washington. The challenge thrown down by Germany, to sink without warning all ships, enemy and neutral, in a vast zone around Great Britain, France, and Italy, was not only of a different order from earlier challenges, it had from the outset an air of irrevocability. Once the challenge was issued, American shippers, without protection, increasingly refused to put to sea. Pressure mounted on the government either to convoy or to arm merchant ships.

In late February, Wilson changed his initial position on armed neutrality. Having initially opposed the government's arming of American merchantmen, on February 26 he wrote to the Congress requesting authority to place naval guns and gun crews on board merchant ships. In doing so, he emphasized that he was not "contemplating war or any step that need lead to it." He continued to hold to the "ideal of peace."[8] Even so, a significant change had occurred in what Wilson now deemed it necessary to do in responding to the German challenge. When Congress failed to give him the authorization sought, by virtue of a Senate filibuster that ended the session, he declared his intention to arm American ships under authority he claimed already to possess.[9]

By the end of February, Wilson had already begun to abandon old positions. While not yet ready to accept the dread alternative, he was steadily moving toward doing so. The news of the Zimmermann telegram undoubtedly helped. On February 24 the president learned through the British government of the proposal made by German Foreign Minister Zimmermann to the Mexican government of an alliance in the event of war with the United States. The German offer, made on January 19, 1917, read in part: "make war together, make peace together, generous financial support, and an understanding on our part that Mexico is to reconquer the lost territory in Texas, New Mexico, and Arizona."[10]

Wilson was shocked and indignant on receiving the news of the German offer. Mexico was a very sensitive issue for him, given the considerable difficulties still attending Mexican-American relations in the winter of 1917. An American military force had only recently been withdrawn from Mexico, and Wilson was confronted with the issue of whether to recognize the Mexican government of Venustiano Carranza despite objectionable features in the new constitution. Yet his severe reaction owed as much to the way in which Berlin had undertaken its move as it did to the proposal itself. The Germans had made their offer to Mexico while they were still engaged in peace negotiations with Washington. Moreover, in sending Zimmermann's proposal to the German minister in Mexico City, they had used American communications facilities that, on their request, had been provided them for the secure and expeditious conduct of the negotiations. Wilson viewed Germany's behavior as a case of bad faith. His attitude toward the government in Berlin hardened perceptibly. The episode served to reinforce the shift reflected in his decision to move to armed neutrality.[11]

Wilson's embrace of armed neutrality proved to be very brief. In his second inaugural address, on March 5, he declared that "we stand firm in armed neutrality."[12] In the days immediately following, days in which Wilson was confined to his private quarters with a bad cold, measures were initiated by the government to implement the new status. On March 18, two days after the president returned to his office, Washington learned that German submarines had attacked and sunk three American vessels, one with considerable loss of life. This was the event that Wilson had earlier said would alone be sufficient to persuade him that the Germans intended to carry out their declaration against American vessels.

Did it persuade him as well to accept war? On the day following the news of the sinkings, Wilson's secretary of state indicated that it had not. In a letter to the president, Lansing wrote, in summary of a conversation of that day with Wilson, that he was in "entire agreement with you that the recent attacks . . . do not materially affect the international situation so far as constituting a reason for declaring that a state of war exists between this country and Germany."[13] Lansing's letter was a fervent and forceful summary of the case for immediate war on Germany, a case Wilson was to make liberal use of in his subsequent war address. It was written, however, because Lansing assumed that the president was still holding out. Indeed, Wilson did seem determined to keep to armed neutrality. On the same day, March 19, his secretary of state pleaded with him to accept belligerent status, Wilson instructed Secretary of the Navy Josephus Daniels that he "wished everything possible done in addition to Armed Guards to protect American shipping, hoping this would meet the ends we have in view."[14] On March 19 as well, a despairing Lansing wrote to Colonel House: "If you agree with me that we should act now, will you not please put your shoulder to the wheel?"[15]

In the event, there was no need for House to respond to Lansing's appeal. The presidential conversion to war came, to all outward appearances, very suddenly. On March 20, the day following the above events, Wilson held a meeting of his cabinet devoted to the issue of war with Germany. The questions the president put to his cabinet were whether he should summon Congress to meet in special session at an earlier date than he had already called for (April 16) and once Congress was assembled, what he should lay before it. The cabinet was unanimous in the view that war was inevitable and that Congress should be called in extraordinary session as soon as possible.

Scarcely more than three weeks had elapsed since the stormy cabinet meeting of February 26, in which Wilson had bitterly reproached some of his cabinet for wanting war.[16] In the March 20 meeting the Wilson of February—often defensive, even querulous—was gone. According to the most detailed account of the later meeting we have, by Secretary of State Lansing, the president greeted his cabinet "smiling as genially and composedly as if nothing of importance was to be considered." At the close of the meeting, Wilson "in his cool, unemotional way" thanked the cabinet members for their advice. "No one could be sure that he [Wilson] would echo the same opinion and act accordingly," Wilson having given no specific indication of what course he would adopt.[17] The secretary's uncertainty was as much a measure of his own anxiety as it was of the president's silence. Wilson's equanimity in receiving the views of his cabinet was indicative of a mind no longer tortured by doubt and indecision over the necessary course to pursue. It was instead a mind searching for justification for a course it had already determined to take.

The day following the cabinet meeting of March 20, the president called Congress to meet in special session on April 2.[18] His reason for doing so was to "advise" the Congress that a state of war existed between Germany and the United States.

Wilson's war address brought to an end the long and increasingly difficult period of American neutrality. It afforded to a divided nation release from an uncertainty and tension that had become almost unendurable. It marked for the first time since the period of independence the country's participation in a European war, thereby breaking a long tradition of isolation from the old continent's politics. Both supporters and opponents of intervention agreed that once America had entered the war, the nation's destiny would be radically altered. In his popular history *Our Times* Mark Sullivan wrote of the night of April 2, 1917: "To every person present, from members of the cabinet in the front row, to observers in the remote seats in the gallery, that evening was the most-to-be-remembered of their lives."[19]

Its historic character apart, Wilson's war address does not have the eloquence and fervor of some of his other memorable speeches. Apart from the ending, it does not have the felicity of phrase and sheer intensity that marked, for example, his January 22, 1917, peace-without-victory address to the Senate. The statement of January 22, 1917, was pure Wilson. In January, in addressing the nation and, even more, the European belligerents, Wilson had articulated long-held and deeply felt convictions about the war, the peace that must follow the war, and the American role in the international order of the future. The peace-without-victory address was quintessential Wilson in its uninhibited idealism, its air of utter detachment from the passions and claims of the warring parties, and its startling expression of hope that despite the terrible sacrifices the belligerents had made, they would nevertheless be willing to give up the prospect of victory.

The January appeal had been the work of a man who had come willingly to his task. Its terms had been fashioned by Wilson alone; neither House nor Lansing had made or been asked to make a contribution. The April declaration was the work of a man who had been unexpectedly forced to set out on a course he dreaded and one for which he was still emotionally and intellectually unprepared. It was perforce a message of war and death and, though only barely voiced, of repression at home. It heralded the beginning of everything Wilson detested. This is why he spoke of the "tragical character of the step" he was taking in asking Congress to accept the "status of belligerent which has thus been thrust upon it" and why he found his duty in addressing Congress "distressing and oppressive."[20] To be sure, the president also held out the promise of a new and better world that victory would bring. But this was the promise. The certainty was suffering and destruction in the greatest war the modern world had yet experienced.

This was one reason for the distinctive tone of the war address. Yet another reason must be found in the awkwardness of the position in which the events of the preceding two months had placed the president. The world that "had suddenly reversed itself" on Wilson had to be explained; it had to be explained, moreover, partly in terms the president had previously rejected. In groping for a new explanation, Wilson turned, not surprisingly, to ideas that had long been urged upon him by Lansing and House. This could not have been congenial to a man of Wilson's intellectual pride. Particularly in the case of Lansing, it must have been difficult and unwelcome. Wilson had never had a very high regard for his secretary of state. What modest esteem he had once entertained toward Lansing had disappeared by the winter of 1917. House records a conversation with the president on the eve of the war address in which Wilson complained "that Lansing was the most unsatisfactory Secretary in his Cabinet; that he was good for a second place but unfitted for the first. That he had no imagination, no constructive ability, and but little real ability of any kind." This harsh judgment was no doubt owing in part to Wilson's conviction that Lansing had virtually sabotaged the president's policies on more than one occasion in the past, a conviction that accounts for Wilson's statement to House that he was afraid of Lansing because the secretary often undertook to launch policies Wilson subsequently had to reverse. Clearly, as House noted in his diary, "their minds are not sympathetic."[21]

In part, however, Wilson's attitude toward Lansing at this time must have reflected the president's chagrin and resentment over the outcome of his long-standing differences with the secretary of state respecting American policy toward the belligerents. The simple fact was that in these differences, and particularly in those arising over the president's last great effort at mediation, the outcome had shown Lansing to have been right, or very nearly so, and Wilson to have been wrong. Lansing had shared none of the president's hopes that the conflict might somehow be ended before America would be forced to intervene. He viewed

Wilson's peace-note initiative of December 1916 as misguided and even dangerous in the opening it gave to Germany to drive a great wedge between the United States and the Allies, a view House shared with Lansing. Lansing was persuaded that the German government would resort to unrestricted submarine warfare once circumstances were judged propitious by Berlin. When Lansing's expectations came to pass, he not unnaturally felt vindicated. He shed a measure of his former inhibition in pressing his views on a president who did not share his general outlook and who no longer desired his retention in office. An ever more insistent Lansing could only have been a great burden to Wilson by March 1917. Even the far more cautious and subtle House must have begun to wear on Wilson after the disagreements of the fall of 1916. Although House had been supportive of the president's last efforts at mediation, once the Germans had shown their hand he was as determined on war as Lansing and did not hide this from the president.

Whatever Wilson's initial reluctance to do so, he had little alternative in preparing his war address but to take quite heavily from the views of Lansing and House. In going to war he was confronted with the need to invest the conflict with a new meaning and significance. Wilson had long contended that America was not concerned with the war's "causes and objects." In saying this, he was widely understood both at home and abroad as placing the two sides in the war on the same moral plane, something that was intensely resented in Great Britain and France. House had repeatedly objected to Wilson's attribution of moral equivalence to the belligerents, warning the president of the resentment and ill will it created in the Allied states, but to no avail. "He seems obsessed with the thought," House wrote in his diary of the peace note Wilson sent to the neutrals and belligerents in December 1916, "and he cannot write or talk on the subject of the war without voicing it."[22] The peace note had said that the president still did not understand precisely what it was the belligerents were fighting for. Their objects had been stated only in "general terms." "But, stated in general terms," the president's appeal observed, "they seem the same on both sides."[23] As good a friend as the United States had in Great Britain, James Bryce, had complained to Wilson that this implied "the moral position and aims of the Allies can be put on the same plane as those of Germany and Austria and the Turks."[24]

Nor did Wilson's moral equation of the two sides come to an end even with the German resort to unrestricted submarine warfare. In February 1917 he was still voicing the wish that neither side would win, that both had been equally indifferent to the rights of neutrals—though

Germany had been brutal in taking life, and England only in taking property. To a famous French philosopher, Henri Bergson, he posed the question "whether one could find on either side anything other than national egoisms struggling with one another."[25]

This view of the war had to be changed once Wilson determined to intervene. It would no longer do to insist that the United States did not know what the conflict was about other than "to see who is strong enough to prevent the other from fighting better," as Wilson had remarked in August 1916 to members of the American Neutral Conference.[26] If the war was little more than a struggle for power between a nation that had the earth (England) and a nation that wanted it (Germany), another favorite Wilson explanation,[27] all that remained as a justification of intervention was the defense of neutral rights and national honor. Even if this were to prove sufficient for the nation at large, it could scarcely satisfy the nation's president. What had brought Wilson to the verge of war had to be transcended by purposes more compelling.

One such purpose lay ready at hand in the view that the war was essentially one between democracy and absolutism. This view had long been pressed on Wilson by his advisers. Both Lansing and House, as well as the American ambassador in London, Walter Page, had cast the great conflict as a struggle between freedom and despotism since the first year of the war. Wilson had never really rejected their argument; he had simply refused to embrace it. That Germany stood for absolutism he was much more disposed to accept than that Great Britain (and France) stood for democracy. And even if one did accept the equations urged by others, Wilson appears to have seen little reason to understand the war in such terms. While acknowledging to Page in September 1916 that "the German system is strictly opposed to everything American," he added that "this didn't seem to me to carry any very great moral reprehensibility."[28] It suddenly did just that, however, in March 1917.

Wilson's conversion was undoubtedly helped by events occurring at the time in Russia. On March 15 came news from Petrograd that the Russian parliament had voted to depose the czar and establish a democratic and constitutional order. Moreover, the fall of the Romanov dynasty appeared to affect developments in central Europe, which pointed in a similar direction. The president was increasingly persuaded that the old order of autocracy was at last giving way to democracy. Within a week he decided to recognize the provisional Russian government.

———

The war message to Congress thus marked the beginning of a new Woodrow Wilson. The old Wilson had seen the war as essentially a conflict to determine who would dominate. The meaning of the war was that it had little meaning other than as a struggle for power, a terrible contest whose principal object was primarily to determine who would be first in Europe and in the world. This is the implicit premise that informs Wilson's revealing, though unpublished, prolegomenon to his peace note of December 1916. What distinguished World War I from most previous wars, Wilson wrote, was not the purposes or objects of the present war but its unprecedented suffering and destruction. It was in the growing awareness of this "fact," this terrible truth, that the president then based so much of his hopes for a permanent peace. If the belligerents could only be brought to see "the uselessness of the utter sacrifices made," this would give to a future peace "the essential basis of endurance—the psychological basis. Deprived of glory, war loses all its charm; when the only attribute of it is suffering, then it is something to be detested."[29]

The peace note of December 1916 must be understood in the light of this reasoning. So, too, must the peace-without-victory address of late January 1917. In the prolegomenon Wilson had concluded that with the experience of the world war before them, "the aim of far-sighted statesmen should be to make of this mightiest of conflicts an object lesson for the future by bringing it to a close with the objects of each group of belligerents still unaccomplished and all the magnificent sacrifices on both sides gone for naught. Only then would war be eliminated as a means of attaining national ambition. The world would be free to build its new peace structure on the solidest foundation it has ever possessed."[30]

In setting forth his peace-without-victory proposal to the belligerents, Wilson necessarily disguised this thought. The warring parties were urged to conclude a peace without victory for prudential and moral reasons. "Victory," Wilson declared before the Senate in January, "would mean peace forced upon the loser, a victor's terms imposed upon the vanquished. It would be accepted in humiliation, under duress, at an intolerable sacrifice, and would leave a sting, a resentment, a bitter memory upon which terms of peace would rest, not permanently, but only as upon quicksand. Only a peace between equals can last."[31] Put in these terms, a peace without victory appeared as the inspiration of an outsider, who could view the interests of the belligerents and their suffering sympathetically yet also dispassionately. The appearance was not a deception. Wilson did believe that only a peace between equals could last. But he also believed, and perhaps even more deeply so, that a peace with-

out victory was indispensable for driving home the lesson to all the belligerents of "the uselessness of the utter sacrifices made." "It seems to
me incredible," Henry Cabot Lodge, a severe critic of the president, observed in commenting on the peace-without-victory address, "that people who have made such awful sacrifices as have been made by the belligerents should be content to forego the prospect of victory, in the hope
of bringing the war to an end, with everything left just as it was. In such
a result they might well think that all their efforts and losses . . . were a
criminal and hideous futility."[32]

Senator Lodge had divined with precision what Wilson intended.
Peace without victory was the ultimate expression of the conviction that
the motives and objects of the belligerents did not warrant substantial
differentiation, that they were morally equivalent. In going to war two
months later, this view had to be discarded. In setting forth "our motives
and our objects" as a belligerent, moral differentiation from the enemy
was indispensable. That the sacrifices entailed by belligerency could be
justified by a peace whose principal purpose was to show the utter uselessness of these sacrifices was unthinkable.

The war address held out a new understanding of the meaning and
significance of the great conflict. What had been a struggle for power
now became a conflict between democracy and autocracy. Wilson intro-
duced his new understanding by denying its novelty. "Our motives and
our objects" in entering the war remained unchanged. "I have exactly
the same things in mind now," he insisted, "that I had in mind when I
addressed the Senate on the twenty-second of January last."[33] With these
words Wilson began his effort to revise the past, an effort that roused
the ire of opponents to new heights. "What is perfectly impossible, what
really represents nauseous hypocrisy," Theodore Roosevelt wrote some
months later to William Allen White, "is to say that we have gone to war
to make the world safe for democracy, in April, when sixty days previously we had been announcing that we wished a 'peace without victory,'
and had no concern with the 'causes or objects' of the war."[34]

The charge of hypocrisy was misplaced. Wilson was no hypocrite.
Had he been one, he would have been far less effective as a leader. His
ability to change while remaining in his own mind the same, to reinvent
himself politically though without being conscious of having done so,
was one of his great strengths. He had shown this strength in making
his pilgrimage from the conservative wing of the Democratic Party to
the leadership of progressive forces. Once that pilgrimage was completed, Wilson would not and could not acknowledge that he had ever
been anything but a progressive. Similarly, having once moved from

neutrality to intervention, Wilson was subsequently unwilling and unable to recognize that he had ever been anything but an interventionist. His insistence after March 1917 that he had always been an interventionist was cut from the same cloth as his insistence before March 1917 that he had ever been anything but strictly neutral. Wilson was throughout his life an awesome example of the power of belief. Being a true believer, he had no need of hypocrisy.

At the same time, Roosevelt was on solid ground in pointing to the disparity between Wilson's war address and his earlier peace-without-victory speech. In both, it is true, a vision is held out of a postwar international order based on the principles that governments derive all their just powers from the consent of the governed, that great nations and small enjoy an equality of rights, and that no nation should henceforth extend its polity over another nation or people. But here the similarity in the two utterances ceased. In January, Wilson the impartial mediator had inveighed against a peace that only established a new balance of power. Such a peace, he had warned, could not last. "There must be, not a balance of power, but a community of power; not organized rivalries, but an organized common peace." The peace-without-victory speech was devoted to the elaboration of an enduring common peace, the only peace, Wilson had warned, that would gain America's approval and enjoy America's support. Of the prerequisites to this peace, a settlement of the war that was based on "equality and a common participation in a common benefit" was the most important.[35]

By April the emphasis had changed. From a peace without victory, Wilson, the soon-to-be war leader, had moved to a peace without autocracy, a goal that could be realized only through victory. The president now understood the principal cause of the war, just as he understood the way to prevent war's recurrence. This war, he explained, was one "determined upon as wars used to be determined upon in the old, unhappy days when peoples were nowhere consulted by their rulers and wars were provoked and waged in the interests of dynasties or of little groups of ambitious men who were accustomed to use their fellow men as pawns and tools."[36]

Wilson's explanation of the origins of the war had a familiar ring. It had been given before by Thomas Paine and Thomas Jefferson. "Why are not republics plunged into war," Paine had asked, "but because the nature of their government does not admit of an interest distinct from that of the nation?"[37] Paine's answer was given again by Wilson: "Self-governed nations do not fill their neighbor states with spies or set the course of intrigue to bring about some critical posture of affairs which will give them an opportunity to strike and make conquest." Only when the decision for war rested on the will of the community rather than on the will of an unrepresentative government, Paine and Jefferson had insisted, would this ever-present specter of Europe's old diplomacy recede and a great step toward permanent peace be taken. Wilson's war message embraced this view: "A steadfast concert for peace can never be maintained except by a partnership of democratic nations. No autocratic government could be trusted to keep faith within it or observe its covenants."[38]

The war address did not expressly abandon the vision of a peace without victory. Not only did it emphasize that toward the German people, as distinct from the German government, America had only a feeling of "sympathy and friendship" but it pledged that in conducting the war America would fight "without rancor and without selfish object, seeking nothing for ourselves but what we shall wish to share with all free peoples." Once liberated from their government, these words plainly implied, the Germans too would be reckoned among free peoples. At that moment, Wilson's peace without victory, "a peace the very principle of which is equality and a common participation in a common benefit," would presumably apply.[39]

These were the words of a visionary who still stood outside the great conflict. When Wilson uttered them, the effects of war were but foreseen, not experienced. Only the experience could test the resolve to "fight without rancor" and to "conduct . . . operations as belligerents without passion."[40] Involvement was bound to alter Wilson's pledge. It had always done so before in the lesser political battles he had waged, battles he had never conducted without passion or rancor. Wilson had not been insincere in his earlier commitment to a peace without victory, but he had made the commitment as an outsider, when he had seen the war as a mere struggle for power, not as a struggle for justice. Once the war was seen as a struggle for justice, peace without victory would recede into a forgotten past.

Why did Wilson finally go to war? What led him in the end to take a course he had seemed determined to avoid, a course whose consequences he so dreaded? In his war address Wilson's answer was simple and direct. "We enter this war," he stated toward the end of his message to Congress, "only where we are clearly forced into it because there are no other means of defending our rights." The "other means" of armed neutrality were rejected as "impracticable," though the principal reason given for reaching this conclusion—that armed neutrality was "practically certain to draw us into the war without either the rights or the effectiveness of belligerents"—had scarcely been put to a serious test.[41] This was the burden of one of Wilson's chief lieutenants in the Senate, Gilbert Hitchcock, of Nebraska, who wrote the president when it was apparent the decision for war had been made that if armed neutrality was wrong at the end of March, it had been wrong at the beginning of March, when the president had come to Congress requesting its authorization. The sinking of a few ships, he argued, did not constitute a change in conditions. Armed neutrality had been neither tried nor tested. America had not lost an armed merchantman or even finished arming the ships. Armed neutrality, Hitchcock pointed out, might yet prove sufficient to protect America's commerce and vindicate her neutral rights. If it failed to do so, war would appear more acceptable as the only alternative to those who still opposed belligerency.[42]

Wilson turned Hitchcock's argument aside. He did so in part for reasons he gave in his address. As he wrote at the time to another advocate of armed neutrality, "To make even the measures of defense [against submarines] legitimate we must obtain the status of belligerents."[43] While this argument was open to question, and in any event should have been apparent at the outset, Wilson undoubtedly became convinced of it. Persuasion was made all the easier by the view the president apparently took toward armed neutrality virtually from the start. Despite his initial commitment, armed neutrality seems never to have been more than a temporary solution for Wilson; more than anything it served as a psychological way station between the determination to remain neutral and the acceptance of war. It facilitated the adjustment to a course he detested and feared, but one he became increasingly convinced he had to take.

The rights that could not be surrendered, and in defense of which America went to war, were of course the rights of a neutral state. Whatever their intrinsic significance, Wilson may be understood as saying, they could not be surrendered. Rights must be defended, if necessary through force, because they are rights. The point is easily obscured and occasionally was so by Wilson himself. Explaining in the war address the "choice we cannot make, we are incapable of making," Wilson declared that "we will not choose the path of submission and suffer the most sacred rights of our nation and our people to be ignored or violated. The wrongs against which we now array ourselves are no common wrongs; they cut to the very roots of human life."[44] But neutral rights were not "the most sacred rights of our nation." Their violation did not "cut to the very roots of human life." Germany's destruction of American ships and lives clearly did do so. But such destruction was entirely the consequence of the exercise of neutral rights and could have been avoided by forgoing such an exercise. It was Wilson's refusal to sacrifice the exercise of neutral rights, his insistence that these rights be defended whatever the cost, that left him with no alternative but war.

Rights, whether neutral or otherwise, could not be surrendered from fear of war. Although it was "a fearful thing to lead this great peaceful people into war, into the most horrible and disastrous of all wars . . . the right is more precious than peace."[45] In this concluding passage of the war address, Wilson succinctly laid bare the point he had earlier obscured: the right is more precious than peace. Not simply neutral rights, though it was neutral rights that were at issue, but right. A nation that failed to defend its rights lost its honor. It also forfeited its prestige and respect, qualities held to be inseparable from honor. Nor did it matter that the rights, which went undefended, expressed less than vital interests. What did matter was the motive that led to their sacrifice. What also mattered were the consequences to which such a sacrifice would lead. Once a nation's rights were abandoned through fear of the price required to defend them, its very sovereignty would be placed in jeopardy.

Wilson was committed to these beliefs. He had expressed them at length in his well-known letter of February 1916 to Senator Stone, chairman of the Senate Committee on Foreign Relations. On that occasion the issue had been the "right" of American citizens to travel on belligerent armed merchant vessels. Opposing any attempt by the Congress to quality this right, Wilson had equated its preservation with the nation's "honor and self respect" and had gone on to declare: "Once accept a single abatement of right and many other humiliations would certainly follow, and the whole fine fabric of international law might crumble under our hands piece by piece. What we are contending for in this matter is of the very essence of things that have made America a sovereign nation. She cannot yield them without conceding her own impotency as a nation and making virtual surrender of her independent position among the nations of the world."[46]

At the time, Wilson was intent on putting down a growing opposition in Congress to his neutrality policy. Even so, these were strong words. They were spoken, the president assured Stone, "in deep solemnity, without heat, with a clear consciousness of the high responsibilities of my office."[47] Although not devoid of rhetorical excess—certainly they constitute the most extreme expression of the domino theory made in the twentieth century by an American president—once uttered they formed a procrustean bed from which, when they were taken together with his other commitments in defense of right, Wilson could not readily escape, if at all.

Wilson decided upon war in March 1917, then, simply because he could see no viable alternative to war. If armed neutrality was "impracticable" and if America was "incapable" of submission, there was no course left save war. Wilson did not expressly invoke the nation's honor and self-respect in the war address; nor did he hold up the nation's prestige and standing, which were inseparable from his own prestige and standing. There was no need to do so. In his calculus, all would have been jeopardized by submission. That consideration, and that consideration alone, formed the compelling reason for intervention.

It did so despite Wilson's almost desperate desire to remain out of the war. Of that desire the agony he went through from early February to mid-March 1917 is eloquent testimony. Even after he had made the decision for war, he could scarcely reconcile himself to what he had done. This is why he continued almost obsessively to seek justification, both from others and from within himself. In his famous conversation with Frank Cobb, of the *New York World,* Wilson left a striking record of his desire to stay out of the European conflict and his sense of impotence in being unable to do so. War, Cobb quoted Wilson as saying, "required illiberalism at home to reinforce the men at the front. We couldn't fight Germany and maintain the ideals of Government that all thinking men shared. . . . Once lead this people into war and they'll forget there was ever such a thing as tolerance."[48] Wilson expressed doubt that the Constitution would survive war. He thought freedom of speech and the right of assembly would be sacrificed. He believed that war would also put an end to domestic reform. To Josephus Daniels the president reportedly said: "Every reform we have won will be the last if we go into the war."[49]

Nor was this all. Wilson thought the prospects of a peace without victory would all but vanish with America's entrance into the war. War, he told Cobb, "would mean that Germany would be beaten and so badly beaten that there would be a dictated peace, a victorious peace." Once America became a belligerent, there would be no one left to lead a war-ravaged world to a just peace, for at the end of such a war "there will be no bystanders with sufficient power to influence the terms." The most terrible and disastrous of all wars would be followed by a vindictive peace. In varying degree, all of these consequences came to pass. Though foreseeing them, Wilson nevertheless took the nation to war. He did so because he believed that he had no alternative. "What else can I do?" he asked Cobb. "Is there anything else I can do?"[50] He asked the same of House.

The Cobb interview is important. It testifies not only to Wilson's detestation of war and to his great fear of war's consequences, a fear that in a number of respects proved self-fulfilling, but to his sense of entrapment. In the almost despairing questions he put to Cobb he plainly sought justification for the neutrality course he had followed, a course that was to end in war. He had asked himself time and again, he told Cobb, what he might have done and what he might still do to avoid war. He could find no other way out: "What else can I do?" Cobb sought to assure him, as did House and Lansing, that there was nothing else he could do, that the German government had left him no alternative but war. Although Wilson sought that assurance, it failed to satisfy his deep need of justification for taking the nation to war.

Nor did this need find complete satisfaction in the ends for which war was to be waged. In concluding the war address Wilson summarized these ends: "for democracy, for the right of those who submit to authority to have a voice in their own government, for the rights and liberties of small nations, for a universal dominion of right by such a concert of free peoples as shall bring peace and safety to all nations and make the world itself at last free."[51] These were the ends of war, not the compelling occasion for war. To Frank Cobb, Wilson had expressed skepticism that war could serve as a means for achieving the ends set forth in the war address. Wilson was soon to shed this skepticism. His excessive pessimism over the undesirable consequences of war was soon transformed into an excessive optimism over what war might accomplish. Still, Wilson's profound pessimism in going to war is apparent. It accounts for his characterization of the step he was finally taking as having a "tragical character." The tragedy consisted in the realization not only that evil means would have to be employed on behalf of good ends but also that the ends themselves were likely to be defeated by the means.

Wilson found it a "distressing and oppressive duty" to advise the Congress of a state of war between Germany and the United States. Although he believed war to be seldom justified, although until almost the very end he refused to consider the great European war an exception to this belief, and although even on the eve of America's entrance into the war he harbored the gravest doubt that the good resulting from U.S. participation might outweigh the evil, he nevertheless took the path of war. "What else can I do?" The issue was no longer how Wilson got to the position he found himself in after January 31, 1917. It was no longer whether he might have avoided this position by taking a different course. He was where he found himself, and where he found himself left no alternative save war.

Wilson went to war in defense of neutral rights. The oldest explanation of America's entrance into World War I remains the most satisfactory. It was the challenge of the submarine to America's right as a neutral that left no alternative save war. In the absence of that challenge, the country would in all likelihood have remained a nonparticipant in the war. It would have remained a nonparticipant despite the prospect of being excluded from the peace settlement and despite even the prospect of Allied defeat. In a nation deeply divided over the war the president's was the deciding vote. Wilson desired almost above all else to keep America out of the war.

Only the right could not be sacrificed to peace. Only the right was more precious than peace, its defense being considered inseparable from honor and, in turn, prestige. Without prestige America would have no standing among nations. Submission to the German challenge would lead the Allies to dismiss America from those states whose voice and interests must be given serious consideration. The Germans, having faced Wilson down, would look upon the president and the nation he represented with still greater contempt than they had shown in the past.

These consequences just possibly could have been accepted had Wilson been intent solely on reaffirming the nation's prewar isolation from Europe's politics. Even then, submission would have proven very difficult given the president's past record of commitment. Step by step he had narrowed what freedom of action he had enjoyed at the outset of the war until it had virtually disappeared. By 1917 Wilson had defined a position on submarine warfare that left him very little room for maneuver. Had he given way then, he would have found himself isolated, ridiculed, and reviled as never before. The division in the country, already perilous, would have deepened still further. With the predictable desertion of many high officials in the administration, the stability of the government might well have been threatened.

The president could only have shrunk from these prospects, and this despite his proud claim that he had no fear of standing alone in defense of a cause he considered just. In fact, Wilson had seldom stood alone in his political career. His period of indecision in February and early March 1917 had been a reflection less of a willingness to take the position of lonely leadership than of a momentary inability to accept an outcome he dreaded but could no longer escape.

Wilson could not escape the decision to go to war because of the positions he had taken on neutral rights, as well as because he was unwilling to return to the nation's prewar policy of isolation from Europe's politics. To submit to the German challenge would have been possible, if at all, only on the assumption of such return. But Wilson had since discarded the assumption that he had still taken for granted at the beginning of the war. In coming to office he had given no indication of an intention to break from or substantially modify the policy of isolation. Despite his earlier views on the inadequacy of isolation in the twentieth century, he had been quite content to follow in the path marked out by others. The outbreak of the European war had not altered his readiness to adhere to a policy encrusted in tradition and generally seen as expressive of an almost permanent condition.

The policy of isolation could be rejected in practice only as a result of some great and compelling event that appeared to alter the features of the political universe and to demonstrate for those with eyes to see the need to break from the past. The European war proved to be such an event for Wilson, not in the beginning, but over time as he followed its destructive course and experienced the growing difficulties of preserving the nation's neutrality in a conflict involving all of the other great powers.

In the years 1915–17 Wilson undertook to transform the nation's historic policy. The war had revealed that America could no longer isolate itself from the world. While "abandoning" isolation, Wilson nevertheless remained intent on keeping the country out of war. Until March 1917, however, the abandonment of isolation did not imply for him the acceptance of war. To the contrary, it was only by remaining out of the war, he insisted, that America's newly assumed role of partner could be fulfilled. It was only by remaining outside the conflict that America could remain a disinterested party, competent to speak on "behalf of humanity" and able to mediate a peace without victory.

The relative ease with which Wilson abandoned isolation, as compared with his difficulty in abandoning neutrality, reflected more than the difference between a decision that did not entail an immediate and painful price and one that did. It also reflected his unwillingness to equate the abandonment of isolation with the acceptance of those prospects—alliances and war—that such an abandonment would normally be considered to hold out. The system of diplomacy that enshrined those prospects had led to the war. Wilson was intent on substituting a new system that avoided the consequences inherent in the old, consequences he saw as holding out the greatest threat to the nation's institutions and values. The conviction that war—the kind of war being fought in Europe—was the great nemesis, the prospect most to be feared, lay at the center of his thought. The principal aim of his transformed policy was the prevention of future wars. More immediately and more importantly, however, that policy sought to prevent America's active involvement in the current European conflict.

Wilson's dilemma, then, was how to reconcile the abandonment of isolation with the avoidance of those consequences to which abandonment could normally be expected to lead. The war had shown the inadequacies of a policy of isolation that decreed nonparticipation in Europe's wars. Neutrality was also undesirable, if not intolerable, because an isolated America could expect to have little voice in the peace settlements that followed Europe's wars. Such exclusion, Wilson came to believe, would now hold out a threatening prospect. An isolated America confronted by a postwar system that resembled the prewar system would likely have to maintain a level of arms in time of peace that could prove threatening to her domestic institutions.

While acknowledging and even urging these considerations, Wilson also emphasized the risks entailed in abandoning isolation, if abandonment meant participation in the system that had led to the catastrophe of the world war. These risks, he made clear from the outset, were unacceptable. America's partnership with the world, Wilson declared in his first statement marking the transformation of traditional American foreign policy, depended on the world's acceptance of the principles Americans believed in: that governments derive all their just powers from the consent of the governed, that great nations and small enjoy an equality of rights, and that no nation should henceforth extend its polity over another nation or people. The reformation of the international system was made the essential condition of the reformation of America's historic policy of isolation.[52]

The nation's participation in the affairs of the world required that the world first be made, if not safe, then at least much safer. What had been implicit in Wilson's May 1916 address to the League to Enforce Peace was explicit in his January 1917 appeal for a peace without victory. "The question upon which the whole future peace and policy of the world depends is this: Is the present war a struggle for a just and secure peace, or only for a new balance of power?" If the latter, he asked "who will guarantee, who can guarantee, the stable equilibrium of the new arrangement?"[53] The president's words allowed little room for misunderstanding. If the war was followed by a return to the old diplomacy, the United States would not participate. It would do so only if a community of power took the place of a balance of power, if an organized common peace succeeded the organized rivalries of the past.

America would become a partner to the world only if the world accepted "American principles." The identification of those principles with "the principles of mankind," principles that "must prevail," could only be interpreted as a claim to world leadership.[54] It was a startling pretension for a nonparticipant in the great struggle. Wilson advanced it with the utmost seriousness, basing it on the conviction that America was the world's greatest power and its only disinterested power. The theme of disinterestedness was a constant one in Wilsonian diplomacy. Its core meaning is apparent: America had no particular interests at stake in the conflict, only the common interest of the international community. Considerations of power apart, the claim to leadership was seen to follow from that fact. In this manner the benefits of isolation, with its corollary of unilateralism, were partly preserved through an internationalism that took for granted American leadership.

These were the principal elements of Woodrow Wilson's new policy, his larger peace policy. It expressed a reason of state evoked by the experience of the European conflict. It embodied a view of the requirements of American security in a world transformed by modern global war. Those requirements as they related to the Western Hemisphere did not break from the past. Wilson's appreciation of the security needs of the United States in the Caribbean region remained entirely conventional. It was in the world beyond that he broke from his predecessors, both in the interests he increasingly saw as critical for the nation's security and well-being and in the means he considered essential for realizing interest. Noninvolvement in the war then raging and the prevention of future wars formed the core of interest, while the reformation of international society constituted the indispensable means for realizing interest.

Wilson's larger policy, it cannot be emphasized too strongly or repeated too often, was predicated on peace. What Henry Adams said of Jefferson—"The essence and genius of his statesmanship lay in peace"[55]—could be said with equal justice of Wilson. To peace all else was subordinated. Yet Wilson had followed a neutrality policy that brought him ineluctably to the point of war. Although at the time utterly convinced that he had pursued a completely neutral course, he had not done so. His reluctance to break with Germany did not show the depth of his commitment to neutrality; it only testified to his fear of becoming a belligerent. Whether in law or in fact, Wilson had not been impartial. The characterization of his policy by many sympathetic contemporaries as one of "benevolent neutrality" toward the Allies was, if anything, an understatement. House entertained no illusions on this score; it was the basis of his frequent complaints about Allied ingratitude.[56] Lansing shared House's attitude. The influential *New Republic*, whose editors were at the time among Wilson's more ardent supporters, best summarized the president's neutrality: "We have in fact permitted the Allies to cut off Germany, we have been in fact prepared for war to deliver munitions and food stuffs to the Allies."[57]

In its essential features Wilson's course was set in the first ten months of the war. By the summer of 1915 Wilson had committed the nation to a neutrality policy that pointed to war with Germany. For the first time, he looked into a future that filled him with dread. A willingness to accept almost any outcome of the war provided that he could keep America out made its appearance alongside the insistence that America's neutral rights be respected. Wilson was to spend the following year and a half attempting to avoid both war and the surrender of the neutrality to which he had committed the nation. His effort resembled the proverbial attempt to square the circle. To resist German encroachment dictated measures that made war ever more likely. To avoid war required a course that made the surrender of right almost a certainty. This choice might have been forestalled at the outset of the war had the president chosen a course that struck a more even balance between the two sides and had he not resisted arming the nation until long past the time war with Germany first clearly threatened. Even when he did reluctantly accept the need to arm, the measures he proposed were altogether modest.

The president's reluctance to arm is easier to understand than his failure to strike a more even balance between the two sides. That balance did not imply the denial of advantages accruing to Great Britain by virtue of geography and naval superiority. It did require impartiality in the enforcement of neutral rights against the two sides, for only by such enforcement might Germany have had the incentive to restrain its conduct of naval warfare. From the outset, however, Wilson failed to enforce America's neutral rights against the Allies as he did against Germany. When, in the spring of 1916, Germany relinquished almost the entirety of the conditions it had previously drawn to justify the effective use of the submarine, it attached the condition that the American government take measures to ensure the observance of rules governing warfare at sea by Germany's enemies. But Wilson summarily rejected the condition attached to the so-called *Sussex* pledge.[58]

It was, as the president must have known, an unsustainable position. While Wilson could not be at all confident that Berlin would in any event abide by its pledge to abandon past methods of submarine warfare, he could be quite sure that it would not do so for long unless significant change was made in the British blockade of Germany. But London showed no disposition to ease Wilson's difficulties. By the spring of 1916 the Allied blockade of Germany had been in place for more than a year. It was an established fact, one against which the world's largest neutral state had made formal protests yet had failed to take, or even threaten, serious measures of reprisal.

These were the circumstances in which Wilson began a determined search for a way to stay out of the war. The Allies proved uncooperative. London made it unmistakably clear that it had no interest in furthering the president's efforts to mediate an end to the war.[59] Consequently, the president's predicament, one that would only grow sharper with the passage of time, became apparent. His neutrality policy was at war with his larger peace policy, which expressed his true reason of state. Wilson's neutrality policy could only further estrange him from the Allies, since it presupposed an impartiality at odds with the course to which Wilson had long committed the nation. The dilemma was as simple as the prospects for overcoming it were meager.

Yet Wilson would not acknowledge what should have been apparent. When the British refused to cooperate by supporting his efforts, Wilson was angered. He saw in the refusal an act of bad faith and a turning point in relations with Grey and his government.[60] The suspicions he already entertained of Allied war aims deepened, never to be entirely erased. In the summer of 1916 he began to see the Allied blockade of Germany in a new light. He obtained from Congress authority to take severe retaliatory measures against any nation discriminating against American firms or interfering with American mail.[61] These measures were aimed at Great Britain and registered the president's growing frustration and anger over London's persistent efforts to tighten ever further its control of neutral trade. Having swallowed the camel of Great Britain's regulation of neutral trade, Wilson now strained at the gnat of its annoying refinements. His new-found desire not only to appear to be but to actually be even-handed reflected his deepening anxiety over the fragility of his standoff with Germany following the *Sussex* crisis. In the summer of 1916 the pledge Germany had given was already showing signs of erosion.

It was too late. Even had Wilson been committed to a greater degree than he was to strike a more even balance between the two sides, it was too late. The die of his neutrality policy could not be recast. Nor could the threat of reprisals do what recasting the nation's neutrality policy might have done had it been possible. The British could also play the game of reprisals. Moreover, there was always the prospect that however hard Wilson might push the Allies, Germany still would not respect the *Sussex* pledge. In that event, the president would have found himself at swords' point with both sides but with no greater assurance of remaining a nonparticipant in the war.

Thus matters stood in the fall of 1916. Although it was already very late in the day for any peace move, Wilson delayed initiating his last effort to put an end to the war before America was drawn in. In a presidential election period, he was sensitive to the charge of playing politics with the war. When his peace note to the belligerents was finally sent on December 18, the Germans had badly compromised his effort by anticipating him with their own peace proposal.

The essential idea on which the December peace initiative rested was quite simple. Wilson had articulated it months earlier in an exchange with a peace group. If the belligerents "once stop fighting and begin to parley," he had explained, "they will never begin fighting again."[62] In appealing to the belligerents to define their war aims, not in abstract but in concrete terms, Wilson's hope was that by defining their aims they would set the stage for the suspension of hostilities and that once they were suspended, as a pleased William Jennings Bryan wrote the president, "neither side will consent to assume responsibility for continuing the unspeakable horror of this conflict, if any reasonable terms can be secured."[63]

What pleased Bryan, however, alarmed Lansing and House. The note left open the possibility that Germany might respond favorably, while the Allies would not. In that event, House had earlier argued with the president, Germany might feel she could begin unrestricted submarine warfare. If Wilson were then to break with Germany, the public might not follow, considering Germany's move more or less justified. Alternatively, if Germany were to act with restraint, House observed, "we would inevitably drift into a sympathetic alliance with her, and if this came about, England and France might . . . declare war against us."[64]

Wilson seemed undeterred by what his advisers agreed would be "stupendous folly" were the latter scenario ever to arise. If the Allies wanted war, House reported him as responding, "we would not shrink from it."[65] But the president quickly added that he did not think that the Allies would dare to resort to war against America. In this view, Wilson was almost certainly right. War with the United States could only have wors-

ened the Allies' position, vitally dependent as they still were on America. Yet if war with the Allies could be safely dismissed, House's vision of
a United States drifting into a "sympathetic alliance" with Germany could
not. For several months the German government had urged President
Wilson to undertake his peace move. The Allies, in contrast, had been
strongly opposed to any peace move since the spring of 1916. Wilson had
no way of knowing how the belligerents might respond to his initiative.
The acceptance of Germany as a partner in the peace negotiations and
a worsening relationship with the Allies could not be ruled out.

Wilson never had to face these possible consequences of a policy that
subordinated almost all interests to the interest in peace. Neither side
was willing to take the president's path to peace. The Germans might
have done so in the fall of 1916 had they been assured that in the event
that the Allies did not respond to Wilson's appeal and declare a willingness to end the war roughly on the basis of the status quo ante, the
United States would have radically altered its neutrality policy to Germany's advantage. But of this they could not be assured. And even if
they could have been, there were always their own war aims, aims that a
German government could abandon only at great peril in 1916.

All this is but speculation. What is not is that to the very end, Wilson's
neutrality policy remained at war with his peace policy. His neutrality
policy provided neither side with the necessary incentive to follow his
peace policy. The Allies had no incentive to follow his peace policy
because they knew, as Walter Lippmann had observed in writing of the
earlier House-Grey negotiations, "that if they maintained their blockade, Germany would either starve or resume submarine warfare."[66] The
key was Wilson's continued acceptance of the blockade. So long as this
could be relied upon—and the events of the fall had not placed it in
real doubt—the Allies could continue to pursue their course rather
than the president's.

The Germans also had little incentive, and largely for the same reason: they could have little confidence that an Allied rejection of Wilson's peace note would result in radical change in the neutral course
the United States had been committed to since the first year of the war.
The Germans badly erred in refusing to do what the president asked
them to do, namely, to entrust their fate to him. Had they done so, they
might well have escaped the disaster that awaited them. Had they done
so, they might well have found themselves in a position of "sympathetic
alliance" with the United States. But the previous wartime course of
German-American relations scarcely supported the act of faith Wilson
now asked for. The Germans went on to make their great mistake,

thereby quite possibly saving Wilson from a fate far worse than the fate he was to experience. The note Lansing made to himself on New Year's Eve 1916, that he had "great confidence in the President's lucky star," was not inappropriate.[67]

The logic of Wilson's neutrality policy made America's participation in the war virtually certain. The logic of his peace policy made his vision of a lasting peace increasingly elusive. Wilson's peace policy was based on the distinction between the peace settlement and the postwar organization charged with the maintenance of peace. America's "partnership" with the world extended to the latter though not to the former. "We have nothing material of any kind to ask for ourselves," the president declared in his historic address of May 1916, "and are quite aware that we are in no sense or degree parties to the present quarrel. Our interest is only in peace and its future guarantees."[68] The belligerents had made the war; the belligerents must make the peace. The United States would limit its new role to participation in the creation and maintenance of the organization designed to keep the peace that was made.

What would happen, however, if the peace settlement proved to be unjust and left some of the parties to it dissatisfied and resentful? If the causes and objects of the war were as obscure and suspect as Wilson had so often depicted them, what assurance was there that from this tainted well the waters of a just and lasting peace would flow? There could be no assurance. Yet Wilson had articulated a postwar policy that tied America's future to a peace settlement in which the nation would have no role.

Aware of the dilemma thus created, Wilson moved in late 1916 to join what he had earlier made separate. A willingness to play a new role in the postwar world was made conditional upon a peace settlement that satisfied America's minimal expectations. This was the burden of Wilson's peace-without-victory address in January 1917. "We shall have no voice in determining what those terms [i.e., peace terms] shall be," the president acknowledged, "but we shall . . . have a voice in determining whether they shall be made lasting or not by the guarantees of a universal covenant." The belligerents were put on notice: they might conclude the war by a peace that served the "several interests and immediate aims of the nations engaged" rather than a peace that would "win the approval of mankind" because it expressed principles of justice to which all peoples could subscribe, but if they did, America would not join in guaranteeing its maintenance. America would not and could not do so because such a peace would not satisfy even the belligerents themselves, let alone win the support of other nations. "If the peace presently to be made is to endure," Wilson declared, "it must be a peace made secure by the organized major force of mankind." Only a community of power could guarantee a tranquil and stable Europe. In turn, only a peace without victory, "only a peace the very principle of which is equality and a common participation in a common benefit," could create the necessary basis for an effective community of power.[69]

This was an ambivalent, even contradictory, message. Although the war had presumably shown that America could no longer isolate herself from the world, the threat of doing just that was held out if the world did not abandon the system that had led to the war. The ambivalence was overcome by events: a week following the president's peace-without-victory address, the Germans declared unrestricted submarine warfare. The declaration signaled the beginning of Wilson's reluctant turn toward war. The distinction he had clung to until the end of January 1917, between the peace terms and the postwar security organization, was abandoned. With America's entrance into the war, the nation's participation in the peace settlement was all but taken for granted. What else could have been the meaning of the promise in the president's war address to "vindicate the principles of peace and justice in the life of the world as against selfish and autocratic power and to set up amongst the really free and self-governed peoples of the world such a concert of purpose and of action as will henceforth ensure the observance of those principles"?[70] How else could this promise have been realized save by a peace settlement that Wilson had earlier laid down in calling for a peace without victory?

The Allies were not committed to Wilson's vision of the peace settlement. To the contrary, their opposition in principle to a peace without victory had been made unmistakably clear. What had not been made clear was the agreements they had concluded among themselves, agreements that were the antithesis of a Wilsonian peace settlement. Although having no specific knowledge of these secret undertakings before becoming a belligerent, the president had long suspected their existence. Given his outlook, Wilson could have been in no doubt that the Allies' secret engagements threatened, if they did not make impossible, the realization of a peace without victory.

Yet the record shows that at the time, Wilson did next to nothing to bind the nation's soon-to-be partners in the war to the principles of a peace without victory. While having no illusions about Allied purposes during the several months preceding America's entrance into the war, he made no effort to exact a price for the nation's participation in the conflict, despite the need in which the Allies stood at the time. Quite the contrary, the American move in November 1916 to squeeze the British on the prospects for obtaining private loans in the United States was quietly reversed in February and early March 1917.

Why did Wilson fail to exact a price for America's participation in the war? The answer can scarcely be that the idea of laying down terms to the Allies simply never occurred to him.[71] More plausible is that Wilson believed he could force the Allies to do his bidding at the end of the war, when American power would be very great. In the meantime he would see no evil, hear no evil, and speak no evil. This may well account for his otherwise mystifying reaction when given the Allied secret agreements by the British foreign secretary, Lord Balfour, in May 1917. Although Wilson insisted after the war that he had not known of the secret agreements, he undoubtedly did know of them. At the time, he must have decided simply to ignore their existence, to put them from his consciousness, an exercise in which he was adept. The time would come when he might confront the Allies and insist upon having his way, a time when, as he once remarked to House, the Allies would be "financially in our hands."[72] Until that day, the need for unity outweighed the demands of principle.

There remains yet another, simpler explanation for Wilson's failure to exact a price for America's participation in the war: timing. Before January 31, 1917, Wilson was determined not to go to war. After that date, he had little alternative to going to war. This being the case, before the end of January the Allies had nothing to buy, given Wilson's insistence on staying out of the conflict. After the end of January Wilson had little to sell, since it must have been apparent to the Allies that he was being forced into the conflict. The Allies had then no incentive, or at most a diminished incentive, to yield. Wilson's opportunity had been in the brief period—at most, three to four months—before the end of January, but he had never been more resolutely set against war than in that period.

Thus Wilson and the nation went to war. A long period in America's history came to an end. The war address pronounced a benediction on this past and proclaimed a radically different future. The just peace it looked forward to was no longer one to be gained without victory. Woodrow Wilson had now put his faith in force. Speaking on the anniversary of the nation's declaration of war, he expressed that faith in these words: "Force, Force to the utmost, Force without stint or limit, the righteous and triumphant Force which shall make Right the law of the world, and cast every selfish dominion down in the dust."[73]

Notes

Preface

1. Earl Latham, ed., *The Philosophy and Policies of Woodrow Wilson* (Chicago: University of Chicago Press, 1958), 176.

2. Woodrow Wilson, quoted in Herbert Bruce Brougham, memorandum of interview with the president, 14 Dec. 1914, in *The Papers of Woodrow Wilson*, ed. Arthur S. Link, 69 vols. (Princeton, NJ: Princeton University Press, 1966–94), 31: 458–59 (hereafter cited as *PWW*).

3. Wilson, address to joint session of Congress, 2 Apr. 1917, ibid., 41:523.

4. These themes are well articulated in Robert E. Osgood, *Ideals and Self-Interest in America's Foreign Relations* (Chicago: University of Chicago Press, 1953), 195–304.

5. Wilson, address to joint session of Congress, 2 Apr. 1917, *PWW*, 41:523.

Introduction

1. "For Wilson 'honor' meant more than chivalrous sentiments or ideals. It was closely tied up with the preservation of historically sanctioned rights. These rights were the rock on which rested the stability of the international order and the integrity of the nation itself." August Heckscher, *Woodrow Wilson* (New York: Macmillan, 1991), 377–78.

2. Secretary of State William Jennings Bryan to James W. Gerard, 19 July 1915, in *PWW*, 33:547; U.S. Department of State, *Foreign Relations of the United States* (Washington, DC: USGPO, 1915), 1915 suppl., 481 (hereafter cited as *FRUS*).

3. Diary of Edward M. House, 30 Sept. 1914, Edward M. House Papers, Manuscripts and Archives, Yale University Library, reprinted in *PWW*, 31:109.

4. House, Diary, 4 Nov. 1914, ibid., 31:263–66.

5. David M. Esposito writes that while Germany did not pose a direct security threat, "what people overlooked then, and overlook now, was the threat to American institutions and ideals implicit in a German victory." *The Legacy of Woodrow Wilson: American Aims in World War I* (Westport, CT: Praeger, 1996), 5.

6. Woodrow Wilson, Fourth of July address, 4 July 1914, *PWW*, 30:248–55.

7. On the relationship between Wilson's conception of neutrality and civilizational concerns, see Frank Ninkovich, *The Wilsonian Century: U.S. Foreign Policy since 1900* (Chicago: University of Chicago Press, 1999).

8. Woodrow Wilson, remarks to Associated Press, New York, 20 Apr. 1915, *PWW*, 33:37–41.

9. Lloyd E. Ambrosius captures this twofold character of Wilson's neutrality in *Wilsonian Statecraft: Theory and Practice of Liberal Internationalism during World War I* (Wilmington, DE: Scholarly Resources, 1991), 27: "Wilson's response to the European war alternated between his twin impulses to avoid and to redeem

the Old World. . . . The president was, paradoxically, at once isolationist and internationalist."

10. Thomas Jefferson to Edward Rutledge, 4 July 1790, in *The Papers of Thomas Jefferson*, ed. Julian P. Boyd et al., 28 vols. to date (Princeton, NJ: Princeton University Press, 1950–),16:601.

11. Woodrow Wilson to Edith Bolling Galt, 9 Aug. 1915, *PWW*, 34:151.

12. Franklin Knight Lane to George Whitefield Lane, 16 Feb. 1917, ibid., 41:239.

13. Edward Grey, Viscount Fallodon, to Edward Mandell House, 14 July 1915, ibid., 34:145.

14. Wilson to House, 21 Aug. 1915, ibid., 34:271.

15. House, Diary, 30 Mar. 1916, ibid., 36:388.

16. See Ross A. Kennedy, "Woodrow Wilson, World War I, and an American Conception of National Security," *Diplomatic History* 25 (Winter 2001): 1–31.

17. Woodrow Wilson, address to League to Enforce Peace, Washington, DC, 27 May 1916, *PWW*, 37:113.

18. House, Diary, 28 May, 23 June 1916.

19. Woodrow Wilson, colloquy with members of the American Neutral Conference, 30 Aug. 1916, *PWW*, 38:115.

20. Woodrow Wilson, address, Omaha, NE, 5 Oct. 1916, ibid., 38:347.

21. Woodrow Wilson, luncheon address to women in Cincinnati, OH, 29 Oct. 1916, ibid., 38:531.

22. Woodrow Wilson, unpublished prolegomenon to a peace note, ca. 25 Nov. 1916, and appeal for a statement of war aims, 18 Dec. 1916, ibid., 40:67–70, 273–76.

23. Appeal for a statement of war aims, 18 Dec. 1916, ibid., 40:275.

24. House, Diary, 29 June 1916.

25. Ibid., 15 May 1916.

26. Wilson, luncheon address to women in Cincinnati, OH, 29 Oct. 1916, *PWW*, 38:531.

27. Woodrow Wilson, campaign address, Shadow Lawn, Monmouth, NJ, 14 Oct. 1916, ibid., 38:436.

28. Wilson, address, Omaha, NE, 5 Oct. 1916, ibid., 38:348.

29. Wilson, address to League to Enforce Peace, Washington, DC, 27 May 1916, ibid., 37:113–15.

30. Wilson "wanted America to play a great role in the international order, but without it having anything to do with the conflict of interests in Europe. America would participate and still remain unique, it would stay pure and yet bear responsibility." Jan William Schulte Nordholt, *Woodrow Wilson: A Life for World Peace* (Berkeley and Los Angeles: University of California Press, 1991), 172.

31. Woodrow Wilson, address to the Daughters of the American Revolution, Washington, DC, 11 Oct. 1915, *PWW*, 35:49.

32. Woodrow Wilson, address to joint session of Congress, 2 Apr. 1917, ibid., 41:523.

33. Woodrow Wilson, address in the Denver Auditorium, Denver, 25 Sept. 1919, ibid., 63:496.

34. Wilson, address, Omaha, NE, 5 Oct. 1916, ibid., 38:349.

1 Woodrow Wilson and His Advisers

1. Jefferson to Thomas Leiper, 12 June 1815, in *The Works of Thomas Jefferson*, ed. Paul Leicester Ford, 12 vols. (New York: G. P. Putnam's Sons, 1904–5), 11:477–78.

2. A. J. P. Taylor, *The Struggle for Mastery in Europe, 1848–1918* (London: Oxford University Press, 1954), xxiv.

3. Edward Grey, Viscount Fallodon, *Twenty Five Years, 1892–1916*, 2 vols. (New York: Frederick A. Stokes, 1925), 2:107.

4. Woodrow Wilson, *Constitutional Government in the United States*, intro. Sidney A. Pearson Jr.(New York: Columbia University Press, 1908), 24 Mar. 1908, reprinted in *PWW*, 18:120.

5. Wilson to Robert Lansing, 13 July 1915, ibid., 33:500.

6. Patrick Devlin, *Too Proud to Fight: Woodrow Wilson's Neutrality* (New York: Oxford University Press, 1975), 659.

7. Woodrow Wilson, address on Abraham Lincoln to assembled guests, Hodgenville, KY, 4 Sept. 1916, *PWW*, 38:144.

8. House, Diary, 15 Apr. 1914, ibid., 29:448–49.

9. House, Diary, 12 Apr. 1916, relating Cary Grayson's characterization, with which House agreed, ibid., 36:402.

10. Devlin, *Too Proud to Fight*, 432; Burton J. Hendrick, *The Life and Letters of Walter H. Page*, 3 vols. (London: Heinemann, 1923–25), 3:281.

11. Winston S. Churchill, *The World Crisis*, 6 vols. (London: Thornton Butterworth, 1923), 3:229.

12. House, Diary, 12 Apr. 1916, *PWW*, 36:402. See also House, Diary, 17 May, 23 Dec. 1916.

13. Wilson to Mary Allen Hulbert, 8 Nov. 1914, *PWW*, 31:280.

14. Roy Stannard Baker, *Woodrow Wilson: Life and Letters*, vol. 6, *1915–1917* (New York: Doubleday, 1937), 265.

15. House, Diary, 14 Dec. 1916, *PWW*, 40:240.

16. [Walter Lippmann], "The Other-Worldliness of Wilson," *New Republic*, 27 Mar. 1915, 194–95.

17. House, Diary, 3 Dec. 1914, *PWW*, 31:384–85.

18. Wilson to Galt, 8 June 1915, ibid., 33:366.

19. William Jennings Bryan to Wilson, 19 Sept. 1914, ibid., 31:56–57.

20. Bryan to Wilson, 1 Dec. 1914 and 23 Apr. 1915, ibid., 31:378–79, 33:66–67.

21. Bryan to Wilson, 15 Feb., 6, 23 Apr., 1 May, 3 June 1915, ibid., 32:235–36, 487, 33:66–67, 91, 321–26.

22. Wilson to Galt, 9 June 1915, ibid., 33:377.

23. Wilson to Nancy Saunders Toy, 31 Jan. 1915, ibid., 32:165.

24. House, Diary, 14 June 1915, ibid., 33:397; House to Wilson, 16 June 1915, ibid., 33:397, 409.

25. House, Diary, 24 June 1915, ibid., 33:448–49.

26. House, Diary, 14 June 1915. "He [Lansing] will be barred from complaining at the President's method of using me in the way he does."

27. Robert Lansing, "Consideration and Outline of Policies," 11 July 1915,

Confidential Memoranda and Notes, 26–30, Manuscript Section, Microfilm Collection, Library of Congress, Washington, DC.

28. Robert Lansing, *War Memoirs of Robert Lansing* (Indianapolis: Bobbs-Merrill, 1935), 128.

29. Lansing, "Consideration and Outline of Policies," 27–29.

30. Robert Lansing, "The President's Attitude toward Great Britain: Its Dangers," Sept. 1916, Confidential Memoranda and Notes, 40.

31. Brougham, memorandum of interview with the president, 14 Dec. 1914, *PWW*, 31:459.

32. Robert Lansing, "Note on a War with Germany," 19 Mar. 1917, Confidential Memoranda and Notes, 76.

33. Lansing, *War Memoirs*, 177–78.

34. Ibid., 47.

35. Robert Lansing, "Embarrassment of Action in the *Arabic* Case," 23 Aug. 1915, Confidential Memoranda and Notes, 31–32.

36. Edward M. House, *The Intimate Papers of Colonel House*, ed. Charles Seymour, 4 vols. (New York: Houghton Mifflin, 1926–28), 1:114. For a recent biography of House see Godfrey Hodgson, *Woodrow Wilson's Right Hand: The Life of Colonel Edward M. House* (New Haven, CT: Yale University Press, 2006).

37. House, *Intimate Papers of Colonel House*, 1:46.

38. House, Diary, 10 Mar. 1916.

39. House, *Intimate Papers of Colonel House*, 1:176–77.

40. House, Diary, 6 Aug. 1914.

41. Ibid., 30 Apr. 1914.

42. Ibid., 7 Feb. 1915.

43. Joyce Grigsby Williams, *Colonel House and Sir Edward Grey: A Study in Anglo-American Diplomacy* (New York: University Press of America, 1984), 61.

44. House, Diary, 22 Aug. 1915.

45. Ibid., 17 Nov. 1916.

46. Ibid., 24 June 1915, *PWW*, 33:450.

47. Ibid., 4 June 1915.

48. Ibid., 10 July 1915.

49. Galt to Wilson, 26 Aug. 1915, *PWW*, 34:336, 338.

50. Wilson to Galt, 28 Aug. 1915, ibid., 34:350, 352–53.

51. House, Diary, 22 May 1916.

52. Wilson to House, 27 Dec. 1915, *PWW*, 35:387.

53. House, Diary, 6 Mar. 1916, ibid., 36:262–63.

54. Baker, *Woodrow Wilson*, 6:129.

55. House, Diary, 14–18 Nov. 1916, *PWW*, 38:645–47, 656–61, 668–69.

56. Wilson to Galt, 18 Aug. 1915, ibid., 34:241.

57. House, Diary, 29 Mar. 1916, ibid., 36:381.

58. Lansing, "President's Attitude toward Great Britain," 40–42.

2 Isolation and Neutrality

1. Woodrow Wilson, "Democracy and Efficiency," *Atlantic Monthly*, Mar. 1901, 289–99, and idem, "The Ideals of America," ibid., Dec. 1902, 721–34, reprinted in *PWW*, 12:6–20, 208–27.

2. Woodrow Wilson, address on Commodore John Barry, 16 May 1914, ibid., 30:34–35.

3. Wilson, address to League to Enforce Peace, 27 May 1916, ibid., 37:113–16.

4. Woodrow Wilson, Memorial Day address, 30 May 1916, ibid., 37:123–28.

5. Woodrow Wilson, appeal to the American people, 18 Aug. 1914, ibid., 30:393–94.

6. Wilson, address to joint session of Congress, 2 Apr. 1917, ibid., 41:523.

7. A general survey of the neutrality legislation of the period is given by Frances Deak in "The United States Neutrality Acts," *International Conciliation*, no. 358 (Mar. 1940). See also U.S. Naval War College, *International Law Situations, 1939* (Washington, DC, 1940), 101–54.

8. From a very large literature, the following works on neutrality have been used: Philip C. Jessup and Frances Deak, *Neutrality: Its History, Economics, and Law,* 4 vols. (New York: Columbia University Press, 1935–36); John Bassett Moore, *A Digest of International Law*, vol. 3 (Washington, DC: USGPO, 1906); Carlton Savage, ed., *Policy of the United States toward Maritime Commerce in War,* 2 vols. (Washington, DC: USGPO, 1934–36); Green H. Hackworth, *Digest of International Law*, vol. 7 (Washington, DC: USGPO, 1943); Oppenheim-Lauterpacht, *International Law,* 7th ed., vol. 2 (London: Longmans, Green, 1952); H. A. Smith, *The Law and Custom of the Sea,* 2nd ed. (London: Stevens, 1950); Julius Stone, *Legal Controls of International Conflict* (London: Stevens, 1954); and Robert W. Tucker, *The Law of War and Neutrality at Sea* (Washington, DC: USGPO, 1957). A valuable analysis of developments in neutrality in the years before World War I and during the first eight months of the war may be found in John W. Coogan, *The End of Neutrality: The United States, Britain, and Maritime Rights, 1899–1915* (Ithaca, NY: Cornell University Press, 1981).

9. Wilson, appeal to the American people, 18 Aug. 1914, *PWW*, 30:394.

10. Jefferson to R. Livingston, 9 Sept. 1801, in Savage, *Policy of the United States,* 1:235.

11. Jefferson to William Short, 3 Oct. 1801, in *The Writings of Thomas Jefferson,* ed. Paul Leicester Ford, 10 vols. (New York: G. P. Putnam's Sons, 1892–99), 7:95.

12. U.S. Naval War College, *International Law Topics and Discussions* (Washington, DC, 1903); Savage, *Policy of the United States,* 1:495–98.

13. In the interwar years, among the many defenses of neutrality as an institution were John Bassett Moore, *International Law and Some Current Illusions* (New York: Macmillan, 1921), 1–80; Philip C. Jessup, *Neutrality: Today and Tomorrow,* vol. 4 of Jessup and Deake, *Neutrality: Its History, Economics, and Law,* 58–85; and Edwin Borchard and William Potter Lage, *Neutrality for the United States* (New Haven, CT: Yale University Press, 1937), 1–32.

14. Smith, *Law and Custom of the Sea,* 75.

15. Lansing, *War Memoirs,* 120.

16. Coogan, *End of Neutrality,* 104–47, contains an illuminating historical analysis of the Declaration of London.

17. Gerard to Secretary of State Lansing, 4 May 1916, *FRUS,* 1916 suppl., 259–60.

18. Secretary of State Lansing to Gerard, 8 May 1916, ibid., 263.

19. *Stigstad* (1918), 5 *Lloyds Prize Cases,* 393, cited in Hackworth, *Digest of International Law,* 7:152.

3 Interpretations

1. Charles C. Tansill, *America Goes to War* (Boston: Little, Brown, 1938), 134.

2. A review of the extensive interwar literature on American intervention, both revisionist and conventional, may be found in Richard W. Leopold, "The Problem of American Intervention, 1917: An Historical Retrospect," *World Politics* 2 (1950): 404–25.

3. Ernest R. May, "Emergence to World Power," in *The Reconstruction of American History*, ed. John Higham (New York: Harper & Row, 1962), 180–81.

4. Roy Stannard Baker, *Woodrow Wilson: Life and Letters*, vol. 5, *1914–1915* (New York: Doubleday, 1934), 156, 211.

5. Ibid., 5:180, 211.

6. Ibid., 5:208–9.

7. Ibid., 5:193.

8. For a review of the post–World War II literature, see Richard L. Watson Jr., "Woodrow Wilson and His Interpreters, 1947–1957," *Mississippi Valley Historical Review* 44 (1957–58): 207–36; and Daniel M. Smith, "National Interest and American Intervention, 1917: An Historiographical Appraisal," *Journal of American History* 54 (1965): 5–24.

9. Edward H. Buehrig, *Woodrow Wilson and the Balance of Power* (Bloomington: Indiana University Press, 1955), 103.

10. Ernest R. May, *The World War and American Isolation, 1914–1917* (Cambridge, MA: Harvard University Press, 1959), 53. To similar effect, see Daniel M. Smith, *The Great Departure: The United States and World War I, 1914–1920* (New York: John Wiley and Sons, 1965), 29.

11. Arthur S. Link, *Wilson: The Struggle for Neutrality, 1914–1915* (Princeton, NJ: Princeton University Press, 1960), 127.

12. Ibid., 129.

13. Arthur S. Link, *Wilson: Campaigns for Progressivism and Peace, 1916–1917* (Princeton, NJ: Princeton University Press, 1965), viii.

14. Theodore Roosevelt to John Callan O'Laughlin, 13 Apr. 1917, in *The Letters of Theodore Roosevelt*, ed. Elting E. Morrison et al. (Cambridge, MA: Harvard University Press, 1954), 1173.

15. Woodrow Wilson, conversation with members of the Senate Foreign Relations Committee, 19 Aug. 1919, *PWW*, 62:390.

16. With the notable exception of Coogan, *End of Neutrality*, the issue of Wilson's neutrality has seemingly ceased to interest historians over the last generation. This has been owing in part to the exhaustive studies of the post–World War II historians, but perhaps in greater part to the seemingly inevitable character of America's activist role as a world power. The idea that fueled the revisionism of the 1920s and 1930s—that America might return to its historic policy of isolation—appeared increasingly unthinkable as the United States continued to embrace its role as "world leader." Even public disaffection with particular instances of intervention, such as the war in Vietnam, did not seriously call into question a close relationship with Western Europe, and it was especially the refusal of entangling alliances with the European powers that had animated the isolationists. Instead, the attention of historians writing in the last generation

has been on the role that Wilson played in fashioning the Versailles peace settlement and the League of Nations. While his first administration has not been neglected, the focus there has been on his various acts of intervention in Mexico and the Caribbean. It is, in short, the ways in which Wilson prefigured the future, not the possibility of returning to a pristine past, that has excited attention in the last generation. See Thomas J. Knock, *To End All Wars: Woodrow Wilson and the Quest for a New World Order* (New York: Oxford University Press, 1992); Kendrick A. Clements, *The Presidency of Woodrow Wilson* (Lawrence: University Press of Kansas, 1992); Frederick S. Calhoun, *Uses of Force and Wilsonian Foreign Policy* (Kent, OH: Kent State University Press, 1993); idem, *Power and Principle: Armed Intervention in Wilsonian Foreign Policy* (Kent, OH: Kent State University Press, 1986); David Steigerwald, *Wilsonian Idealism in America* (Ithaca, NY: Cornell University Press, 1994); Robert D. Johnson, *The Peace Progressives and American Foreign Policy* (Cambridge, MA: Harvard University Press, 1995); Esposito, *Legacy of Woodrow Wilson;* Frank Ninkovich, *Modernity and Power: A History of the Domino Theory in the Twentieth Century* (Chicago: University of Chicago Press, 1994); idem, *Wilsonian Century;* John Milton Cooper Jr., *Breaking the Heart of the World: Woodrow Wilson and the Fight for the League of Nations* (Cambridge: Cambridge University Press, 2001), idem, *The Warrior and the Priest: Woodrow Wilson and Theodore Roosevelt* (Cambridge, MA: Harvard University Press, 1983); Lloyd E. Ambrosius, *Wilsonianism: Woodrow Wilson and His Legacy in American Foreign Relations* (New York: Palgrave/Macmillan, 2002); idem, *Woodrow Wilson and the American Diplomatic Tradition: The Treaty Fight in Perspective* (Cambridge: Cambridge University Press, 1987); and John A. Thompson, *Woodrow Wilson* (London: Pearson, 2002).

17. Coogan, *End of Neutrality,* 255: "Evaluation of American maritime rights policy during World War I rests essentially on the answer to one question: could the United States have blocked a German victory while preserving its own neutrality within the existing system of international relations, avoiding identification with Allied aggrandizement, and preventing the innocent deaths and suffering caused by the blockade?" Although Coogan is unwilling to answer the question with "certainty," his view is that had the United States combined a strict neutrality with measures of preparedness, "the promise of American mediation and a compromise peace does not seem totally unrealistic." To this extent, the position taken here does not substantially differ from Coogan's. It does differ in the analysis of Wilson, however. Wilson, Coogan writes, "believed that German victory in Europe would endanger American national security, that neutral rights were not sufficiently important to justify a clash with Britain, and that American public opinion must not be allowed to become so outraged by the blockade that it compromised his leadership as it had compromised that of James Madison in 1812" (249). The president's actions presumably followed from these beliefs. I see a different Wilson.

18. Brougham, memorandum of interview with the president, 14 Dec. 1914, *PWW,* 31:458–59.

19. House, Diary, 4 Nov. 1914, ibid., 31:265.

20. Link, *Wilson: The Struggle for Neutrality,* 129.

21. Ibid., 127.

22. Lansing to Wilson, 27 Sept. 1914, Papers of the Department of State, National Archives, Washington, DC.

23. On preparedness, see esp. Esposito, *Legacy of Woodrow Wilson*, 40–56; and Thompson, *Woodrow Wilson*, 105–7, 115–17.

24. Grey to Cecil Spring Rice, 3 Sept. 1914, *PWW*, 30:473.

25. Grey, *Twenty Five Years*, 1:107.

26. House, Diary, 10 Feb. 1915.

27. Wilson to House, 29 Jan. 1915, *PWW*, 32:158.

28. House, Diary, 28 Sept. 1914, ibid., 31:95.

29. House to Wilson, 16 June 1915, ibid., 33:406.

4 German Submarines and the Long-Distance Blockade

1. Spring Rice to Grey, 3 Sept. 1914, *PWW*, 30:472.

2. Spring Rice to Grey, 25 Aug. 1914, in *The Letters and Friendships of Cecil Spring Rice*, ed. Stephen Gwynn (London: Constable, 1929), 218–23.

3. Brougham, memorandum of interview with the president, 14 Dec. 1914, *PWW*, 31:458–60.

4. House, Diary, 30 Aug. and 4 Nov. 1914, ibid., 30:461–67 and 31:263–66.

5. Brougham, memorandum of interview with the president, 14 Dec. 1914, ibid., 31:458–60.

6. Wilson to Galt, 18 Aug. 1915, ibid., 34:240–44.

7. Gerard to Bryan, 4 Feb. 1915, *FRUS*, 1915 suppl., 94.

8. Robert Lansing, "Memorandum on Relations with Germany and Possibilities," 15 Feb. 1915, in U.S. Department of State, *Papers Relating to the Foreign Relations of the United States: The Lansing Papers, 1914–1920*, 2 vols. (Washington, DC: USGPO, 1939–40), 1:367–68.

9. This and the following several paragraphs draw from Arno Spindler, *La guerre sous-marine*, trans. René Jouan, 3 vols. (Paris: Payot, 1933–35), 1:11–122; and May, *World War and American Isolation*, 113–36.

10. Gerard to Bryan, 4 Feb. 1915, *FRUS*, 1915 suppl., 94.

11. Count Johann von Bernstorff to Bryan, 7 Feb. 1915, ibid., 95–97.

12. Lansing to Wilson, 7 Feb. 1915, *PWW*, 32:195–96.

13. Bryan to Gerard, 10 Feb. 1915, *FRUS*, 1915 suppl., 98–100; *PWW*, 32:207–10.

14. *New York Times*, 11 Feb. 1915.

15. *Wall Street Journal*, 4 Jan. 1916, quoted in Alice Morrissey, *The American Defense of Neutral Right, 1914–1917* (Cambridge, MA: Harvard University Press, 1939), 54.

16. Wilson to Lansing, 11 Feb. 1915, *PWW*, 32:216–18. Dickinson's "clear and firm declaration in advance" was addressed to the destruction of "American ships while legitimately under the protection of the American flag." This may well have been the "right way" of dealing with the German move, but it was not Wilson's way.

17. Bryan to Walter H. Page, 10 Feb. 1915, *FRUS*, 1915 suppl., 100–101.

18. Bryan to Page, 16 Feb. 1915, ibid., 107.

19. For the British declaration of Nov. 3, 1914, and the diplomatic correspondence, see ibid., 1914 suppl., 463–70.

20. Coogan, *End of Neutrality*, 236.

21. See Lansing, Confidential Memoranda and Notes, esp. "War General," 15 Apr. 1915, "War Conditions and Violations," 3 May 1915, and "Cruel and Inhuman Acts of War," 25 May 1915.

22. Page to Bryan, 15 Mar. 1915, *PWW,* 32:382.

23. Lansing to Floyd Clarke, 16 Feb. 1915, in Lansing Papers, Library of Congress, Washington, DC.

24. "Our Diplomacy at Its Best" (editorial), *New York Times,* 18 Feb. 1915; *New Republic,* 13 Feb. 1915, 35.

25. Chandler Anderson, Diary, Jan. 4–Feb. 13, 1915, Diary and Papers of Chandler P. Anderson, Library of Congress, Washington, DC. Anderson felt that the note of February 10 "would have been improved by stating more explicitly that American citizens on belligerents' vessels were entitled to the protection of the rule of international law requiring that the passengers and crew on merchant vessels must be removed to a place of safety before the ships could be sunk."

26. Spring Rice to Bryan, 1 Mar. 1915, *FRUS,* 1915 suppl., 127–28.

27. Page to Bryan, 15 Mar. 1915, ibid., 143–45.

28. Bryan to Page, 30 Mar. 1915, ibid., 152–56.

29. Page to Lansing, 24 July 1915, ibid., 168–71.

30. Page to Wilson, 10 Mar. 1915, *PWW,* 32:357–63.

31. Page to Bryan, 3 Mar. 1915, ibid., 32:313.

32. "Are American Protests Vain?" *New Republic,* 10 Apr. 1915, 247–48.

33. Page to Bryan, 21 Mar. 1915, *FRUS,* 1915 suppl., 146–47.

34. Ibid.

35. Gerard to Bryan, 21 Mar. 1915, ibid., 354–55.

36. Wilson to Bryan, 24 Mar. 1915, *PWW,* 32:424–25.

37. In a cabinet meeting of March 19, 1915, Garrison had taken exception to the president's apparent intention to accept the British order in council as establishing a formal blockade, protesting on a case-by-case basis when the British exceeded the rights of a blockading belligerent power. On March 20 he sent a memorandum to Wilson outlining his position. Until Great Britain proclaimed a formal blockade, Garrison wrote, "I think that her whole order in council contravenes international law and she should be so notified and be told that we will hold her to 'strict accountability,' that being the same phrase which we used to Germany." Lindley Miller Garrison to Wilson, 20 Mar. 1915, ibid., 32:404–8. Garrison's memorandum pointed to countermeasures against Great Britain should the long-distance blockades persist, though of what severity is uncertain. Wilson did not acknowledge the memorandum.

38. Robert Lansing, "Memorandum by the Counselor for the Department of State on Proposed Reply to the British Note of March 15, 1915, and Order in Council," 24 Mar. 1915, in *Lansing Papers,* 1:290–91.

39. Wilson to Bryan, 24 Mar. 1915, *PWW,* 32:424–25. Wilson's use of the phrase *strict accountability* here must be discounted.

40. Bryan to Page, 30 Mar. 1915, *FRUS,* 1915 suppl., 152–56; Wilson to Lansing, 28 Mar. 1915, *PWW,* 32:443–49.

5 The *Lusitania*

1. *New Republic,* 13 Feb. 1915, 35; "Dealing with Germany," ibid., 15 May 1915, 27.

2. On March 28, 1915, the small British liner *Fabala,* outward bound from Liverpool, was sunk by a German submarine, with the loss of more than one hundred

lives. An American citizen, Leon Thrasher, had drowned. The sinking was at once seen by the press as a test case of the position the American government had taken in its note of February 10, 1915. On April 22 Wilson sent to Bryan the outline of a note to the German government. The outline substantially reaffirmed the contents of the February 10 note and thoroughly alarmed an already anxious secretary of state, who feared that the proposed note would "very much inflame the already hostile feeling against us in Germany." In the brief period between this exchange and the sinking of the *Lusitania* a perplexed Wilson did nothing. The days of silence suggest that the *Fabala* case would be allowed to drift in the hope that it might simply fade away. *PWW*, 33:61–62, 66–67.

3. Lansing to Wilson, 17 May 1915, ibid., 33:214–16.

4. House to Wilson, 11 May 1915, ibid., 33:158.

5. William Howard Taft to Wilson, 10 May 1915, ibid., 33:150–52.

6. Joseph P. Tumulty, *Woodrow Wilson as I Knew Him* (London: Heinemann, 1922), 233.

7. Gerard to House, 1 June 1915, *PWW*, 33:407.

8. Baker, *Woodrow Wilson*, 5:368.

9. Bryan to Gerard, 13 May 1915, *FRUS*, 1915 suppl., 393–96.

10. Woodrow Wilson, address to newly naturalized citizens, Philadelphia, 10 May 1915, *PWW*, 33:147–50.

11. Woodrow Wilson, press conference, 11 May 1915, ibid., 33:153–54.

12. Wilson, remarks to Associated Press, 20 Apr. 1915, ibid., 33:37–41.

13. Gerard to Bryan, 15 and 17 May 1915, *FRUS*, 1915 suppl., 396, 398.

14. Bryan to Wilson, 12 May 1915, *PWW*, 33:165–66.

15. Bryan to Wilson, 9 May 1915, ibid., 33:134–35.

16. Lansing to Bryan, 9 May 1915, *Lansing Papers*, 1:387–88.

17. Wilson to Bryan, 11 May 1915, *PWW*, 33:154.

18. House to Wilson, 25 May 1915, ibid., 33:253–54.

19. House, Diary, 3 Dec. 1914, ibid., 32:384–85.

20. Lansing to Wilson, 17 May 1915, ibid., 33:214–16.

21. Link, *Wilson: The Struggle for Neutrality*, 384.

22. Wilson to House, 14 July 1915, *PWW*, 33:505.

23. Hendrick, *Life and Letters of Walter H. Page*, 2:26.

24. Gerard to Bryan, 28 May 1915, *FRUS*, 1915 suppl., 419–21.

25. Lansing to Bryan, 1 June 1915, *Lansing Papers*, 1:417.

26. Lindley Miller Garrison, memorandum, 1 June 1915, *PWW*, 33:294–95.

27. Lansing to Gerard, 9 June 1915, *FRUS*, 1915 suppl., 436–38.

28. Gerard to Lansing, 8 July 1915, ibid., 463–66.

29. Lansing to Gerard, 21 July 1915, ibid., 480–82.

30. Devlin, *Too Proud to Fight*, 314.

31. *Literary Digest*, 22 May 1915, p. 197; 24 July 1915, p. 143.

32. Wilson to Lansing, 13 July 1915, *PWW*, 33:500.

33. Wilson to Toy, 23 May 1915, ibid., 33:241.

34. The American proposal was made to the belligerents on February 20, 1915. For the correspondence, see *FRUS*, 1915 suppl., 119–27.

35. House to Wilson, 14 and 19 May 1915, *PWW*, 33:197–98, 222.

36. Wilson to House, 20 May 1915, ibid., 33:223.

37. Wilson to Gerard, 23 May 1915, ibid., 33:238.

38. House to Wilson, 25 May 1915, ibid., 33:253.

39. Wilson to House, 23 May 1915, ibid., 33:239.

40. Bryan to Gerard, 23 May 1915, *FRUS*, 1915 suppl., 406; House to Wilson, 25 May 1915, *PWW*, 33:253–54.

41. Bernstorff to Theobald von Bethmann Hollweg, 29 May 1915, *PWW*, 33: 283–84. Although nothing came of Wilson's effort, the episode is revealing. In a lengthy note to this document, the *PWW* editors find the episode significant in illustrating Wilson's "search for an alternative to war," while acknowledging that this search encompassed "efforts to . . . persuade Germany to join hands with the American government in establishing freedom of the seas for neutral vessels and non-contraband cargoes." (ibid., 33:282). In fact, Wilson was not to make a comparable effort again until late 1916.

42. Bernstorff to Theobald von Bethmann Hollweg, 29 May 1915, ibid., 33: 283–84.

43. Bernstorff to Bethmann Hollweg, 2 June 1915, ibid., 33:316–20.

44. The incident of the *Armenian* was reported on July 1, 1915, and attracted some attention in the press. The American muleteers were employed by the British government; their death drew no protest from Washington. Page duly reported the incident. Page to Lansing, 30 June and 3 July 1915, *FRUS*, 1915 suppl., 457–59.

45. Gerard to Lansing, 24 June, 3–5 July 1915, ibid., 453, 457–62; Lansing to Gerard, 8 July 1915, ibid., 462; Gerard to Lansing, 15 July 1915, ibid., 474; Lansing to Gerard, 19 July 1915, ibid., 477.

46. Lansing, *War Memoirs*, 40.

47. Lansing to Wilson, 13 Sept. 1915, *Lansing Papers*, 1:480–81.

48. Bryan to Wilson, 3 and 5 June 1915, *PWW*, 33:321–26, 342; Wilson to Bryan, 5 June 1915, ibid., 33:343.

6   The Maritime Blockade and Submarine Warfare

1. Bernstorff to Lansing, 1 Sept. 1915, *FRUS*, 1915 suppl., 530.

2. Lansing to Gerard, 8 May 1916, ibid., 1916 suppl., 232, 267.

3. Lansing, *War Memoirs*, 115.

4. Gerard to Lansing, 4 May 1916, *FRUS*, 1916 suppl., 257–60.

5. Woodrow Wilson, remarks at a luncheon in New York, 17 May 1915, *PWW*, 33:209–11.

6. On December 8, 1941, the day following the Japanese attack on Pearl Harbor, the U.S. chief of naval operations ordered American naval forces in the Pacific to execute unrestricted submarine and aerial warfare. Thirty years separates the reprisal measures at sea taken by Germany and the destruction of Japanese cities by conventional and atomic weapons.

7. In the case of noncombatant lives lost at sea through German submarine warfare, statistics vary. At the most, however, the number did not exceed ten thousand. Noncombatant deaths attributable to the blockade remain to this day a matter of uncertainty and controversy if only because German casualties were not the result of starvation as such but of malnutrition. Postwar German estimates, the result of detailed study, concluded that the deaths attributable to the British

blockade numbered approximately five hundred thousand. The figure is accepted by the interwar British historian of the blockade, A. C. Bell, in *A History of the Blockade of Germany* (London: HMSO, 1937), 117–18.

8. House to Wilson, 10 July 1915, *PWW*, 33:490–91.

9. House, Diary, 22 May 1916.

10. Savage, *Policy of the United States*, 2:533n.

11. Morrissey, *American Defense of Neutral Right*, 108, citing Archibald Hurd, *The Merchant Navy*, 3 vols. (London: J. Murray, 1920–24), 2:237–38, gives these figures: in May 1915, 149 ships; in December 1915, 766 ships.

12. "In most direct contradiction of international law all distinctions between merchantmen and war vessels have been obliterated by the order to British merchantmen to arm themselves and to ram submarines." Gerard to Lansing, 8 July 1915, *FRUS*, 1915 suppl., 463–66.

13. Lansing to Gerard, 9 June 1915, ibid., 436–38.

14. Ibid., 437. The phrase is Wilson's: "The sinking of passenger ships involves principles of humanity which throw into the background only special circumstances of detail."

15. House to Wilson, 22 Aug. 1915, *PWW*, 34:298–99.

16. Wilson to Galt, 23 Aug. 1915, ibid., 34:298.

17. Lansing to Gerard, 21 July 1915, *FRUS*, 1915 suppl., 480–92.

18. House, Diary, 14 May 1916.

19. Wilson, address to joint session of Congress, 2 Apr. 1917, *PWW*, 41:519.

20. Arthur S. Link, *Woodrow Wilson: Revolution, War, and Peace* (Arlington Heights, IL: Harlan Davidson, 1979), 39–40.

21. Wilson to House, 20 Sept. 1915, *PWW*, 34:493.

22. May, *World War and American Isolation*, 160–78.

23. Ibid., 177.

24. Lansing to Gerard, 21 July 1915, *FRUS*, 1915 suppl., 480–82.

7 The House-Grey Memorandum

1. House, Diary, 8 Oct. 1915, *PWW*, 35:42–44.

2. Ibid.

3. House to Wilson, 9 Feb. 1916, *PWW*, 36:147–48.

4. House to Wilson, 9 Feb. 1915, ibid., 32:205.

5. House, Diary, 10 Feb. 1915.

6. Grey to House, 2 June 1915, House Papers.

7. House, Diary, 22 Sept. 1915, *PWW*, 34:206.

8. Ibid., 13 Oct. 1916. "I told him of my proposal to the President concerning intervention. He was much interested, and agreed with me absolutely." Yet when Wilson asked his opinion of the plan, Lansing's support was certainly less than fulsome. *Lansing Papers*, 1:495.

9. House, Diary, 14 Oct. 1915, *PWW*, 35:61–62.

10. House to Grey, 3 Sept. 1915, House Papers.

11. Grey to House, 22 Sept. 1915, *PWW*, 35:71n3.

12. House, Diary, 15 Oct. 1915.

13. Ibid., 17 Oct. 1915.

14. Wilson to Lansing (enclosure), 17 Oct. 1915, *PWW*, 35:80–82. The "under-

standing" was, of course, a diplomatic lie, Wilson being privy to all that passed between Grey and House. We do not know, of course, how Grey would have responded in these exchanges had he known House was showing them to the president.

15. Ibid., 35:80.

16. House, Diary, 19 Oct. 1915.

17. House to Wilson, 10 Nov. 1915, *PWW*, 35:186.

18. Wilson to House, 11 Nov. 1915, ibid., 35:192.

19. Bernstorff to Bethmann Hollweg, 23 Nov. 1915, ibid., 35:241–43.

20. Wilson, address to League to Enforce Peace, 27 May 1916, ibid., 37:113–16.

21. House to Wilson (enclosure), 25 Nov. 1915, ibid., 35:254–55.

22. House, Diary, 25 Nov. 1915.

23. House to Wilson (enclosure), 25 Nov. 1915, *PWW*, 35:254–56.

24. House, Diary, 28 Nov. 1915, ibid., 35:258–61.

25. Ibid.

26. Ibid., 16 Oct. 1915.

27. House to Page, 12 Dec. 1915, House Papers.

28. House to Grey, 22 Dec. 1915, *PWW*, 35:383n.

29. House, Diary, 8 Dec. 1915.

30. Lansing to Wilson, 29 Nov. 1915, *PWW*, 35:264.

31. House, Diary, 15 Dec. 1915, ibid., 35:356.

32. Ibid., 359.

33. House to Wilson, 22 Dec. 1915, ibid., 35:381–82.

34. Wilson to House, 24 Dec. 1915, ibid., 35:387–88.

35. House, Diary, 25 Dec. 1915.

36. House to Wilson, 26 Dec. 1915, *PWW*, 35:391.

37. House, Diary, 6 Jan. 1916.

38. Ibid., 13 Jan. 1916. "I told [Lord] Bryce of our difficulties with Spring Rice. He counseled not taking them up here, stating if I did so and he was removed, it might lessen my influence and that, he thought, would be a much more serious matter than any good accomplished."

39. Ibid., 6 Jan. 1916.

40. House to Wilson, 7 Jan. 1916, *PWW*, 35:453.

41. Wilson to House, 9 Jan. 1916, ibid., 35:457.

42. House, Diary, 6 Jan. 1916.

43. Ibid., 10 Jan. 1916.

44. House to Wilson, 11 Jan. 1916, *PWW*, 35:465–66.

45. House to Wilson, 10 Jan. 1916, ibid., 35:458–59.

46. Wilson to House, 11 Jan. 1916, ibid., 35:462.

47. Wilson to House, 24 Dec. 1915, ibid., 35:387–88.

48. House, Diary, 11 Jan. 1916.

49. House to Wilson, 13 Jan. 1916, *PWW*, 35:471–73.

50. House to Wilson, 15 Jan. 1916, ibid., 35:484–86. In his diary House noted: "What I was most interested in was George's insistence that the war could only be brought to an end by the President, and that terms could be declared by him which the belligerents could never agree upon if left to themselves. Fantastic as this may seem, there is some truth in it, and if the President had taken my advice

and increased the Army of the United States in the early months of the war, as I strongly urged him to do, he would be in a position today to do what George wishes him to do this coming Autumn." House, Diary, 14 Jan. 1916.

51. House to Wilson, 15 Jan. 1916, *PWW*, 35:483.

52. House, Diary, 15 Jan. 1916.

53. House to Wilson, 16 Jan. 1916, *PWW*, 35:487–88.

54. House to Wilson, 3 Feb. 1916, ibid., 36:122–23.

55. House, Diary, 2 Feb. 1916.

56. House to Wilson, 3 Feb. 1916, *PWW*, 36:125–26. The "hell" that would break loose refers to House's estimate of the impending German offensive at Verdun, which began on February 21, 1916. This would be followed by the Allied counteroffensive in the Somme.

57. "Conversation du Colonel House avec M. Jules Cambon," 2 Feb. 1916, reprinted in *PWW*, 36:126.

58. House, Diary, 7 Feb. 1916.

59. House to Wilson, 9 Feb. 1916, *PWW*, 36:147.

60. Ibid.

61. House, Diary, 7 Feb. 1916.

62. "Deuxieme Entrevue du Colonel House," 7 Feb. 1916, reprinted in *PWW*, 36:148–49.

63. House to Wilson, 9 Feb. 1916, ibid., 36:148.

64. "Deuxieme Entrevue du Colonel House," 7 Feb. 1916.

65. House to Wilson, 10 Feb. 1916, *PWW*, 36:166.

66. House, Diary, 10 Feb. 1916.

67. Lansing to Wilson, 7 Jan. 1916, and Wilson to Lansing, 10 Jan. 1916, *PWW*, 35:448, 457.

68. Devlin, *Too Proud to Fight*, 427.

69. House to Wilson, 10 Feb. 1916, *PWW*, 36:166–68.

70. House, Diary, 10 Feb. 1916.

71. House to Wilson, 10 Feb. 1916, *PWW*, 36:166–68.

72. House to Wilson, 11 Feb. 1916, ibid., 36:170.

73. House, Diary, 11 Feb. 1916.

74. Lansing to Wilson (enclosure), 24 Jan. 1916, *PWW*, 35:516–18.

75. Hendrick, *Life and Letters of Walter H. Page*, 3:281–82.

76. House, Diary, 11 Feb. 1916.

77. Ibid., 14 Feb. 1916.

78. Ibid., 15 Feb. 1916.

79. Ibid., 17 Feb. 1916.

80. The memorandum was dated February 22, 1916, and initialed by Grey.

81. House, Diary, 17 Feb. 1916.

82. Ibid., 21, 22 Feb. 1916.

83. Ibid., 4, 6 Mar. 1916. House did not show the president the memorandum until early evening. Earlier, he had taken a long drive with the Wilsons, during which he had "outlined every important detail of my mission." The president read the memorandum in the light of this expectedly optimistic oral report.

84. House to Grey, 7 Mar. 1916, *PWW*, 36:266.

85. House, *Intimate Papers of Colonel House*, 2:201.

86. Walter Lippmann, *Men of Destiny* (New York: Macmillan, 1928), 132–33.

87. Wilson to House, 12 Feb. 1916, *PWW,* 36:173.

88. Lippmann, *Men of Destiny,* 134.

89. Wilson to William J. Stone, 24 Feb. 1916, *PWW,* 36:213.

90. Lippmann, *Men of Destiny,* 134–35. Lippmann adds: "I do not believe that House and Wilson clearly understood each other here: in this incident we can see that in spite of their apparent agreement they started from different premises about the war, and that their minds worked differently as to the American objective."

91. The president apparently gave no explanation for his action. At least, none is recorded by House. Nor does House comment on the episode.

92. Grey to House, 24 Mar. 1916, House Papers.

93. Grey to House, 7 Apr. 1916, ibid.

94. The principal secret treaties were the agreements France and Great Britain concluded in March 1915 with Russia, which provided that Russia should have the Bosphorus and the Dardanelles as well as Constantinople; the agreement of April 1915 between France and Britain with Italy, promising Italy Trentino, South Tyrol, Trieste, Istria and Dalmatia, and the Dodecanese Islands; the October 1915 Sykes-Picot agreement between France and Great Britain, providing for French supremacy in Syria and British rule in Palestine and present-day Iraq (excluding Mosul, which went to France); and the British commitment in February 1917 to Japan, pledging Britain to support Japan's claim to Kiaochou and the German Pacific islands north of the equator.

95. Lippmann, *Men of Destiny,* 135–36.

96. Hendrick, *Life and Letters of Walter H. Page,* 3:282.

97. Thus the conclusion of a memorandum by E. S. Montague, of the Foreign Office, to the prime minister: "I fear if House could deliver the goods the goods are not good enough. It is not enough that we should secure a partial victory—it is not enough that Germany should be punished by her own self-inflicted material damage. We must win a complete victory and that I think House cannot secure us." E. S. Montague to H. H. Asquith, 18 Mar. 1916, Asquith Papers, Bodleian Library, Oxford, quoted in Arthur S. Link, *Wilson: Confusion and Crises, 1915–1916* (Princeton, NJ: Princeton University Press, 1964), 140.

98. Grey to Lord Bertie of Thame, 5 May 1916, Harding MSS 23, quoted in V H. Rothwell, *British War Aims and Peace Diplomacy, 1914–1918* (London: Oxford University Press, 1971), 36.

8 The "Great Utterance"

1. House, Diary, 3 May 1916, *PWW,* 36:596–602.

2. House to Wilson, 9 May 1916 (enclosure), ibid., 37:6–7.

3. Ibid., 37:6.

4. House to Grey, 11 May 1916 (enclosure), ibid., 37:21.

5. House to Wilson, 14 May 1916 (enclosure), ibid., 37:43–44.

6. House, Diary, 13 May 1916.

7. House to Wilson, 14 May 1916, *PWW,* 37:42.

8. Wilson to House, 16 May 1916, ibid., 37:57–58. Regarding the British government's treatment of Irish rebels, on April 24, 1916, a rebellion led by Sir Roger Casement had broken out in Dublin. It was swiftly put down by the British

government, the insurrectionists being shot. Casement alone was subsequently tried and hanged. The effect of the affair in the United States was to strengthen the forces of isolation. See Link, *Wilson: Campaigns for Progressivism and Peace,* 13–15.

9. House, Diary, 18 May 1916.

10. *FRUS,* 1915 suppl., 578–89.

11. Wilson to House, 24 Dec. 1915, *PWW,* 35:387–88.

12. House to Wilson, 17 May 1916 (enclosure), ibid., 37:62–64.

13. Wilson to House, 18 May 1916, ibid., 37:68. The statement goes on: "They would not in any case have been able, even if willing, to be even-handed with us in the trade rivalries which must inevitably follow the war."

14. House to Wilson, 17 May 1916, ibid., 37:63.

15. House, Diary, 17, 18 May 1916.

16. Ibid., 14 May 1916.

17. Wilson to House, 18 May 1916, *PWW,* 37:68.

18. House to Wilson, 17 May 1916, ibid., 37:64.

19. Wilson to House, 18 May 1916, ibid., 37:68.

20. House to Wilson, 21 May 1916 (enclosure), ibid., 37:88, 91.

21. Wilson to House, 22 May 1916 (enclosure), ibid., 37:93.

22. House, Diary, 24 May 1916, ibid., 37:103–6.

23. House to Wilson, 19 May 1916, ibid., 37:77.

24. Lansing to Wilson, 25 May 1916, ibid., 37:106–8.

25. "President Wilson's Peace Plan," *Literary Digest,* 10 June 1916, pp. 1683–85.

26. "Mr. Wilson's Great Utterance," *New Republic,* 3 June 1916, 102.

27. Wilson, address to League to Enforce Peace, 27 May 1916, *PWW,* 37:113–16.

28. Wilson to House, 29 May 1916, ibid., 37:118.

29. Gerard to Lansing, 9 June 1916, *FRUS,* 1916 suppl., 272.

30. Secretary of State Jagow to Bernstorff, 7 June 1916, in *Official German Documents Relating to the World War,* trans. under the supervision of the Carnegie Endowment for International Peace, 2 vols. (New York: Oxford University Press, 1922), 2:976–78.

31. Memoranda by Walter Hines Page, [c. 23 Sept. 1916], *PWW,* 38:251–55.

32. House to Wilson, 31 May 1916 (enclosure), ibid., 37:131–32.

33. Ibid. Grey's telegram was a rewritten version of an earlier draft by Balfour. In Balfour's draft there is no reference to France, but there is a statement of British war aims: "While no British statesman desires to wage a bloody and costly war in order either to 'destroy' Germany or to be 'revenged' on her, it seems impossible to believe that a peace satisfactory to the Allies can be secured unless Belgium be restored, Alsace and Lorraine given back to France, Poland relieved from German domination, the status of Turkey profoundly modified—*not* in the interests of the Central Powers—and some other changes made in the map of Europe in accordance with the principle of nationality." Quoted in Link, *Wilson: Campaigns for Progressivism and Peace,* 34. Balfour's terms of peace are not unlike those stated in the House-Grey memorandum. Why did Grey omit them? Devlin writes: "The terms of the 'satisfactory peace' outlined by Balfour by no means embraced all of the Allies' recent commitments: what if America replied that she accepted the terms and on the faith of them was ready to go to war?" *Too Proud to Fight,* 493.

34. House to Wilson, 1 June 1916, *PWW*, 37:134–35.

35. House to Wilson, 9 June 1916 (enclosure), ibid., 37:178–80. The correspondence between House and Grey continued during the summer of 1916, though by then it had taken on an increasingly strained character. That it was carried on in a period of deteriorating relations between the two countries did not help matters. Grey closed it out in a letter of August 28, in which he noted: "The continual reports that public opinion in the United States is determined at all costs to keep out of the war, makes people ask whether even with a League of Nations the United States could be depended upon to uphold treaties commitments by force. . . . And yet unless the United States is a member of the League of Nations and a member that could be depended upon to intervene, the peace of the world would be no more secure in future than it was in 1914. These are the thoughts and doubts that check response here." Ibid., 38:89–92.

36. House to Grey, 27 May 1916, House Papers.

37. House, Diary, 23 June 1916. House added: "It would mean the end of militarism but it would also mean an end of navalism and that perhaps is where the shoe pinches. Great Britain desires to destroy militarism and at the same time perpetuate navalism, when the war has shown that of the two navalism might be made the more oppressive of the two branches of military service."

38. Ibid., 29 June 1916.

39. Wilson to House, 22 June 1916, *PWW*, 37:280–81.

9 Woodrow Wilson's War Address

1. Wilson, address to joint session of Congress, 2 Apr. 1917, ibid., 41:521.

2. Wilson to House, 24 Jan. 1917, ibid., 41:3.

3. House, Diary, 1 Feb. 1917, ibid., 41:87.

4. Wilson to Stone, 24 Feb. 1916, ibid., 36:213–14.

5. Woodrow Wilson, address to joint session of Congress, 3 Feb. 1917, ibid., 41:111.

6. These efforts were set off by a message from the Austro-Hungarian foreign minister, Count Ottokar Czernin, to Lansing. Sent on February 5, the note responded to Wilson's wish to maintain relations with Austria if possible and to his call for a negotiated peace in which "there should be neither victor nor loser." What prevented Austria from talking about peace, Czernin declared, was the Allied "program which aims at the dismemberment of Austria-Hungary." Penfield to Lansing, 5 Feb. 1917, *FRUS*, 1917 suppl. 1, 38. The message aroused hope in a desperate president. A note written by Wilson was sent to Page in London on February 8 and presented to Lloyd George. The British government was told that the president was trying to avoid breaking with Austria in order to keep open channels of official intercourse but that the chief obstacle to doing so was the Allied stated peace terms calling for the dismemberment of Austria-Hungary. Wilson asked for the Allied abandonment of Austria's radical dismemberment. Lansing to Page, 8 Feb. 1917, ibid., 40–41. Lloyd George, however, refused to give any assurances regarding Austria. Denying that the Allies had a policy of "sheer dismemberment," he nevertheless insisted upon applying the principle of nationality to the demands of the Rumanians, Slavs, Serbians, and Italians. Page to Lansing, 11 Feb. 1917, ibid., 41–44. A change in the British position soon followed. On

February 20 Lloyd George told Page that he had discussed the matter with some of his associates, and if Wilson formally submitted a peace proposal on behalf of Austria-Hungary, his government would be glad to consider it provided the utmost secrecy was kept. Page to Lansing, 20 Feb. 1917, ibid., 55–56. But nothing was to come of the affair, Austria being unable to consider a separate peace. German Foreign Minister Zimmermann, on hearing of Czernin's February 5 feeler, wrote to his ambassador in Vienna: "Although I appreciate Count Czernin's wish to avoid a break with the United States, nevertheless I believe that too friendly an attitude on the part of the Austrian Government would be objectionable, in view of the openly announced efforts on the part of the President to differentiate between us and Austria-Hungary." *Official German Documents Relating to the World War,* 2:1324–25.

7. Henry Cabot Lodge to Roosevelt, 2 Mar. 1917, in *Selections from the Correspondence of Theodore Roosevelt and Henry Cabot Lodge, 1884–1918,* ed. Henry Cabot Lodge, 2 vols. (New York: Charles Scribner, 1925), 2:409.

8. Woodrow Wilson, address to joint session of Congress, 26 Feb. 1917, *PWW,* 41:283–87.

9. Woodrow Wilson, statement, 9 Mar. 1917, ibid., 41:367.

10. Page to Lansing, 24 Feb. 1917, *FRUS,* 1917 suppl. 1, 147.

11. The effect of the telegram on the public proved even greater perhaps than its effect on the president. On February 28 Wilson released a copy of the telegram to the Associated Press, and on March 1 the story appeared in the nation's press. Its impact was immediate and overwhelming. Only doubt over the authenticity of the telegram held back a nearly unanimous public response of indignation and outrage. All doubt was removed on March 3, however, by Zimmermann's admission that he had indeed sent the telegram to the German ambassador to Mexico. We can only speculate over why Wilson decided to publish the Zimmermann telegram. Arthur Link has written that the president arranged for publication because "he thought that the American people had a right to know the facts" and because he felt that once they knew the facts, both they and "Congress as well, would then support him in the risky course of armed neutrality once it was put into force." Link, *Wilson: Campaigns for Progressivism and Peace,* 353. Wilson's decision may also have been one of the first signs that he was looking beyond armed neutrality and contemplating the prospect of war.

12. Woodrow Wilson, second inaugural address, 5 Mar. 1917, *PWW,* 41:332–35.

13. Lansing to Wilson, 19 Mar. 1917, ibid., 41:425–27.

14. Josephus Daniels, Diary, 19 Mar. 1917, reprinted in ibid., 41:430.

15. Lansing to House, 19 Mar. 1917, ibid., 41:429–30.

16. The cabinet meeting of February 26 had been acrimonious, according to Franklin Lane, Wilson's secretary of interior, the president having accused Lane, Secretary of the Treasury William G. McAdoo, Secretary of Agriculture David F. Houston, and Secretary of Commerce William C. Redfield of wanting war. "We couldn't get the idea out of his head that we were bent on pushing the country into war. Houston talked of resigning after the meeting. McAdoo will—within a year, I believe. I tried to smooth them down by recalling our past experiences with the President. . . . He comes out right but he is slower than a glacier—and things are mighty disagreeable, whenever anything has to be done." *The Letters of Franklin*

K. Lane, ed. Anne W. Lane and Louise H. Hall (Boston: Houghton Mifflin, 1922), 239–41, quoted in ibid., 41:282–83.

17. Lansing, memorandum, 20 Mar. 1917, ibid., 41:436–44.

18. Woodrow Wilson, proclamation, 21 Mar. 1917, ibid., 41:446.

19. Mark Sullivan, *Our Times: America at the Birth of the Twentieth Century*, ed. Dan Rather (New York: Charles Scribner, 1996), 512.

20. Wilson, address to joint session of Congress, 2 Apr. 1917, *PWW*, 41:519–27.

21. House, Diary, 28 Mar. 1917, ibid., 41:496–98.

22. House, Diary, 20 Dec. 1917, ibid., 40:304–5.

23. Wilson, appeal for a statement of war aims, 18 Dec. 1916, ibid., 40:273–76.

24. James, Viscount Bryce, to Wilson, 22 Dec. 1916, ibid., 40:317.

25. Henri Bergson, "Mes missions (1917–1918)," *La revue hommes et mondes* 3 (July 1947) 359–75, quoted in ibid., 41:315–16.

26. Wilson, colloquy with members of the American Neutral Conference, 30 Aug. 1916, ibid., 38:115.

27. Walter Hines Page, memorandum, 23 Sept. 1916, ibid., 38:241.

28. Ibid.

29. Wilson, unpublished prolegomenon to a peace note, ca. 25 Nov. 1916, ibid., 40:69.

30. Ibid., 40:70.

31. Woodrow Wilson, address to Senate, 22 Jan. 1917, ibid., 40:536.

32. Henry Cabot Lodge, "The President's Plan for a World Peace," speech delivered in the Senate, 1 Feb. 1917, in Lodge, *War Addresses, 1915–1917* (Boston: Houghton Mifflin, 1917), 251.

33. Wilson, address to joint session of Congress, 2 Apr. 1917, *PWW*, 41:523.

34. Roosevelt to William Allen White, 3 Aug. 1917, in *Letters of Theodore Roosevelt*, 1216–17.

35. Wilson, address to Senate, 22 Jan. 1917, *PWW*, 40:536.

36. Wilson, address to joint session of Congress, 2 Apr. 1917, ibid., 41:523.

37. Thomas Paine, "The Rights of Man" (1791), in *The Writings of Thomas Paine*, ed. Moncure Daniel Conway, 4 vols. (New York: G. P. Putnam's Sons, 1894–96), 2:388.

38. Wilson, address to joint session of Congress, 2 Apr. 1917, *PWW* 41:523–24.

39. Wilson, address to Senate, 22 Jan. 1917, ibid., 40:536.

40. Wilson, address to joint session of Congress, 2 Apr. 1917, ibid., 41:525.

41. Ibid., 41:521, 526.

42. Gilbert M. Hitchcock to Wilson, 29 Mar. 1917, *PWW*, 41:498–500.

43. Wilson to Matthew Hale, 31 Mar. 1917, Papers of Woodrow Wilson, Library of Congress, Washington, DC, quoted in Link, *Wilson: Campaigns for Progressivism and Peace*, 412.

44. Wilson, address to joint session of Congress, 2 Apr. 1917, *PWW* 41:521.

45. Ibid., 41:526.

46. Wilson to Stone, 24 Feb. 1916, *PWW*, 36:213–14.

47. Ibid., 36:214.

48. John L. Heaton, *Cobb of "The World"* (New York: Dutton, 1924), 268–69. There is nothing in Wilson's papers that validates Cobb's account of the conversation he had with Wilson. But Cobb was a responsible journalist, and the account

he gave of a tortured president rings true. On one point he appears to have mis-led posterity: Cobb reported the conversation as having taken place in the early morning of April 2, whereas Arthur S. Link has established the date as March 19. Link, *Wilson: Campaigns for Progressivism and Peace*, 399.

49. Daniels, Diary, 20 Mar. 1917, *PWW*, 41:444.

50. Heaton, *Cobb of "The World,"* 269.

51. Wilson, address to joint session of Congress, 2 Apr. 1917, *PWW* 41:526–27.

52. Wilson, address to League to Enforce Peace, 27 May 1916, ibid., 37:115–16.

53. Wilson, address to Senate, 22 Jan. 1917, ibid., 40:535–36.

54. Ibid., 40:539.

55. Henry Adams, *History of the United States of America during the Administration of Jefferson and Madison*, 9 vols., 2nd ed. (New York: Charles Scribner's, 1903), 1:445.

56. See House, Diary, 3 Dec. 1916.

57. [Walter Lippmann], "The Defense of the Atlantic World," *New Republic*, 17 Feb. 1917, 59.

58. *FRUS*, 1916 suppl., 263.

59. Grey to House (enclosure), 7 Apr. 1916, and Grey to House (enclosure), 12 May 1916, *PWW*, 36:511–12, 37:43–44.

60. Wilson to House, 16 May 1916, ibid., 37:57–58.

61. *Congressional Record*, 64th Cong., 1st sess., 13485, 13488, 13792–94.

62. Wilson, colloquy with members of the American Neutral Conference, 30 Aug. 1916, *PWW*, 38:117.

63. Bryan to Wilson, 21 Dec. 1916, ibid., 40:314.

64. House, Diary, 15 Nov. 1916, ibid., 38:658–59.

65. Ibid., 38:658.

66. Lippmann, *Men of Destiny*, 135.

67. Desk diary of Robert Lansing, Library of Congress, Washington, DC, 31 Dec. 1916.

68. Wilson, address to League to Enforce Peace, 27 May 1916, *PWW*, 37:114.

69. Wilson, address to Senate, 22 Jan. 1917, ibid., 40:535–36.

70. Wilson, address to joint session of Congress, 2 Apr. 1917, ibid., 41:523.

71. "The idea of laying down terms to the Allies for American participation never seemed to have occurred to Wilson at this time." Link, *Campaigns for Progressivism and Peace*, 409.

72. Wilson to House, 11 July 1917, House Papers, quoted in Hodgson, *Woodrow Wilson's Right Hand*, 105.

73. Woodrow Wilson, address, Baltimore, 6 Apr. 1918, *PWW*, 47:270.

Index

Adams, Henry, on Jefferson and Peace, 207

Ambrosius, Lloyd E., twofold character of Wilson's neutrality, 215n9

American Neutral Conference, 195

Ancona, 152, 153

Anderson, Chandler P., 98; account of ambiguity of February 10, 1915 note to German government, 100

Arabic, 36, 37, 38, 43, 141, 144, 146; sinking of, 128; American government's threat to break relations with Germany, 128; pledge of Germany, 131

Armenian incident, 126–27

Asquith, Herbert, 164, 166, 167, 169

Austria, 151, 153, 231n6

Baker, Ray Stannard: persuaded there had never been clear understanding between Wilson and House, 48; Wilson as the arbiter of the war, 74; president's neutrality doomed by circumstances over which he had little control, 74–75; law governing neutral-belligerent relations characterized by great uncertainty, 75; fatality of Wilson's course, 75

balance of power: persisting dilemma of American diplomacy, 1; issue in Napoleonic War and World War I, 17; United States as holder of, 18; ordering principle of international society, 53

Balfour, Arthur J., 156, 159, 160, 163, 164; terms of peace and Patrick Devlin's comment, 166–67; gave Wilson Allied secret agreements in May 1917, 214

Balkan wars, 64

Belgium, invasion of, effect on Americans, 97, 108

Bergson, Henri, 195

Bernstorff, Johann von, 39, 42, 43; determined to avoid war, 37; writes to Bethmann Hollweg of Wilson's proposed mediation, 125; reports on terms of Wilson's proposed mediation, 126; promises to do what he can to satisfy Lansing's demand, 128; "best of the lot" in House's opinion, 151; told by House that blockade must be left alone, 179

Bethmann Hollweg, Theobald von, 160, 177; reluctantly consents to unrestricted submarine warfare, 94; fears diplomatic break with United States, 122

Boer War, 64

Briand, Aristide, 162, 167, 172; asks House for his views conditions of peace, 163; rejected call for peace conference, 164, 168

Bryan, William Jennings: Wilson entertains possible resignation of, 26; had no qualifications for position as secretary of state, 27; difference with Wilson raised by neutrality, 28; resigns, 28; assessment of character, 29; logic led generation later to American policy of "renunciatory" neutrality, 78; expresses criticism of British refusal to allow *Wilhelminia* to proceed to German port, 97–98; refused to protest British mining of North Sea, 98; opposes note to Germany of May 13, 1915, 113–14; seeks Wilson's support for postponement of accounting with

son from pursuing plan, 148; writes to
Grey that time may soon come when
American government should intervene and demand that peace parleys
begin, 149; offers to go to Europe,
152; writes Grey on need for better
understanding between Washington
and London, 152; finds president not
as belligerent as he was before, 152;
reluctant to undertake trip to Europe,
153; writes president of invitation he
had received from Germany, 153; asks
for instructions on what to say in London and Berlin, 154; interprets president's letter as giving him a "free
hand" to act, 155; abandons almost
immediately in London errand upon
which he was primarily bound, 155;
acquaints Grey with "real purpose" of
visit, 155; assumed Grey's support for
his plan, 155–56; assured Grey and
Balfour that president more powerful
than any sovereign in Europe, 156;
discovers British immovable on blockade, 158; made no progress on his
plan, 158; cables Wilson not to send
any note to England concerning shipping troubles, 159; told by Grey and
Balfour that the questions they discussed could go no further, 159; in
Berlin, sees signs of growing struggle
over submarine policy, 160; in Paris,
seeks to impress upon Cambon
gamble war represented, 160–61; tells
Wilson that by fall of 1916 he could
mediate end to war, 161; French
accounts of meeting of February 7,
1916, promising American intervention, 162; reports to Wilson that he
had brought Grey around on continuing *Lusitania* controversy, 164; assures
Grey that Lansing's modus vivendi
would be dropped, 164; convinced
Grey has agreed to president's calling
peace conference, 164; meeting with
Asquith, Balfour, and Grey to discuss
proposed peace conference, 164–65;
dinner meeting, February 14, 1916,

regarded by House as determinative
for peace plan, 165; affirms that peace
terms would have to conform to Wilsonian standards of justice, 166–67;
disputes French memorandum of conversation House had with Briand and
Cambon, 167; Grey draws up House-
Grey memorandum, 167–68; dis-
cusses with Grey best time to act on
memorandum, 169; president accepts
memorandum with qualifications,
169; sends telegram, written by Wilson, to Grey, 169–70; receives letter
from Grey that Allies are not interested in peace conference, 171–72;
encourages Wilson's peacemaking
propensities, 174; urges Wilson to
reconsider invitation to address
League to Enforce Peace, 175; writes
Grey that America's entrance into war
would not be good thing for England,
175; cables Grey that "America has
reach crossroads," 177–78; expresses
doubt about course he and Wilson
were following, 178; tells Bernstorff
that blockade cannot be changed,
179; suggests to Wilson desirability of
coming out again for strong navy, 179;
writes Wilson that he would not make
calling of peace conference any more
definite, 180; writes Grey that Jusserand warned him again making
peace proposal, 186; remains puzzled
by Allied response, 186; on Wilson
and Lansing, 193; repeatedly objected
to Wilson's moral equivalence, 194;
alarmed over Wilson's December 1916
peace initiative, 210; on Lloyd George
and preparedness, 227n50; correspondence with Grey during summer
1916, 231n35

international law: belligerent acts of
retaliation against enemy, 66–71; traditional blockade of Germany all but
impossible, 101–2; American claim
that its citizens had right to safety on
Allied merchant ships, 132–33; Amer-